THE BIG BOOK OF

OVERHEARD IN DUBLIN

DUBLIN WIT FROM OVERHEARDINDUBLIN.COM

Gill & Macmillan

To Eithne and Gerry

We'd like to thank all those people who have posted overheard stories to our website. Without you, there would be no 'Overheard in Dublin'!

Gill & Macmillan Ltd
Hume Avenue, Park West, Dublin 12
with associated companies throughout the world
www.gillmacmillan.ie
© Gerard Kelly and Sinéad Kelly 2009
978 07171 4538 6

Print origination by TypeIT, Dublin
Illustrations by Eoin Coveney
Printed in the UK by Cox and Wyman, Reading

This book is typeset in 10pt Garamond Book on 11pt.

The paper used in this book comes from the wood pulp of managed forests. For every tree felled, at least one tree is planted, thereby renewing natural resources.

A CIP catalogue record for this book is available from the British Library.

5 4 3 2 1

Marty Whel(of Fortune)

Was on the way home from the Ireland versus Sweden match last week on the DART when a random drunk spots Marty Whelan. A lot of banter went back and forward and then the drunk starts shouting at Marty, 'Wheel of Fortune'.

He was having so much fun and was loving the sound of his own voice so much I don't think anyone had the heart to tell him Marty hosts 'Fame and Fortune'.

Overheard by Ali, northbound DART
Posted on Tuesday, 7 March 2006

Ray D'Arcy crisps

Walking down Nassau Street the other day, I was passing a billboard ad for Walkers crisps (it's just a picture of Gary Lineker holding a bag of crisps). Two D4 type girls were walking in front of me. On seeing the picture:

Girl#1: 'Why is there a picture of Ray D'Arcy holding a bag of crisps?'

Girl#2: 'I dunno, it's a bit stupid alright isn't it?'

… I agree, there's an awful lot of stupid going around.

Overheard by Val, Nassau Street
Posted on Monday, 6 March 2006

Smelly bum

On the bus a while ago. A rather large woman with a bit of a B.O. problem gets on. Cue little boy, sniffing, 'Wot's dat smell? Wot's dat smell!'

His mam tries to get him to shut up. No luck. He continues, 'I tink it's her (pointing to the large woman). Yeah, it's her. She's got a smelly bum!'

Needless to say, that's when the mam chose to get off the bus.

Overheard by CC, no. 3 bus
Posted on Friday, 3 March 2006

Hong Kong Elvis

A girl in work said she has an Elvis CD that you can only buy in Hong Kong. One of her fellow employees asked,

'What's it called, wok and roll?"

Genius!

Overheard by Anonymous, George's Quay
Posted on Friday, 3 March 2006

A Crumblin poet

Sitting outside Redz on Thursday night. A young one and this fella were having a chat.

Girl: 'Where ye from?'

Fella: 'Crumblin. Where ye from?'

Girl: 'Ballyfermot.'

Fella replies, 'Ballyfermot people pick your pockets!' Turns to walk away, shouting, 'Watch yer pockets, boys, Ballyer Birds in the House!'

Leaving a very shocked girl on the corner of O'Connell Street.

Overheard by Mary, Redz, O'Connell Bridge
Posted on Thursday, 2 March 2006

Get out more!

I used to work in a pub in Lucan (where everybody thinks they're a D4 head) and here was the order I got one night:

'Pint of the black stuff (fair enough), pint of Heino (right so), a Shirley Bassey (we'll get to that in a minute), and a bottle of apples.' (Figured it out?)

Here is a legend of what they all translate to:

Pint of the black stuff — Guinness (obviously)
Pint of Heino — Heineken (obviously)
Shirley Bassey — Black Bush
Bottle of apples — Bulmers

When we say that these people need to get out more, it doesn't mean go out and upset the bar staff of their local!

Overheard by Matt, in work, pub in Lucan
Posted on Thursday, 2 March 2006

Kennedy's brain

Listening to 'What's in Kennedy's Head', the prestigious game show on FM104, whereby listeners have to guess what Adrian Kennedy (host of the above game show) is thinking of — i.e., what's in his head — by asking him clues.

Cue the nice lady with the accent straight out of Moore Street, whose question was, 'Is it something in your head?' And who then proceeded to guess, 'Is it your brain?'

It wasn't.

Overheard by David, FM104
Posted on Wednesday, 1 March 2006

A plaice without sole!

While my friend was in a pub he took a picture of some classic graffitti on the wall in the bathroom, saying, 'A city without a chipper is a plaice without sole.'

Good to see there are some poets left in Dublin!

Overheard by Naomi, city centre pub
Posted on Tuesday, 28 February 2006

Funny riot!

Overheard at the riots in town on Saturday:

'Stones five for 50, Helmets €1'

Ah, the Dublin humour even in times of strife!

Overheard by Linda, O'Connell Street
Posted on Tuesday, 28 February 2006

Rioters

Conversation between two masked rioters on Saturday:

Rioter #1: 'Did ya hear me sister's having twins?'

Rioter #2: 'No way, dat's brilliant ...'

And then they continued to fire rocks at the police ... classic Dublin.

Overheard by Steff, O'Connell Street
Posted on Tuesday, 28 February 2006

Leinster House moves to Dame Street

Three scumbags running over O'Connell Bridge during the riots.

Scumbag #1: 'Leg it, we gotta geh to Leinster House.'

Scumbag #2: 'Where's dat?'

Scumbag #3: 'Down be Dame Street.'

Overheard by Dan, O'Connell Bridge
Posted on Monday, 27 February 2006

Drinks round

I used to work in a busy city centre bar and I once got the following order from a customer (of D4 persuasion):

'Hi, could I have a Heino, a Probs, an AG, a VRB, a JDC and a GT.'

AKA: A Heineken, a Carlsberg, a Guinness (as in Arthur Guinness), a vodka and Redbull, a Jack

Daniels and Coke, and a Gin and Tonic (that
one's fair game).

Overheard by Amy, pub, Dublin 2
Posted on Monday, 27 February 2006

I predict a riot

A man loudly shouts into his mobile phone on
the Saturday afternoon of the Love Ulster parade
riots:

'I'm going down to O'Connell Street to throw a
few bricks at the coppers.'

Overheard by Swench, Exchequer Street, Dublin 2
Posted on Saturday, 25 February 2006

Use the sink!

While in Mother Redcaps pub I overheard this
girl who returned from the ladies toilet saying to
her friends, 'I don't like washing my hands in
that toilet.'

Quick as a flash the barman said, 'Most people
use the sink.'

Overheard by Max, Mother Redcaps
Posted on Thursday, 23 February 2006

Ballymunners

Written on the back of the no. 77A bus:

'Ballymunners rob yer runners.'

Overheard by John, no. 77A bus
Posted on Thursday, 23 February 2006

An offer you can refuse

Seen, not heard. Poster in hairdresser's window, offering a root-dyeing service for people whose highlights were starting to grow out:

'Come in and let us touch you up.'

Overheard by Flan, Hair-braid shop, Marlborough Street,
Parnell Street

Posted on Tuesday, 21 February 2006

Babyface O'Reilly

A group of boys were hanging around a small park in Dublin 12. Another teenage boy rides up on a flash pushbike.

Small boy: 'Where did you rob that?'

Teen: 'Didn't. I bought it.'

Small boy: 'Nah, you couldn't'a. Where'd you rob it?'

Teen: 'I told you I bought it at [cycle shop].'

Small boy: 'And here I thought you were some sort of gangster. What kind of gangster does that?'

Overheard by Anonymous, St Martin's Drive, Dublin 12

Posted on Saturday, 18 February 2006

Sectarian songs

Was busking in Temple Bar late last Saturday night. A group of lads, total Dubs, came up and started singing with me. One of them turned to me and asked me to play 'some sectarian songs'! His friends got very enthusiastic. 'Yeah play some sectarian songs!'

I didn't, and I didn't play any racist or anti-Semitic songs either!

Overheard by Anonymous, Temple Bar
Posted on Friday, 17 February 2006

The ref's ma ...

Standing on Hill 16 at a Dublin match, when the referee made a terrible call. A guy shouts out, 'Ref, do ye know hew bleedin ugly yer ma is?' He continues, '… she's so bleedin ugly, she couldn't gerra DART in Connolly Station!'

Everyone was in hysterics.

Overheard by JG, Hill 16
Posted on Tuesday, 14 February 2006

Strawberries

On a school trip from the North down to Dublin there was a Dub selling strawberries. 'Stra-brees, stra-brees,' she shouted. My friend from Tyrone turned to me and asked, 'What did she say?' And before I had a chance to answer, my other friend said, 'Er, something about a strong breeze.'

Overheard by Carmel, Grafton Street
Posted on Monday, 13 February 2006

High four!

I was cycling home from work the other day, and as I passed a packed bus stop a woman put her hand out to stop the bus. The cyclist in front of me slapped her hand while shouting 'High Five!'

The girl, with a rather heavy Dublin accent, screamed after him, while holding her fingers in the air, 'I've only got four fingers you bastard!'

The people standing at the bus stop erupted with laughter.

Overheard by Pablo, bus stop outside Connolly DART Station
Posted on Thursday, 9 February 2006

Vicious words

Scribbled on the no. 13 bus stop on O'Connell Street:

'Finglas heads wet their beds.'

Overheard by Brian.K, no. 13 bus stop on O'Connell Street
Posted on Wednesday, 1 February 2006

Gotta know the lingo around here!

Security guard, foreign national probably Nigerian, gesturing with his walkie-talkie to dealer bloke to tidy up pallets and boxes near shopping centre doorway.

Dealer: 'Der's no problem, mate. Get yer gaffer on the blower and I'll have a chinwag wih 'im, he knows the jackanory.'

Retreats one very confused security guard!

Overheard by Anonymous, Ilac entrance, Moore Street
Posted on Tuesday, 24 January 2006

Kittens ... fussy little bastards!

One day I was too lazy to go shopping so I decided to do an on-line Superquinn order rather than having to get ready and drive in traffic etc. While ordering my groceries I realised I had no kitten food so I added two boxes of Whiskas Kitten to my order.

Later on I received a phone call from Superquinn saying there were a few things they were out of stock on ... one of which was the kitten food. Here's the conversation:

Girl: 'We're out of the kitten food ... would de Adult wan be OK?'

Me: 'Ah no, sure, I'll leave it.'

Girl: 'Are ye sure? I have de Wiskis Adult food here.'

Me: 'No, really it's OK cos they're only three months old they can't eat the Adult food.'

Girl: [Thinks for a few seconds] 'Wha abou the Kite Kat Adult ... will dey eat da?'

Me: 'No, honestly it's OK they're only kittens.'

Girl: 'Jaysus, dem cats, fussy little bastards aren't they!'

Overheard by catlady, on the phone to Superquinn
Posted on Friday, 20 January 2006

The honesty of a schoolboy

In a school science class a 'well built' female teacher was talking about heat travelling from one thing to another.

Teacher: 'And what would happen if I sat down on this radiator, boys?'

Student: 'You'd break it miss!'

It was worth him getting suspended for — we laughed for hours after.

Overheard by daithi, a school that shall remain un-named!
Posted on Friday, 20 January 2006

Irish generosity ...

Saw a sign above a promotional 'offer' in a Centra:

'Buy one, get one!'

So typical of Ireland today …

Overheard by Paul, Centra beside Temple Bar
Posted on Thursday, 19 January 2006

Motor tax problems

While in the motor tax office in Nutgrove I overheard a woman who was struggling to fill in her motor tax renewal form ask her friend, 'How the fecking hell are you supposed to remember the chastity number?'

Overheard by Sinead, Motor Tax Office, Nutgrove
Posted on Wednesday, 18 January 2006

Drunken philosophy

Written inside one of the ladies toilets in The Bleeding Horse on Camden Street:

'Seriously, the hokey pokey, really what is it all about?'

Overheard by Anonymous, The Bleeding Horse
Posted on Wednesday, 18 January 2006

Bus aerobics

On the bus heading out of town an elderly woman in a wheelchair is wheeled on by her husband. She asks him to wheel her further down the bus, and he says, 'We're only staying on for two stops, will ye just sit there,' to which she replies nice and calmly with an auld Dub twang, 'Well I'm not going to get up and do aerobics around the bus, am I?'

Overheard by SC, no. 20B bus
Posted on Saturday, 14 January 2006

Raffle ticket

Overheard in the Hole In The Wall pub, raffle ticket seller from local GAA club is selling tickets. He approaches a drunk at the bar.

'Do you want to buy a raffle ticket?'

'Is it for the local GAA club?' replies the drunk.

'No,' says the ticket seller, 'it's for a portable telly and a feckin ham ... do you want one or wha?'

Overheard by Anonymous, Hole In The Wall, Blackhorse Avenue
Posted on Tuesday, 10 January 2006

Clever blonde

Blonde, sitting in an office in Ballymount where she has worked for the last eight months, asks: 'Where is Dublin 12?'

Manager: 'You've been working in it for the last eight months.'

Overheard by Matt, office in Ballymount, Dublin 12
Posted on Tuesday, 10 January 2006

Sharon's OK, no cause for concern

Standing in the queue at a sandwich bar in town. There's a TV monitor on the wall to keep the queue folk from getting restless. Sky News is on with no sound, and the main story and newsflash info bar are regarding Israeli Prime Minister Ariel Sharon's health. The headlines strap line reads, 'Sharon's health declines further'. Two girls in front of me seem baffled by this and one says to the other, 'Who's Sharon, is she the one from X Factor, Osbourne, what happened her?'

I nearly wet myself, but had to step in when they kept questioning each other, making assumptions about what could have happened.

'He's the Israeli Prime Minister,' I said.

To which the same girl replied, 'Ah, sure then I don't care.'

Celebrity vs Politics, brilliant. Brightened up my January no end.

Overheard by Larry, Rathmines Inn
Posted on Thursday, 5 January 2006

Pot kettle black

At the Leinster v Munster Rugby match, I overheard a Munster fan shouting at the Leinster players, 'You're a bunch of langers!'

Overheard by Tim, RDS
Posted on Wednesday, 4 January 2006

Mr Happy at Glenageary Station

Me: 'Can you tell me the time of the next train to Greystones?'

Glenageary ticket clerk: 'The wallllll!'

Me: 'Excuse me, the wallllll? I want to know the time of the next train to Greystones.'

Glenageary ticket clerk: 'The wallllll!'

Me: 'The wallllll ... what's a wallllll?'

Glenageary ticket clerk: 'The wallllll! The wallllll! Timetable ... (on) the wallllll!'

Overheard by Damian, at Glenageary Railway Station
Posted on Wednesday, 4 January 2006

Mothers, ya gotta love em!

During a very distressing situation, my mother was faced with a man who entered her workplace, threatening to burn the place to the ground. He had some petrol with him and began to pour the contents about the place. My mother immediately pushed a panic button, alerting the guards, and all was fine in the end.

However, later on while talking about the ordeal with my sister, she came out with this gem:

My sister: 'So, Mam, how did you react so fast, I mean, was it the adrenalin?'

My mother amazingly replies, 'No, no, it was definitely the petrol!'

Overheard by Graeme, at home in Dublin
Posted on Thursday, 29 December 2005

Dry or greasy skin, sir?

At a beautician in Stillorgan, I ran into an old friend buying his girlfriend's Christmas present — some fancy moisturiser. After much thought he picked up one of the numerous varieties of moisturiser and brought it to the counter. Still unsure, he sought advice from the lady behind the counter:

Guy: 'Pardon me, but do you think this is a good moisturiser for my girlfriend?'

Lady: 'Well that depends, what type of skin does she have?'

Guy: 'I dunno … Caucasian?!'

Overheard by darkhorse, Stillorgan
Posted on Thursday, 29 December 2005

Male or female?

In school a few years ago, a very well-spoken teacher was getting us to fill out a form. In a very clear and loud voice he said, 'Now where it says sex, do not write yes please or no thank you.'

Cue uproarious laughter from the entire year.

Overheard by Wilbo, southside school
Posted on Thursday, 22 December 2005

The important issues of the day

While sitting upstairs on the no. 77 bus (air full of hash smoke as usual) we pass by the new Lidl supermarket on the Greenhills Road.

Stoned guy #1: 'Look ders de new Lidl!'

Stoned guy #2: 'Ah yeah, der popping up everywhere.'

Stoned guy #1: 'Is it Liddle or Leedle or Loidle?'

(They ponder on this for a couple of seconds.)

Stoned guy #2: 'I dunno but I know de other one's called Aldi.'

Stoned guy #1: 'Anyway the beer's durt cheap it is …'

Overheard by G, no. 77 bus
Posted on Wednesday, 21 December 2005

Frozen

There were a few lads working in the frozen section of Dunnes Stores, throwing frozen turkeys into the fridge with some force, when some old dear turns around to them and says, 'Ah be careful with them turkeys, boys, they'll bruise when they thaw out.'

To which a reply came, 'Don't worry about it, luv, they can't feel a thing …'

Overheard by Orlando, Dunnes Stores
Posted on Tuesday, 20 December 2005

Using your head

In college, the angry janitor was trying to push some kind of trolley past everyone in the canteen queue, but no one was paying any attention to him.

Janitor: 'Sorry, sorry, excuse me, excuse me …'

No one is listening.

Janitor: 'Jaysus, ah look, ders €20 on the ground.'

Everyone looks towards the imaginary money.

Janitor: 'Yiz f**kin heard that!'

Overheard by John, Ballyfermot College
Posted on Sunday, 18 December 2005

Sick bus?

Man to bus driver: 'Is this bus going to the Mater Hospital?'

Bus driver: 'Well, I dunno, it was fine when I took it ourra da garage dis morning ...'

Overheard by Nicantuile, Chapelizod, Dublin
Posted on Saturday, 17 December 2005

Everyday Luas talk

On the Luas a group of 15–16 year old boys coming from school got on at Bluebell. One of them complained to his mates that his girlfriend had dumped him the night before by text! Highly indignant at this insult he said he was better off without her anyway; all she was doing was costing him money. He went on to detail all the money he had spent on her, bringing her out and buying her presents.

'I must have spent at least €400 on her,' he announced to his mates, at which one of them piped up, 'Jaysus for that kind of money I'll be your girlfriend.'

Overheard by Anonymous, Luas to Tallaght
Posted on Monday, 12 December 2005

Viva le euros

While at the bureau de change in the Bank of Ireland this old lady in front of me went to the counter and said to the girl behind the desk, 'Hello love, I'm going to France this weekend so I just want to change my Irish euros into French euros.'

Overheard by Sean, Bank of Ireland, Tallaght
Posted on Thursday, 8 December 2005

Is there a doctor in the house?

In the Omniplex a while back, a particularly boring bit of the movie was on, when a cry came from the dark.

Shadow at the front (shouting): 'Anyone! Is there

a doctor here? Is there a doctor here?'

(Shock. Confusion.)

Voice from the back: 'Here, I'm a doctor.'

Voice from the front: 'Sh*te film, isn't it?' ... and sat back down.

Voice from the back: 'Little bastard, if I find ya I'll rattle ya.'

Overheard by YoYoBoy, Santry Cinema
Posted on Sunday, 5 December 2005

A delicate legal matter

In Court No. 4 at the Four Courts, a woman who alleged a serious verbal assault was in the witness box, and was asked by defence counsel,'Can you tell the court what the defendant said?'

Woman: 'I'm a respectable woman; I couldn't possibly say those words in public.'

Kindly judge: 'Perhaps it might preserve everyone's dignity if the witness wrote the alleged word on a piece of paper.'

Having been given the piece of paper and a pen, the woman still appeared to be in difficulty, and the judge intervened to ask her, 'Is everything alright?'

To which the redoubtable Dublin woman replied, 'Is there one or two 'l's in bollix?'

Overheard by Gary, Court No. 4 at the Four Courts
Posted on Saturday, 4 December 2005

Sound as a euro

Man shouts over to elderly woman in a bar in Ballyfermot, 'How's it going there, Patsy, keeping well?' to which the woman replied loudly,

'Sound as a euro, sound as a euro.'

Overheard by Anna, Ballyfermot
Posted on Saturday, 4 December 2005

French literature for dummies

On the way home from work on the no. 46A bus. It's packed, it's hot and everyone is well and truly pissed off (including the driver). The UCD stop comes up and the bell rings. Then the bell rings again and again and again and again. Obviously each person getting off thought they were the first to do it. Suddenly the bus driver slams on the brakes, turns on the intercom and roars at the entire bus …

'Will yis stop ringing the bleedin' bell, who the f**k do yis think I am? I'm not f**kin Quasimodo!'

Overheard by Jessica, on the no. 46A bus
Posted on Saturday, 4 December 2005

AIB security doors – fit for a prison!

Withdrawing money at the AIB bank in Tallaght. On the way out there was a bit of a queue due to the new doors they've installed. They're automatic and take a while to open. People were getting a bit annoyed with the slowness of the doors. One bloke in pure Dublin wit said,

'You'd get outta Mountjoy quicker than yed get outta heor!'

Overheard by Karl, Tallaght
Posted on Friday, 2 December 2005

Spec Savers

At a wedding last Friday night and it was the best man's speech. He says, 'These are the loveliest bridesmaids I've ever seen, just gorgeous.'

Someone shouts out from the crowd, 'Ya should have gone to Spec Savers!'

Overheard by Vikki, at a wedding in Killiney
Posted on Monday, 28 November 2005

So that's how the elite runners always win ...

Running the Dublin City Marathon a couple of weeks back. Running up the North Circular Road, which was closed to all road traffic while the marathon was going through, we went through a series of traffic lights (obviously redundant while the race was in progress) around Doyle's Corner. Smartarse behind me:

'Jaysus, I'd be winning if it weren't for all these feckin' red lights!'

Overheard by Gary, on the Marathon
Posted on Tuesday, 15 November 2005

No age barrier

Overheard two elderly ladies on the no. 2 bus discussing the drug problem in Dublin:

Mary: 'Jaysus, Josie, aren't them drugs terrible?'

Josie: 'Mary, if it wasn't for the Valium, I'd be on drugs meself.'

Overheard by Mark, no. 2 bus
Posted on Saturday, 5 November 2005

You don't have to go home but you can't stay here!

While in Slattery's pub in Rathmines for a few, I noticed a drunken old man hunched over the bar. As the evening went on he got more gargled and even more noisy! Eventually the barman told him to go home and helped him to the door. As he was leaving, he turned and told the barman politely to 'f**k off!' and that he had plenty of other pubs where he could go. Then he left.

All was quiet again for about five minutes when the old codger burst through the side door and stumbled up to the bar. The barman looks at him and says, 'I already told you to go home!'

The oul fella looks at him and while scratching his head in typical oul fogey fashion replies,

'Do you work in every f**kin pub in this town or wat?'

Overheard by Anonymous, Slattery's (Rathmines)
Posted on Thursday, 3 November 2005

Who's the idiot?

Two students talking on the top deck of the no. 3 bus this morning. One, still drunk from the night before, sees a Garda directing traffic.

'Look at that idiot of a guard standing in the road wavin' at cars.'

Overheard by Busman, no. 3 bus
Posted on Tuesday, 1 November 2005

I'm bleedin' crippled! But hey me appetite's good!

Was sitting in A&E in St James's Hospital and a doctor came to chat with the man on the trolley next to me. The doctor asked how he was and the man replied, 'I'm a bleedin' cripple, you let me out (of hospital) and now I'm a bleedin' cripple!'

The doctor could only tell him that he had signed himself out and he had been told not to walk on his legs. The man then proceeded to shout abuse and talk about filing a case. Then when the doctor asked how his wrist was, the man replied, 'Brand new, me wrist's fine.'

The doctor then asked how his appetite was, and the man replied, 'Me appetite's brand new, I love me appetite!'

Overheard by Daniel, St James's Hospital
Posted on Monday, 31 October 2005

No rats allowed!

A corporation tenant complaining to a maintenance foreman, 'I have rats in my house!'

Without blinking the foreman replied, 'Ma'am do you not know it's against the bylaws to keep pets?'

Overheard by Gerry, complaints hatch in Council depot
Posted on Monday, 31 October 2005

On the beat!

My friend, a trainee Ban Garda in Dublin, was called to a disturbance at a city centre pub. She encountered a drunken couple arguing. The following exchange took place after the husband pushed the wife:

Wife: 'Did you see that, you saw that, him pushing me an' all!'

Garda: 'Can we calm down a little and no I didn't see anything.'

Wife: 'Ye're all the f**king same in your fancy f**king uniforms, think yer're bloody brilliant, ya f**king b**ch!'

Husband: 'Don't take it out on her (pointing at the Garda's blue training badges), she's only bleeding training!'

Overheard by Jane, city centre pub
Posted on Sunday, 30 October 2005

It's not unusual

On the DART — terrible Monday morning in bleakest winter, driver makes an announcement about something or other and the drones going into work pay no attention.

The next minute we hear the DART driver singing, with great gusto, 'My my my DE-LI-LAAAH, ahhhhh why why WHY! DE-LI-LAAAh!'

He had forgotten to turn his mike off ... almost made going into work in a rain-storm feel OK.

Overheard by Joey, on the DART
Posted on Wednesday, 26 October 2005

The old Blanch injury

A friend of mine was doing her nursing placement in A&E at James Connolly Hospital in Blanchardstown when a bloke was rushed in covered in blood. Immediately a doctor was called to the scene to inspect the West Dublin patient.

Doc: 'Can you hear me? Where are you bleeding from?'

Injured bloke: 'I'm bleedin' from Blanch ...'

Overheard by Neill, James Connolly Hospital
Posted on Wednesday, 26 October 2005

It's a wok not a pan!

In Lees Kitchen in Dalkey one Friday night, a guy was asking the Chinese guy behind the counter for ribs. Even though the shop was packed, he kept shouting that he wanted ribs, and every time the Chinese guy kept saying, 'No ribs!' With a growing crowd behind him, the guy does a HUGE fart. In the stunned silence that followed for a second, the guy says dead proud,

'Coooook dah in your pan!'

Overheard by Dabuk, Lees Kitchen, Dalkey
Posted on Monday, 24 October 2005

Macker's house ...

I was on a plane over to London sitting in front of a youth soccer team. Just after the take off I overheard one of the young lads looking out the window saying,

'Here, Macker, I can see your house from here, I think it's on fire.'

Overheard by Noddy, Aer Lingus flight to London
Posted on Saturday, 22 October 2005

Any excuse for a pun!

Last Christmas, myself and pal buying our very first REAL Christmas trees for our respective new apartments. We were very excited and proud, and there before everyone else to get the pick of the bunch! After much deliberation we picked out two enormous trees, and as we struggled to get them to the check-out counter, dragging them behind us with difficulty but pride, we heard a broad Dublin accent shout from behind us:

'Jaysis, branchin' out are yis, girls?'

Overheard by Jess, B&Q, Liffey Valley
Posted on Thursday, 13 October 2005

Eyes in me arse

Got on a no. 42 bus heading from Artane to the city. There was a newspaper on the seat and I was too lazy to move it so I sat on it. A fella gets on at the next stop and sits in the seat across from me:

'Are ya readin dat paper yur sittin on?'

Only in Dublin.

Overheard by Owen, no. 42 bus in Artane
Posted on Friday, 7 October 2005

It's not just on Father Ted

Took my English husband to Dublin. Two lads were weaving down the road and one loudly said to the other, 'He has always been a fecking eejit!' My husband roared and said, 'They really do say fecking eejit over here!'

Overheard by Liz, O'Connell Street
Posted on Friday, 7 October 2005

A smack of a lorry

Supermarket checkout. Little old lady buying 30 cans of cat food.

Old lady to checkout girl: 'I have three lovely cats. They are great company for me. I don't know where I would be without them.'

Checkout girl: 'Yeah. I had a cat once but he got a smack of a lorry and that was the end of that.'

Little old lady leaves hurriedly with her mouth still hanging open.

Overheard by ljr, Superquinn Sundrive
Posted on Thursday, 6 October 2005

Loo-azz or Luas

Upon arrival at Heuston Station, having just stepped off the Limerick/Dublin train, I overheard a girl ask a lady where the Luas was.

'They're over there beside the men's Loo-aaz,' she replied, pointing at the ladies toilets.

Hmmm …

Overheard by brian, Heuston Station
Posted on Wednesday, 5 October 2005

Say it slowly

In a restaurant with my kids, food arrives and my eldest girl (four years old at the time) says out loud something that sounds like, 'Where is my f**king knife', to which my wife and I turn around in astonishment and stare at her.

'What did you say?' I ask in shock.

Slowly she says, 'Where is my FORK and knife?'

Overheard by stephen, in restaurant
Posted on Wednesday, 5 October 2005

Soup anyone?

Was at Lansdowne Road for an Ireland game recently, when a guy behind me shouted at one of the soup-selling guys in the red boiler suits, 'Hey bud, have ya any soup left?' At that point the guy turned around and said yeah, and started to walk up towards the man. Then as the terrace was silent he says,

'Serves ya right for making too much of it!'

Classic stuff!

Overheard by Darren, Lansdowne Road
Posted on Sunday, 2 October 2005

Onions all wrapped up

Christmas Eve, 2004, small friendly supermarket in Dalkey.

Struggling holiday temp on checkout: 'What do I ring through the wrapping paper on?'

Exasperated colleague, clearly for the hundredth time: 'Scallions!'

Overheard by maevesther, Dalkey
Posted on Saturday, 1 October 2005

You tool ...

I'll set the scene. It's last period on a Friday afternoon. We're doing Metalwork theory. Everyone wishes they were somewhere else. The teacher mentions the 'bastard file' and everyone erupts into a fit of the giggles. After a five second pause, the teacher says:

'Lads, there are many humorous phrases in

engineering: "bastard file", "bitch callipers".
Laugh now, and laugh hard, because by God you
have to get them out of your system.'

Overheard by Paulie, Metalwork class
Posted on Friday, 23 September 2005

Contagious disease

Picture this. Swimming pool, south west Dublin.
All kids queuing up to have their showers after
swimming lessons, eagerly chatting away to each
other about their upcoming Holy Communion.

Tallaght girl asks quiet child beside her, 'When
are you making yer communion?'

Child answers: 'I can't, I'm Muslim.'

Tallaght child answers: 'Don't worry I had 'em
last week, you only break out in spots for a few
days, sure you'll be better in no time.'

Overheard by Margaret, Balrothery swimming pool, Tallaght
Posted on Tuesday, 20 September 2005

Hope he spares her

I heard an old lady on a bus tell her friend, 'If
God spares me I'll be buried in Balbriggan.'

Overheard by Anonymous, on no. 19 bus
Posted on Thursday, 8 September 2005

Honest Irish

I was standing outside a south Dublin pub with
random regulars. The lounge girl on duty came
out for a quick fag break. One elderly man

looked over towards her and said, 'You shouldn't be smoking, luv, it ruins your skin.' The girl nodded in agreement and smiled. The man spoke again: 'Ruin your skin you will and you have a lovely fat face.'

Overheard by Paddy, pub in Donnybrook
Posted on Tuesday, 6 September 2005

Decent bus driver

I was getting off the bus one day and I thanked the bus driver as he was letting me off and he replies, 'It's alright, I was going this way anyway.'

Cheeky bastard.

Overheard by Kate, no. 48A bus
Posted on Tuesday, 30 August 2005

Sauce

While queuing in McDonald's one afternoon I overheard the lad in front placing his order which went, 'Chicken nuggets an' a large coke, please.'

The girl behind the counter responded, 'What sauce would you like with the nuggets?'

'Ehhhh, what have you?'

The girl went on to list various dips. 'We have barbecue sauce, curry sauce, sweet and sour sauce, garlic mayonnaise …'

To which the lad interrupted, 'Ehhhhh … red.'

Overheard by J, McDonald's, Phibsboro
Posted on Tuesday, 30 August 2005

How far is that?

Standing at a pedestrian light in the city centre I was queried by a confused looking American tourist who was pointing at the large real-time car park information board.

'How far is that?'

'Sorry?' I says.

Then he says a little more exasperated, wagging his digit at the sign again, 'Christ Church, 136 spaces — how far is that?'

Overheard by Derro, city centre
Posted on Monday, 29 August 2005

More cinema exploits

Whilst watching the movie 'The Last of the Mohicans' in the Savoy many years ago. Daniel Day Lewis is just about to jump off the waterfall and turns to his girl and says, 'I will be back.' A young fella at the back of the cinema shouts: 'Good man Christie!'

The whole cinema exploded with laughter and the moment was ruined for the movie.

Overheard by Anonymous, Savoy
Posted on Monday, 29 August 2005

Directions

One evening I was sitting on a bus going to Rathmines to meet a few friends. A few rows in front of me there were two Spanish girls who were a little flustered. One girl turns to a young lad sitting on the row opposite her and says,

'Excuse me, are you Irish?'

He replies, 'Yes.'

'Can you tell me where to get off the bus for Rathmines, please?' she asks.

Clueless, he answers, in a strong American accent, 'Sorry, I'm only half Irish!'

Overheard by Legend, on a bus to Rathmines
Posted on Monday, 29 August 2005

Sometimes it's best just to smile and nod

While working in a heritage centre as a Viking re-enactor, an American tourist asked, 'Do you have reservations for your Vikings like we do for our Indians?'

Needless to say I was stumped.

Overheard by Saoirse, Heritage Centre
Posted on Saturday, 27 August 2005

Quick cyclist

My sister was standing on the Canal bridge on Phibsboro Road, holding her shoe in her hand (the heel had come off). A young Dublin lad cycling along looked at her and without missing a beat says,

'Eh! Howiya Cinderella!'

Overheard by Barry, Phibsboro
Posted on Friday, 26 August 2005

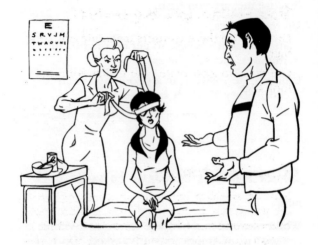

Comic relief

Nurse bandaged up an anxious young woman's injured eye, assuring her it would heal completely, given rest. Her boyfriend broke the tension by asking,

'When does she get the parrot?'

Overheard by Sinéad, in the A&E department
of the Eye and Ear Hospital
Posted on Thursday, 25 August 2005

Sedation

A mother talking to her young child who was running amuck in Topshop:

'Get off the floor for f**k's sake, you should of come with a sedative!'

Overheard by Jackie, Liffey Valley Shopping Centre
Posted on Thursday, 25 August 2005

Does my bum look big in this?

Girl #1: 'Do these trousers make my arse look big?'

Girl #2: 'No, chocolate cake makes your arse look big!'

Overheard by Rob, on the Luas
Posted on Thursday, 25 August 2005

Planning a robbery?

Noticed two 'head-de-balls' approaching me in the street, one in animated conversation, the other listening attentively. Next the speaker stops and puts down his Champion Sports bag, the better to describe something to his friend. All I could glean as I passed was,

'And dere's a gap of about dis much between de counter and de safe ...'

Overheard by Stephen, O'Connell Street
Posted on Wednesday, 24 August 2005

The root cause of bad Irish weather

My Dad was in the barbers in Stillorgan a couple of months ago. He mentioned to the barber that the weather had been terrible recently. The barber replied,

'Must be all this globalisation.'

Overheard by Deirdre, barber shop in Stillorgan
Posted on Tuesday, 23 August 2005

Wow! Window goes up, window goes down, window goes up, window ...

Couple of years ago on a rare sunny Irish day, two of my friends broke down in Glasnevin. Next thing a Garda car pulls up. Seeing as two young lads were driving a Range Rover, they were a bit suspicious.

Garda #1: 'What's goin on here, lads?'

Boy #1: 'We ran out of petrol.'

Garda #1: 'This your car?'

Boy #1: 'No, it's my mum's and yes, she knows I'm out in it.' Then the Garda starts walking around the car checking it out when he sees the back window.

Garda #1: 'What happened here, lads?' The two lads look a bit confused.

Garda #1: 'The back window. It's gone. What did ye do to it?'

Boy #1: 'Eh, nothing, it's electric.'

Garda #2: ?????? So one of the lads shows the Garda how the back window goes up and down.

Garda #1: (Shouts to Garda car) 'Jaysus, Paddy, get outta the car and look at this! Jaysus, lads, that's f**kin brilliant! Right, come on now and we'll get ye some petrol!'

Overheard by Ali, Glasnevin
Posted on Tuesday, 23 August 2005

Long way around

I was listening to the 'Adrian Kennedy Phoneshow' one night and they were talking about people who didn't ever want children. One woman came on the show and said,

'I swear to God, Adrian, if I ever got pregnant I'd swim the Atlantic Ocean to England to get rid of it.'

Amazingly, no one pointed out to her what she'd said!

Overheard by Emma, on the radio
Posted on Tuesday, 23 August 2005

Hospital food

Was in a Dublin hospital in the early hours. A drunk was sitting beside me. When he was called to the counter, presumably the nurse/receptionist asked him personal details such as name, address, etc., to which he replied,

'Batter burger and chips, luv, I've been waiting for f**king ages.'

Overheard by Michael, Mater Hospital
Posted on 23 August 2005

Wife's hairdryer

I was in a Chinese take-away in Phibsboro after the pubs closed. There were the usual drunken racist remarks from a few lads in front of me. Then one of them asked the Chinese man behind the counter where he was from. The man replied that he was from Hong Kong, to which the other guy replied,

'That's a coincidence … my wife's hairdryer is from Hong Kong!'

Overheard by Greg, Phibsboro
Posted on Tuesday, 23 August 2005

Ice-cream, sir?

Whilst working in the ice-cream stall in Stephen's Green Shopping Centre, I was greeted by a rather plump man with a moustache, copious amounts of gold jewellery and a Dublin top.

Me: 'Ice-cream, sir?'

Dub: 'Yeah, cheers Bud, oide loike a plain one.'

Me: 'Vanilla?'

Dub: 'Did you not hear me or sumtin? I said I want a plain!'

I didn't stay too long in the job after that …

Overheard by James, St Stephen's Green
Posted on Tuesday, 23 August 2005

O.J., OK

Little girl in Tesco in Mount Merrion.

Little girl: 'Daddy, can we get some O.J.?'

Daddy: 'We have plenty of O.J. at home.'

Little girl: 'Can we get "Apple" O.J.?'

Overheard by David, Tesco in Mount Merrion
Posted on Tuesday, 23 August 2005

Vaccinate

A father and child came into a hospital emergency department and while giving details to the receptionist about the boy's dog bite the receptionist asked the father, 'Is he up to date with his vaccinations?'

The father replied, 'Jaysus, I don't know, I'll have to ring my next door neighbour.'

The receptionist asked, 'Why your neighbour?'

The father replied, 'Cos she owns the f**king dog.'

Overheard by Paul, St James's Hospital
Posted on Monday, 22 August 2005

Rules made in Ireland

I was in the bus station when I overheard a tourist enquiring about a bus that went to Limerick. She had got a timetable off the Internet that said the bus stopped in Kildare, her destination.

The helpful lady behind the enquiries desk said, 'Ah no, that's wrong, the Limerick bus only picks up passengers in Kildare and it does not drop off passengers.'

To which the tourist said, 'Run that by me again, it does a pick up but no drop off,' to which the reply was,

'That's right, but you could chance your arm with the driver and see if he'll drop you off.'

Overheard by Mary Maloney, Busaras
Posted on Sunday, 21 August 2005

Clarification

I was on one of the no. 41s heading out to the airport (upper deck, bus was packed). A guy answers his phone and within seconds he begins a heated argument with the caller. It gets to the point where he's shouting, exclaiming that he is 'innocent', that he is 'not cheating' and he's 'on the bus out to Swords'.

He grows tired of his partner's accusations, jumps up out of his seat and turns to shout at the entire upper floor, 'My girlfriend on the other end thinks I'm cheating behind her back, everyone say hello!'

Everyone — 'HELLLOOOOO!'

He shouts back into the phone, 'Now are ya f**king happy!?' and hangs up.

Overheard by Martin, no. 41 bus
Posted on Sunday, 21 August 2005

Irish film

I was in the UCI Coolock to see a film recently and when the censor's cert came on some young wan at the front says to her mates, 'Aw jaysus it's in bleedin Irish!'

Overheard by Kenny, UCI Coolock
Posted on Sunday, 21 August 2005

'WHERE IS HE?'

A couple of weeks ago, at an amateur panto, the guy on stage is doing the whole 'HE'S BEHIND YOU' bit. On asking the audience for the last time, 'WHERE IS HE?', a child of no more than seven shouts from the front row,

'He's behind you, ya f**kin b*ll*x!'

Overheard by Gill, Stillorgan
Posted on Sunday, 21 August 2005

He obviously forgot where he was

Whilst travelling on the rush hour Luas line recently, a man's phone began to ring. Man answers loudly,

'Howaya Sharon … yea, yea, on the Luas now … what's for dinner this evening … lasagne … oh lovely … what time will I call over …I'll see you at 6 o'clock so … OK I'll see you later, Sweet Tits! … bye.'

Overheard by Sean, on the Luas
Posted on Sunday, 21 August 2005

Pub grub

Around 1990, mid-afternoon in an old-fashioned bar off O'Connell Street. The owner resents drinkers asking for food, but provides pretty basic sandwiches under duress. An American visitor comes in and asks him for a glass of stout and something to eat. As the owner starts to pull the Guinness, he calls down to the barman at the other end of the (long) bar,

'Hey, Christy, will ye stop scratchin' yer arse there and make this man a sandwich!'

Overheard by Anonymous, the Something Inn
Posted on Sunday, 21 August 2005

Chipper slash emergency

Myself and my wife were in town late Wednesday night and decided to pop into Leo Burdock's for a fish supper on the way home. We parked the car, and proceeded to head towards the chipper. On the way a guy, obviously after a few 'gargles', came running past us in the opposite direction, to which we took no notice. Having installed ourselves in the queue, the same guy re-appeared, duly re-took his place in the queue just ahead of us, and said, 'Jaysus, tanks a million, I had to pop off for a slash ...'

Overheard by Gav, Leo Burdock's
Posted on Sunday, 21 August 2005

Water safety Dublin style

Travelling on the DART from Howth to Connolly Station last winter one cloudy morning, approaching Raheny it started to rain heavily and the speed of the train caused the rain to blow in through an open window.

Woman in seat nearby: 'Oh quick quick close the window I am drowning!'

Male voice from down the carriage: 'Don't worry missus I'm a lifeguard.'

Overheard by Sean, on the DART
Posted on Saturday, 20 August 2005

Leppers?

Shortly after the smoking ban was introduced into Ireland, I was standing outside a pub having

a smoke when I overheard two aul' ones in conversation.

One said, 'Jaysus, this smoking ban is a pain in the arse.'

To which the other replied, 'I know, jaysus, we're like bleedin' leopards out here.'

Overheard by John, outside the A1, Ardlea Road
Posted on Saturday, 20 August 2005

Paradoxical law enforcement

My brother and his girlfriend had pulled over in their car, when a guard came along and tapped on the window:

'If you want to stay here,' he said, 'you better move along.'

Overheard by Leelaa, Pearse Street
Posted on Saturday, 20 August 2005

Baileys sans Irish cream

Two middle-aged American ladies standing at the bar: 'Any idea what you are goin to have?'

'I'm getting the Baileys Irish Cream.'

'Mmmmm can you order one for me too … without the cream.'

Overheard by L, The Temple Bar
Posted on Friday, 19 August 2005

Not religious?

One day my boss (who is a know-it-all) and I were discussing the new bottle of cleaning fluid he'd bought and he asked me what I thought the smell reminded me of. I said white spirits or something like that and he said,

'Oh I know that smell, it's the same stuff they used in the hospital when my daughter was born, to clean her after they cut her UN BIBLICAL cord.'

Overheard by kc, work
Posted on Friday, 19 August 2005

Euro changeover

When I was working in the Allsports café at the time of the euro changeover in Dublin, one of my colleagues had a unique way of asking customers if they wanted money changed from pounds to euro.

Customer arrives at the counter with Irish punts and he would ask,

'Would you like me to "euronate" that for you?'

Overheard by Julyan, Allsports café
Posted on Friday, 19 August 2005

You've got to admire him

I was standin' outside Farringtons havin' a smoke when a taxi was just about to pull away from Fitzsimons. These two English chicks ran to catch it, hailing …'TAXI! TAXI!' … to which the driver lowered his window and roared …'PASSENGER! PASSENGER!' … and drove off!

Overheard by Red, Temple Bar
Posted on Thursday, 18 August 2005

Never stop for a hoodie

Coming past Baker's Corner on the no. 46A, some kid in a hoodie broke into a run to catch the bus. The bus obligingly stopped, and the kid, instead of boarding, stands and asks, 'Are yeh goin' to Dun Laoghaire?' (As if this wasn't printed on the front, as if this wasn't a friggin' 46A coming back from town!)

The driver says yeah, and the kid says, 'That's great for you, Mister! Cause I'm not goin' there!' and runs off.

Overheard by Lee, no. 46A bus in Dun Laoghaire
Posted on Thursday, 18 August 2005

Americans

I was sitting on the Luas at the Four Courts Luas stop. Two American women sitting beside me. Out the window I saw two elderly gents, obviously barristers, horsehair wigs, long black gowns, briefcases, the lot, walking into the courts. One of the Americans pipes up,

'Oh look, they must be graduating!'

Overheard by Robbie, on the Luas
Posted on Thursday, 18 August 2005

Expensive service

In a café on Camden Street. Foreign couple walk in (obvious tourists — camera around neck, sandals with socks etc.) and ask the run-off-her-feet waitress, 'Can we smoke in here?', to which the girl replies,

'Of course you can but it will cost you a €3,000 service charge and you may or may not have to visit Mountjoy!'

The confused look on offending tourist's face was class!

Overheard by J, Café Sofia
Posted on Tuesday, 16 August 2005

Where do you want to have it?

Lad in front of me ordering his food, cashier asks him, 'Are you having it here?' Lad looks around and points down at an empty table,

'Nah, I'll have it over there if that's alright.'

Overheard by Theo, Burger King Coolock
Posted on Tuesday, 16 August 2005

A head fetish

Overheard on the no. 77A from town. Five excited kids get on at the Coombe.

'Come on! Upstairs, the front seat,' one of them shouts, 'We can look at the driver's head!'

Overheard by Johnner, The Coombe
Posted on Saturday, 13 August 2005

Give the child a name!

My sister's friend had a baby boy a couple of weeks ago. After the birth everyone was sitting around discussing the new arrival. The child's grandmother asked the parents what name they were thinking of giving the child.

Mother: 'We're probably going to name him Marc with a "c".'

Grandmother: 'CARK?!'

Overheard by Dermot, Stillorgan
Posted on Thursday, 11 August 2005

The Look of the draw

On the no. 65B bus on the way home. Two 'howyas' talking rather loudly. One girl said to the other, 'I'm after gettin me house.' The other girl replies, 'Bout bleedin time.' The first girl then says, 'Yeah, but no side entrance.' The second girl goes,

'Give tha back, no side entrance, that's takin the piss, how ya supposed to get your wheelie bin out!?'

Overheard by Barbara, no. 65B bus
Posted on Wednesday, 10 August 2005

The way to Amerilla

On the no. 19 bus the other day a young woman gets on with her 6-year-old daughter. After a while the little girl starts singing, 'Is this the way to Amerilo ...' The mother decides to join in, 'Every night I've been huggin' my pilla.' To which the young girl replies in flatist Dub accent,

'Jaysus, Ma, it's not "pilla" it's "pillow", you're real common, d'ya know tha!'

Overheard by Jen, no. 19 bus
Posted on Monday, 8 August 2005

Road rage?!

A taxi pulls out across the path of a car in traffic.
The car driver honks the horn at the taxi driver.
The taxi driver without batting an eyelid shouts
back at him,

'Ah, save yer horn for yer missus!'

Overheard by Ogmios, St Stephen's Green
Posted on Monday, 8 August 2005

What would you like to watch?

Sitting in UGC cinema during the trailers, an
advertisement for Sky Movies came on, talking
about all the movies you can watch. At the end
the voice-over on the ad says, 'WHAT WOULD
YOU LIKE TO WATCH?' to which some little
head-the-ball in front of me shouts at the screen,

'The bleedin film for f**k sake!'

Overheard by Kyra, UGC Cinema
Posted on Monday, 8 August 2005

Confession

One Saturday morning I was standing in a very
long queue in an electrical wholesalers. The
queue was out the door and literally following a
queuing system like that in the airport. Anyway,
this little old lady about 84 years joins the queue
behind me, sighs and says,

'Ah Jaysus! Only one priest on again.'

Overheard by Des, Dublin
Posted on Friday, 5 August 2005

Lamest Luas joke ever!

While waiting at the Luas stop at the Red Cow roundabout the Luas approaches from a distance in its customary snail-pace like fashion. Two impatient guys start criticising the speed of the tram.

One of the guys: 'Jaysus! It's no Carl LEWIS.'

Overheard by Paul, Red Cow Luas stop
Posted on Friday, 5 August 2005

Very affordable housing

I'm in the back of a car with my friends. The front-seat passenger is browsing through the property section of the *Irish Times*:

Driver: 'Did you read that about a fella buyin a parking space in an underground car park in town for 10 grand!?'

Front-seat passenger (thoughtfully): 'Cud ya build on it!?'

Overheard by Seany, in a car in Malahide
Posted on Thursday, 4 August 2005

Paki surprise

I brought an English friend to a Dublin versus Meath match. He's from London but is of Indian origin. As we were leaving the match a bunch of Hill16ers were coming towards us singing, 'I'd rather be a Paki than a royal, I'd rather be a Paki than a royal', by coincidence.

I realised with horror what would happen but it was too late. As they passed my 'Indian' friend they saw him and started to rub his hair and throw their arms around him, singing louder.

As they passed us by all you could hear was one fan shouting, 'That was f**king great ... we were singing about Pakis and then one arrived.'

Overheard, outside Croker by Shane
Posted on Wednesday, 3 August 2005

Bring on the harassment lawsuit ...

Coming up to the counter in McDonald's, I heard the middle-aged manager say to the tired-looking girl sweeping the floor: 'Go on, sweep me off my feet.'

I had to bite my lip ...

Overheard by Anonymous, McDonald's, Blackrock
Posted on Wednesday, 3 August 2005

The effort a Dub will go to ...

Travelling on the no. 79 bus from Ballyfermot into town, we got stuck in mad traffic along the quays. There were two young lads sitting a few seats in front of me on the upper deck. One of the lads looks out the window and spots someone they know walking on the footpath on the other side of the Liffey. He says aloud to his pal, 'Loook — it's bleedin' Anto.'

The lad jumps up on the seat and opens the window (the old slidey type) and for the next few minutes roars as loud as he can, 'ANTO, ANTO, AAAANNNTO!'

Finally, Anto hears them and looks over. To which he continues, 'YOU'RE ONLY A LITTLE BOLLIX!'

Overheard by Max, no. 79 bus
Posted on Wednesday, 3 August 2005

Sorry, no exchanges or refunds

Going into the Coombe with my older sister, helping her carry her 2-month-old daughter who was asleep in one of those car seats with the handle, and this Dub who was outside having a smoke looks me in the eye and says,

'Ahh here bud, you can't give them back you know!'

Overheard by Mick, front steps of the Coombe Hospital
Posted on Wednesday, 3 August 2005

Drink responsibly ...

Myself and a couple of friends were waiting for one of the buses in the centre of Dublin that were organised to take people going to the Oxegen music festival last month. There were Gardaí at the stops making sure the queues didn't get out of hand.

Anyway, everyone there seemed to be carrying crates of beer and such in the hope of smuggling them into the concert area, when this country lad carrying a huge crate of Dutch Gold turns around as he was entering one of the buses that had just arrived and shouts to one of the Guards (clearly happy he's able to flout the anti-public drinking laws),

'Hoi, Guard, just off to do some major binge drinkin', ya know yourself,' followed by a grin and a wink, and soon after followed by nasty frowns by all the Gardaí present.

Overheard by Jim, off O'Connell Street
Posted on Wednesday, 3 August 2005

Beatle with curry sauce, please

After getting their curry off the local curry-shop owner, Ringo, nearly every oul' fella — full of gargle — says,

'Cheers, Ringo, you're a star!'

Overheard by Derek, most weekends in Ballyfermot
Posted on Wednesday, 3 August 2005

Culture vultures

A while back, when the James Joyce bridge (the one down near Guinness) on the Liffey was only opened after about 200 years in the process, I was going by on the bus, half listening to the chitchat. Two oul' ones in front were admiring the bridge.

One says to the other: 'Isn't it gorgeous all the same. It's just like that bridge in Sydney ...'

Exactly like it, if you ask me.

Overheard by Derek, on the no. 79 bus on the quays
Posted on Wednesday, 3 August 2005

A Dublin emergency

I work in a pharmacy and we get many strange incidents but this one tops them all. A 15-year-old lad comes running in one morning looking rushed and out of breath. So I'm thinking, emergency, first aid needed, or he needs an inhaler.

Runs up to counter: 'Do ya sell stationery?' I check to see if I heard him correctly: 'Em sorry this is a pharmacy.' To which he replies,

'Is there nowhere in this f**kin city that sells a rooooler at noyen a clak in da mornin?!'

Overheard by John, at work on O'Connell Street
Posted on Tuesday, 2 August 2005

Everyone has their breaking point

One day walking down our main thoroughfare past the bus-stops outside the BOI, the crowds were heavy. Some girl with a thick Dublin accent, of about 18 or 19, was waiting for her bus. People must have been brushing off her and bumping into her on their way past, for all of a sudden, from out of the general din of the crowd she shouted out to the anonymous pedestrians,

'The next person who bumps into me's gonna get a f**kin diiig!'

Only in Dublin.

Overheard by Kevin, O'Connell Street
Posted on Monday, 1 August 2005

The wrong road to Tallaght

On the Luas to Ranelagh, Friday night around 11. Guy who's totally off his head and mumbling general abuse to all the young ladies around him suddenly bursts out with a tuneless homage to John Denver:

'Country road! Take me home!

To the place where I go!

Tallafornia! [incomprehensible]

Country road, country road!'

Overheard by mojo, the Green Line Luas
(to Ranelagh, not Tallaght)
Posted on Saturday, 30 July 2005

Howaya, Guard

Myself and three of my friends were sitting in my car, just having a laugh, listening to music. When out of nowhere two Gardaí appeared, one at each side of the car (obviously they thought we were up to something). I rolled down the driver window and the Garda said:

'Howaya lads, we're the Guards,' to which my friend could only reply,

'Howaya Guards, we're the lads!'

Overheard by Janey Mac, in my car
Posted on Friday, 29 July 2005

Chicken wings

Guy: 'Do you have any chicken wings there love?'

Girl behind counter: 'Yes.'

Guy: 'Then fly over there and get us a burger will ya.'

Overheard by Mark, Super Macs, O'Connell Street
Posted on Friday, 29 July 2005

Inspiring words

After finishing a match some years ago I decided to stick around to watch another. Standing on the sideline in amongst the locals the match was tight and coming up to the final whistle. One of the players 'Willie' was chasing his marker to win the ball. Cue an over-excited manager shouting at the top of his voice,

'GO ON WILLIE GET UP HIS ARSE!'

Both sidelines erupt into fits of laughter as the play continues on but the manager's face turns a very bright crimson after realising what he had said.

It was lost on some of the younger supporters ... just as well really.

Overheard by Deano, Malahide Castle
Posted on Thursday, 28 July 2005

Bargain Town

Sitting on the no. 39 going into town, two brothers, guessing about seven or eight, hop on with their ma and sit down the back. One of them starts singing the 'bargain town' theme off the radio, 'Hurry on down to bargain town!' again and again. He had a pretty rough accent but strains to make 'town' sound like the radio, more and more each time.

The elder brother goes, 'Will ye shurrup! Yer wreckin' me head! It's "taown"!'

'Hurry on down to bargain town!'

'It's "taowin"!'

'Hurry on down to bargain town!'

'It's "taowin"!'

'Hurry on down to bargain town!'

'F**ksake, ma, will ya tell him, it's "taowin"!'

'Stop annoyin' yer brother. It's "taown".'

'Hurry on down to bargain town!'

Slap! Tears.

Overheard by Anonymous, sitting on the no. 39 bus going into town
Posted on Thursday, 28 July 2005

There's always one

Back in '97 I was in the Ambassador cinema, as it was then, watching the film of the moment, 'Titanic'. We were at the scene where one of the lifeboats returns to the masses of floating bodies, searching for survivors. Everyone of course was very quiet and subdued at this poignant moment, holding their breath for a reply as the officer manning the boat called, 'Is anyone alive out there?'

A guy (real Dub!) up the balcony of the cinema just couldn't bear to leave this question unanswered, and so breaking the dead silence pipes up, 'Over here!' at the top of his lungs.

The whole place erupted! It certainly was worth sitting through the whole three hours for that — there's always one!

Overheard by Aoife, Ambassador Cinema

Posted on Thursday, 28 July 2005

Knickers

In Dunnes Stores underwear department. My sister's boyfriend holds up a pair of knickers and shouts all over the shop,

'Hey, Nora, I see your knickers are coming down in the sale.'

Overheard by Robert, in Dunnes Stores underwear department

Posted on Thursday, 28 July 2005

No love on the line

While queuing in the GPO, I was standing behind a very well dressed gentleman in a suit. The queue line was all over the place and a lady in an equally flamboyant dress pushed in, in front of him. The two started arguing and it almost came to fisticuffs.

In behind the fortified counter the An Post guy winks at me and starts singing and waving his arms above his head from side to side (à la John Lennon):

'And all we are saaaaaying, is give peace a chaaaance ...'

Overheard by Big Gaz, GPO

Posted on Wednesday, 27 July 2005

Fore!

I was sitting on the bus when it pulled up at a stop just outside a public golf course. The doors opened and two fellas threw the golf bags over their shoulders and climbed on to the bus.

'Didn't see it comin' in here lads,' said the driver.

Wasted behind a wheel, I thought to myself!

Overheard by Brian, lower deck of the no. 42 bus
Posted on Wednesday, 27 July 2005

The innocence of a wee one

I was flying into Dublin a few weeks back and we were coming into land. There was pretty much silence on the plane as we were descending. Only the voice of an innocent, young child can be heard. Real excited:

'Yay, we're going to land. Yay, Mammy, we're going to land. Yay, we're going to land. Yay!' (That may not be verbatim, but you get the picture. A giddy child, excited about the plane landing.) Everyone around has a nice little smile, while listening to the happy child.

Just as we are about to hit the tarmac there was a few bounces and a slight struggle to keep control of the plane. Nothing too drastic, but enough for you to instinctively grab the back of the chair in front.

Next thing the same little child, now panicked, is squealing: 'No, Mammy, I don't like it. I've changed my mind. I don't like landing. I don't like. NO! I don't, it's not nice! AAarrrgggghhh!'

It probably was scaring the child, but all on the plane just burst out laughing ...

Overheard by Hungover Child, Ryanair flight coming into land in Dublin Airport
Posted on Tuesday, 26 July 2005

Not from the barrel of a gun

I was waiting for a no. 34 bus in Church Street listening to two old biddies — a long time ago before all but three births per year were to single mothers.

'D'ya see the Foleys' youngest is after gettin married?'

'Gaway, tha was quick, was she pregnant or what?'

'Naa, don't think so.'

'Jayz, there's posh for ya.'

Overheard by Brian, Church Street bus stop
Posted on Monday, 25 July 2005

Don't we all ...

Man in Eddie Rocket's restaurant at 3 a.m., holding on to the counter, intoxicated, proclaiming, 'I love eating, I love it. I love eating ...'

Overheard by Jim, Eddie Rocket's, Dame Street
Posted on Monday, 25 July 2005

Maybe he was really hungry?

On the no. 49 bus going out of town the other night, a pissed aul fella (he had wicked eyebrows, but that's another story) gets on and sits across from a young lad. Nothing unusual till the old man leans over towards the young bloke and slurs,

'Here lad ... do you know the ingredients of soda bread?'

Overheard by GCW, on the no. 49 bus
Posted on Sunday, 24 July 2005

A quite packed Luas ...

Packed sardine-can-like Luas, in the silence of it, one lad shouts out to whoever ... Tony it might have been,

'HEY TONY WHAT'S YOUR FAVOURITE HUMMING NOISE!'

The silent laughter around the Luas is brilliant!

Overheard by Bucky, on the Luas, Connolly Station line
Posted on Saturday, 23 July 2005

Choo choo sardines

I decided to take an extremely crowded Luas
tram to Connolly to head for Croke Park for the
Dublin versus Wexford match. With the Luas
packed to capacity, it pulled up to the Red Cow
roundabout, doors opened, and with that some
smart-arse shouts to the unsuspecting
passengers on the platform,

'Come on, hop on the Bangladeshi express!'

Overheard by Ray, Luas tram
Posted on Friday, 22 July 2005

What every culchie dreads hearing ...

On their way to the Leinster football final last
Sunday, a bunch of lads in Laois jerseys were
walking up Clonliffe Road, trailed by a bunch of
lads in Dublin jerseys. The Dublin lads were
messing around, taunting and jeering the
'culchies'.

A worried flush rose on the back of the Laois
lads' necks when the Dubs started singing, 'We
saw where you parked your car, doo-dah, doo-
dah!'

Overheard by Flan, outside Croke Park
Posted on Friday, 22 July 2005

Dublin barmen ... aren't they great!

Sitting in Mulligans pub on Poolbeg Street
having a pint at the bar, when a Yank came up
and said to the barman, 'Excuse me sir, where is
your bathroom?'

So the barman gave him directions and off went the Yank. A few minutes later the Yank returns and says to the barman, 'Excuse me sir, there's no lock on the door.'

The barman replied without looking up from the pint of Guinness he was pulling, 'As long as I've been here, no one ever tried to rob a shite.'

Overheard by Butty, Mulligans pub

Posted on Friday, 22 July 2005

Dublin Bus ... serving the ENTIRE community a piece of their mind!

A pleasant summer evening, on the lower deck of the no. 90 bus, which is about half full of locals/tourists/culchies.

We're coming up the quays from Heuston Station towards town when the driver slams on the brakes. The whole bus lurches to the right, as a car has driven across its path. Everyone is shocked/startled and silent at this.

The next thing we hear is the bus driver leaning out the window bellowing at the top of his lungs.

'F**KIN' foreigners!'

The whole bus, foreigners and all, erupted in laughter.

Overheard by John, on the no. 90 route to Connolly Station

Posted on Thursday, 21 July 2005

THE LEGS!

One sunny afternoon in Phoenix Park a mate of mine had to relieve himself. He found a quiet spot and attended to nature. Moments later a muppet-mobile (you know the drill, six muppets crammed into an old Toyota Starlet) comes around the corner. The windows lower, standard head-the-ball sticks his head out and roars, 'Heeeere you … with THE LEGS!' and the mobile speeds off.

My mate (bewildered by this stage) stands there confirming, 'Yes, I have legs. Well spotted.'

Overheard by Leno, Phoenix Park
Posted on Thursday, 21 July 2005

Jayo!

Was in the Temple Bar on Dorset Street after a Dublin match, when a Chinese fella in a Dublin jersey crossed the road in front of the jammed pub. With no prompting the whole pub started chanting 'Jayo, Jayo, Jayo' in unison. Obviously the Chinese fella was scarlet and turned a bright shade of red but still managed to raise his arm and acknowledge the crowd and everyone fell about laughing.

Class.

Overheard by D, Temple Bar, Dorset Street
Posted on Wednesday, 20 July 2005

Someone didn't learn their spellings!

I was coming home from college last November, on the no. 65B. As I got upstairs I got a real strong smell of hash! I saw a group of 14-year-old skanger lads sitting at the back talking and smoking away! One lad walked up and said, 'I'm gonna write "JOINT" on the window,' as they were fogged up!

In true skanger style he wrote 'GIANT'. Nice to know that being high didn't affect his ability to spell!

Overheard by Stephen, over the M50, Tallaght

Posted on Tuesday, 19 July 2005

Well, that's alright so!

I was down in the courts recently for work. We were waiting for our case to be heard and had to listen to several young lads who were up for drink driving, theft etc. There was this young lad in particular who stood out; he had smashed up a few cars in a rage and the following was his defence!

Judge: 'So, can you tell me why you smashed up the three cars?'

Lad: 'Coz some bleedin foreigner upset me girlfriend.'

Judge: 'What had that got to do with the owners of the three cars? What had they done to upset you?'

Lad: 'Well, yer man ran off so I couldn't get him.'

Judge: 'So you took it out on the owners of the cars?'

Lad: 'Well I was bleedin mad wasn't I?'

Judge: 'So you just lash out when you're angry?'

Lad: 'No, judge, I don't.'

Judge: 'But you just said you lashed out because you were mad.'

Lad: 'Yeah, but I don't usually.'

Judge: 'So why did you this time?'

Lad: 'Cause I was off me bleedin head wasn't I?'

Overheard by Nuls, in the Four Courts
Posted on Tuesday, 19 July 2005

Fire safety

Our Fire Safety warden at work sent around a survey of what we would do in case of a fire.

One of the questions was, 'What steps would you take if you discovered a fire?'

Some witty so-and-so replied, 'Very big ones.'

Overheard by Andy K, the office
Posted on Monday, 18 July 2005

Face paint issues

Drinking and dancing in Flannagans last Saturday night, I went to the toilet and there was lots of chatting and yapping going on like usually in the ladies. Then suddenly this chick comes out with,

'There is only one problem: I don't have my eyebrow pencil with me!'

The problems that can arise on a night out …

Overheard by Kim, Flannagans pub
Posted on Thursday, 14 July 2005

How romantic …

Old guy in a printshop in Dundrum discussing the new receptionist:

66

'Jaysus, I'd crawl through a mile of glass just to throw stones at her shite.'

Overheard by Mark, Dundrum
Posted on Thursday, 14 July 2005

Holy God!

At my yearly visit to church on Christmas Day. The family in front of me obviously weren't regular Mass-goers either, because when the priest came out onto the altar, the 4-year-old son turns to his mother and yells at the top of his voice,

'There's God! You're in big trouble now!'

Overheard by Anna, in church, Greenhills
Posted on Tuesday, 12 July 2005

Go toilet in a shop???

When my sister was working in a sports shop, she heard a father with son.

Son: 'Da, I need to go toilet, will ye bring me?'

Father: 'Awh jaysus, just go behind dat rail der!'

Overheard by ashy, JD Sports in Liffey Valley
Posted on Saturday, 9 July 2005

Druid man

A drunk with a can of Druids in his hand is chatting up the girls behind the counter. He's blabbing on for ages about how his wife won't get out of bed so he brought her raspberries. Mid-speech he looks closely at one of the girls' breasts and says, 'That's a lovely name!'

Girl peers down at her t-shirt for a minute, then bursts out laughing, 'That's not my name!'

'It is,' said the drunk, peering closer. 'Spar! Where are you from?'

Overheard by Nicola Cassidy, Spar shop on Camden Street
Posted on Thursday, 7 July 2005

A child's logic!

Waiting in long queue to pay for car tax, at the back a young Dublin mother stands with her boisterous 10-year-old son. A Nigerian mother walks in the door dressed in full traditional dress and sandals. The 10-year-old yells up to his mother,

'Ma, that woman over there is black but why are her feet white?'

Overheard by Dermot, Car Tax Office
Posted on Wednesday, 6 July 2005

Escaping exam questions

Three girls outside an O'Brien's Sandwich shop discussing exams. One says, 'I think my problem is that I don't read the question properly,' to which one of the others replies,

'Ooooh my God, that is like, so my problem too. I start answering the question, and then I go off on a tandem …!'

One way of getting out of having to complete the exam!

Overheard by Daisy, O'Brien's Sandwich shop, D4
Posted on Wednesday, 6 July 2005

Girlzandboyz

While unpacking shoe boxes in Dunnes Stores I overheard two women having an argument. After a few heated exchanges, one of them walked over to me and thrust a pair of kid's pyjamas under my nose and said,

'Here! Are dese for young wans or young fellahs?!'

Overheard by Nicola, Dunnes Stores, Ilac Centre, Dublin
Posted on Wednesday, 6 July 2005

Who says chivalry is dead ...

Sitting upstairs on the no. 15A bus out of town. Passing through Rathgar, father and young daughter (five) make their way to stairs. Father is walking in front of little girl. Just as they reach the stairs, little girl screams, 'Ladies first!' Father steps aside ...

Chivalry is alive and well!

Overheard by Chuckster, on no. 15A bus
Posted on Tuesday, 5 July 2005

Ask a stupid question ... in Dublin

In Grogans pub I overhead the following:

Bloke: 'Do yis have a toilet?'

Barman: 'What do you think?'

Barman (after bloke walks off): 'F**kin eejit.'

Overheard by old man, Grogans pub
Posted on Monday, 4 July 2005

Mind the jacket

Shopping in Dunnes Stores in Crumlin a 2-year-old boy toddler was being chased by his 6-year-old sister. The girl proceeds to knock her brother down onto the floor and stomps her feet heavily onto his back, resulting in the child wailing. As I stared in disbelief their father appears.

'Ah, stop that now,' he says to his daughter, 'Ya'll ruin his good jacket!'

Overheard by Grainne, Dunnes Stores
Posted on Friday, 3 June 2005

Just like heaven

On a Ryanair flight to Paris, just as we got above the white, fluffy clouds and it felt like we were walking on them, I heard a little Irish kid's voice squeak matter-of-factly above the din, 'Oh look, we're in heaven!'

Overheard by Alison, Ryanair flight to Paris
Posted on Saturday, 2 July 2005

Funny butcher

Was in a butchers the other day and this girl walks in and says to the fella behind the counter, 'A pound a fillet.'

The fella turns around and says, 'A pound I don't!'

Overheard by Brian, Keoghs butchers in Crumlin
Posted on Saturday, 2 July 2005

Who's Judas?

Was on a no. 10 bus in Dublin last Easter when I overheard these two Dubs in their twenties, going on about all that happened from Holy Thursday till Easter Sunday back in biblical times.

Judas came up in the conversation, to which one of the girls says, 'Judas?' And the other one went, 'Ya, Judas, ya know, yer man dat ratted on Jesus!'

Overheard by Jonathan, on a bus
Posted on Friday, 1 July 2005

Tea and sambos

I was waiting for the Nitelink on Westmoreland Street a few years ago with a few mates and an oul lad came up to us and said, 'Ah jaysus lads can you spare us a pound for a cuppa tea and a sambo?'

Quick as a flash my mate said, 'Feckin' hell, a pound for a cup a tea and a sandwich! I want to know where you're going.'

Overheard by Pete, Westmoreland Street
Posted on Friday, 1 July 2005

Ryanair and its quality staff

While on a Ryanair flight home from Gatwick the plane was on its way to the runway for take off and one of the air hostesses comes over the intercom:

'Cabin crew to landing position,' … two seconds later … 'or take off even!'

Overheard by Deano, London Gatwick
Posted on Thursday, 30 June 2005

Italian stallion

On a packed bus seated second seat from the back upstairs, when a group of school kids start having a conversation about religion.

One of them goes, 'I'm a Catolic!'

Another one goes, 'I'm a Roman Catolic.'

To which another one goes, 'Ya Italian bastard!'

Only in Dublin!

Overheard by Deavo, no. 16A bus
Posted on Thursday, 30 June 2005

Giving account of yourself

A friend told me of an incident that happened to him recently. He was standing in the queue at the Credit Union. When he was almost at the top of the queue, with only one man in front of him, the loudspeaker announced: 'Counter number nine, please.'

The man in front of him did not move. My friend leaned over towards him to indicate to him that it was his turn when he heard the man whispering, 'One, two, three, four ...'

It then dawned on my friend that the man had interpreted the announcement as, 'Count to number nine please'!

Overheard by FJ Murray, Drimnagh
Posted on Thursday, 30 June 2005

Inflation

I went down to Croke Park early before the last U2 concert to see if I could get a ticket. I came across a head-the-ball who was asking, 'Anyone buying or selling a ticket?'

I asked, 'How much are you selling them for?'

He replied, '250.'

I wasn't interested. However a young Asian tourist eagerly approaches the guy and asks, 'You have ticket? How much?'

Head-the-ball (while making sheepish eye contact with me): '300.'

The Asian guy willingly accepts.

Overheard by Paul, outside Croke Park
Posted on Tuesday, 28 June 2005

Revealing graffiti

Some brilliant graffiti I saw on my way to work one morning and it still cracks me up to this day:

'Willo Murphy does the sunbeds.'

Overheard by Mel, Coolock
Posted on Monday, 27 June 2005

Rashers

In a butchers in town a girl asked for a pound of rashers. The butcher asked her what type of rashers. The girl replies, 'The ones that you fry!'

Overheard by Ms Silly, butchers in town
Posted on Monday, 27 June 2005

Love is not blind!

Coming out of the U2 concert on Saturday night, there were lots of women going ga-ga over the Garda horses. One girl says, 'Aaaah look at the horse, isn't it beautiful?'

To which her boyfriend replies, 'Well it's better looking than you!'

Overheard by Neil, outside Croke Park after U2 concert
Posted on Monday, 27 June 2005

Tis not Russia you're in now boy ...

While waiting patiently to ask a member of the Garda Síochána directions to get to the Canal End, an English gentleman had approached him also looking for directions. Here is how the conversation went:

English guy: 'Hi mate can you tell me which way I go to get to the Kossack Stand?'

Guard staring blankly for a minute, but couldn't help himself: ''Tis not Russia you're in now, boy, keep going down there and it's on the right-hand side.'

Meanwhile I stepped up to ask my question, and I was trying to keep a very straight face, when the Guard said, 'I suppose you're looking for the Hoggan Stand.'

A Guard with a sense of humour, who would have thought it …

Overheard by Nicola, U2 concert
Posted on Monday, 27 June 2005

Big Knockers

One day in an Economics lecture we were all dozing off until this one-liner promptly awoke us. As our lecturer explained the natural ups and downs of an economy, he says,

'Lads, there is always going to be big knockers in society.'

As we all struggled to keep the laughter in, it must have clicked with him what he had said, so he told us to get it out and have a good laugh, to which we obliged! We didn't realise he was being sarcastic and told us all to shut up and stop being so immature.

Overheard by Laura, UCD
Posted on Friday, 24 June 2005

Sun or sunbeds?

While in the changing rooms in Penneys in Rathfarnham I overheard two women who were trying on three-quarter length pants.

One said to the other: 'Mary would you not try on a pair of shorts, you'd get a lovely tan in the sun in Spain?'

To which Mary replied: 'Ah no, sure I wouldn't be bothered with the sun, I'll just do the sun beds when I get back!'

Wonders never cease!

Overheard by Eithne, Penneys in Rathfarnham
Posted on Friday, 24 June 2005

Internet difficulties

This happened in a BESS lecture, perhaps proving that the lecturers are just as dumb as the students doing the course ...

While explaining the different ways to contact her if there were any problems, the lecturer has greatly endorsed using the Internet. Then she came out with,

'However, if any of you have trouble using computers or the Internet, please email me and we'll arrange a time to sort it out.'

Hmmm, didn't think that one through, did she?

Overheard by Boxty, in a Trinity lecture theatre
Posted on Thursday, 23 June 2005

A Spaniard's farewell to Ireland

Just before departing on a flight to Madrid, a young Spanish student sitting behind us made a last-minute call. It went something like this (you'll have to imagine the Spanish accent):

'Hello, Eileen. I am on the plane and we are just about to leave. I have something to say to you, Eileen. This is very important to me. F**k off, Eileen.'

And she hangs up.

Overheard by Dave, on flight El 594
Posted on Thursday, 23 June 2005

Is Marley Park outdoors?

Going to the Coldplay concert last night at Marley Park, in the pub before the gig with my girlfriend. I was looking out the window at the sun shining and said, 'This is some day for the gig.'

She replies, 'Is Marley Park outdoors?'

Should I keep seeing this girl …

Overheard by Mac, Temple Bar
Posted on Thursday, 23 June 2005

Ask a stupid question …

Young lad in court for minor offence. Judge asks him, 'Are you working at the moment? Lad replies, 'Yes.' Judge asks, 'Who do you support?' Lad answers, 'Man Utd.' Judge, not amused, says, 'WHO do you support at home?'

'Oh you mean me Ma?!' came the reply.

Overheard by Bab, courthouse in Kilmainham
Posted on Wednesday, 22 June 2005

Explaining the rules

In Quinn's, during Longford-Dublin match. Guy is explaining the concept of hurling and football to his girlfriend (who *is* Irish!).

Guy: 'If it goes between the posts and below the bar it's a goal, and that's worth three points; and if it goes between the posts and over the bar, that's a point.'

Girl: 'O right, yea, and what's a try …?'

Overheard by Edel, Quinn's Drumcondra
Posted on Wednesday, 22 June 2005

Horse for sale

I was sitting on the no. 39 bus with a friend on our way home from town, talking to these lads who just decided to strike up a conversation. Just as we come to the dual carriageway a couple of head-the-balls get on and sit down beside us (we were sitting at the back) and started talking to the lads we had been making small talk with. When one of the lads, only about 12, turns around and says, 'D'ye wanna buy a horse?'

One of the lads turns around and says, 'What would I bleedin want with a horse?'

Another one of the lads decides to amuse the little lad and says, 'How much are ye sellin yer horse for?'

To all our shock and amusement the little lad turns to him and says, 'Well I don't know, I havta f**kin rob him first, don't I?'

Amazing!

Overheard by Tanya, on the no. 39 bus
Posted on Tuesday, 21 June 2005

Women drivers

On a flight from Liverpool to Dublin on Aer Lingus, the pilot came on to give the usual pre-flight chat. Turns out it was a female pilot, much to the amusement of a group of middle-aged Dubs sitting at the back of the plane! Cheers went up, like 'Go wan ya good thing!' etc.

Anyway, the flight was relatively uneventful, but the landing was particularly bumpy. After bouncing off the tarmac about three times and finally shuddering to a halt, the pilot came on and apologised for the bumpy landing.

With that, one of the lads at the back shouts up, 'Ah jaysis, missus, I'd hate ta see yer bleedin parallel parkin!'

Overheard by Barry, Aer Lingus flight
Posted on Tuesday, 21 June 2005

Duvets

One evening waiting for a friend outside Clery's, a group of three middle-aged, fake-tanned, make-up-caked-onto-their-faces women walk past. As they pass the Clery's entrance, one of them goes,

'Oh hang on Mary, I'll come to Ann Summer's with ya but I want to have a look at duvets in Clery's first.'

Bet she's a real tiger in the bedroom ...

Overheard by Squiggles, O'Connell Street
Posted on Monday, 20 June 2005

Team worker

About a year ago a young lad started work in the office I work in, let's call him John. John and I were in different departments, however due to a shortage of desks he sat at the desk beside mine for the first two or three days.

John spent those first days asking me questions about what he should be doing etc. and I spent those first days responding that I was sorry but I worked in another department and could not help him, he should ask someone in his department.

A couple of weeks later at a staff night out, John, about a dozen co-workers and I were sat around a table. I asked John, 'So how are you getting on? All settled in?'

John eagerly answered, 'Oh, yeah thanks. The first few days I was sitting beside a right bitch, but I like where I am now.'

I never saw so many people decide to go get a round at the same time!

Overheard by Teresa, work night out

Posted on Thursday, 16 June 2005

It pays to think before you speak, especially after watching Sky news!

My grandson was being christened in a church in Lucan. His name is Sam Adam. The priest held him up to the congregation and said,

'We would like to welcome Saddam into our church.'

The church rattled with laughter, as the red faced priest made the correction.

Overheard by Anonymous, St Mary's Church, Lucan

Posted on Saturday, 11 June 2005

Two accents?

Some schoolgirl on her mobile on the Luas:

'Outside the school? Yeah I'm on the Luas, I'll be two minutes like. Yeah I'll be there. I'm fookin comin alrigh?! Will ya hold on ...Yeah, outside the school. Will ya fookin hold on! I'm comin! Jaysus! Fookin givin' me hassle.'

She gets off the phone to whoever it was and makes another call (in a blatant southside accent):

'Hello, yes, yes, I'm on my way. OK, excellent. Alroysh, heh, see you then.'

Overheard by Rob Gallagher, on the Luas between Charlemont and Windy Arbour stops

Posted on Friday, 10 June 2005

Sober munch

My mate was on the DART last Holy Thursday having a good snigger at some 'rock boys' talking about how wasted they were going to get that night. When one of them mentioned that the pub would be closed tomorrow the other said in disbelief,

'No way! Does that mean that loike Abrakebabra will close as well?'

When the others said, 'No, why do you ask?' he replied,

'Cos loike no one would eat that food sober.'

Overheard by claire b
Posted on Wednesday, 8 June 2005

'Car minding'

Up for a game at Croke Park a few weeks back. Paid the €10 to the local 12-year-old 'head-the-ball'-to-be so he'd look after the car. A BMW parked behind and the young lad roars, 'Giz €10 an' I'll mind yer car.'

Yer man replied, pleased as punch, 'No, that's OK. I'm leaving my dog in the car. He's a German shepherd.'

Without blinking the young entrepreneur replies, 'Yea, sound. Here, can your dog put out fires?'

Savage!

Overheard by Barry, Croke Park
Posted on Wednesday, 8 June 2005

The very confident salesman

While relaxing on the Boardwalk along the Liffey on a sunny June bank holiday afternoon, my attention was drawn to a few animated head-the-balls who stopped nearby. One of them was taking packets of rashers out of an Elvery's sports shop plastic bag. He took out two packets at a time. For each time he took out a pair he declared,

'5', '10', '15', '20' etc., up to '50'.

I couldn't make sense of his mathematics. Why was he adding '5' for every two packets he pulled out? Then when he was finished he put all the packets of rashers back in the bag and headed off enthusiastically with his two mates, exclaiming,

'Sorted! That's €50 worth we have there — two packets for €5.'

A bargain!

Overheard by Pearse, Boardwalk at Eden Quay
Posted on Tuesday, 7 June 2005

Where are the animals?

On a recent visit to a packed Dublin Zoo, we had an hour-long queue before we got in. Because it was the afternoon after the animal feeding time, all the animals were panned out in long grass and hence, out of sight. It was increasingly frustrating for the paying public.

One old couple I saw summed it up. The old man approached the window of the lion cage, had a quick look, threw his eyes up to heaven and walked on. His wife, just behind him asks,

'Anything in there, Charlie?'

Charlie replies sarcastically, 'Yeah, more f**kin straw!'

Overheard by Anonymous, Dublin Zoo
Posted on Tuesday, 7 June 2005

That's all they asked

British tourist: 'Do you know which side of the Liffey we are on?'

Dub: 'Yeah.'

Overheard by Aspro, Tara Street DART station
Posted on Monday, 6 June 2005

Spot on

A friend was working in a Finglas Spar when two aul' ones came in, catching up with each other's weekend.

'We got a new video player and watched a few films.'

'Jaysis, that's great! What make is it?'

'Christ! I forget ... it begins with a "P".'

'Is it a Mitsubishi?'

'That's it!'

Overheard by PoC, Finglas
Posted on Tuesday, 7 June 2005

Better value

An irate Dublin bus driver, roaring out the window at a bad driver:

'WHERE D'YA GET YER LICENCE? Tesco? Or
Dunnes Stores?'

Overheard by Mark, Portobello Bridge

Posted on Friday, 3 June 2005

Lassies in danger

While walking up North Great George's Street I
noticed that the movie 'Lassie' was being shot.

There were Guards, directors, loads of actors in
old-fashioned clothes and of course the dog
Lassie. There were actually two Lassies —
probably just in case something happened to the
other one.

They were in their kennels in a white van and
the door was open so you could see both of
them. The van was surrounded by a group of
skangers who were trying to pet the dogs and
take pictures of them with their camera phones,
while they had a fag in their hands.

The two American women sitting in the front of
the van noticed what was happening after a
while. The one in the passenger side said, 'Em,
excuse me, sir, please don't do that, please leave
the dogs alone,' in her high-pitched American
accent.

The skanger replied, 'OK, OK, missuz, iym only
tryin to av a look a' dem.'

Then the woman said, 'OK, sir, you can look but
please do not put your hands anywhere near
them!'

'Alri!' he replies. After this the skanger repeated
what he had done, filling the back of the van
with smoke. The woman in the driver's seat got
out and slammed the door shut and once again

told him that he was told not to do that and he
replied, 'OK, I'm sorry, I'm sorry, I wos only tryin
to see de lovely little doggie.'

Overheard by Mr.b, North Great George's Street
Posted on Wednesday, 1 June 2005

Clairvoyant auld ones

On the bus to Finglas yesterday an auld one got
on and immediately spotted another auld one in
front of me and they carried on with their
greetings of 'Oh I haven't seen you in ages'. The
conversation went from grandkids to health to
the 'good old days'.

Auld one #1 says, 'Do you remember Mrs Kelly
down the street who died in 1953?'

'Oh I do,' replies auld one #2, 'I went up to the
house to see her laid out but sure I didn't know
her till AFTER she was dead!'

Auld one #1 just said, 'Oh, that's a pity, she was
a lovely woman!'

Overheard by Jennifer, no. 40C bus
Posted on Wednesday, 1 June 2005

Apathetic response

I used to work part-time in Atlantic Homecare in
Blanchardstown Centre as a shelf technician.
One day, while stacking paint, I was asked a
question that anyone who has worked in these
kinds of service jobs is familiar with: 'Excuse me,
luv, but do you work here?'

Having heard the question for the thousandth
time that week, I lost interest in saying yes I do

and replied, 'Oh sorry, I'm just wearing the official Atlantic Homecare replica jersey,' and walked off, leaving the woman apologising in my wake.

Overheard by NM, Atlantic Homecare

Posted on Wednesday, 1 June 2005

Sex and the city ... hardly!

Three classy birds ordering cocktails last Friday evening in the Vaults. After much debating, they decided to go with cosmopolitans. They ordered from the rather stressed looking barman who proceeded to line up the glasses on the bar. The good looking blonde one said to her friend, 'Jaysus, there's loads of ice in them glasses, sure he won't fit any gargle into them.'

Her friend (from Cork I think) then said, 'Someone should say it to him that we don't want all that ice.'

She shouldn't have opened her mouth as her friends jostled her up to the bar and forced her to say it to him. She over-the-top politely called the barman over, apologised 17 times and asked him if he could take some ice out of the glasses.

The barman looked at her with disdain and disgust and replied, 'I'm cooling the glasses.'

Mortified Cork lass or wha!

Overheard by Reyo, Vaults Bar, IFSC

Posted on Wednesday, 1 June 2005

Toto the chip man

The scene: An Italian-run chipper throbbing with people before a Dublin match in Croke Park.

One Dub (fresh out of the boozer after a
morning's drinking) barely squeezes in the door
and is at the back of a very long line. Not content
with being at the back of the queue he starts to
shout his order at the overrun Italian employees:

'BATTER BURGER AND CHIPS PLEASE.'

Clearly he is wasting his time so he tries a
different angle to try and get their attention, so
he shouts:

'HERE, SCHILLACI, GET ME A BLEEDIN BATTER
BURGER WILL YA.'

Cue thunderous laughter from the rest of the
line …

Overheard by Darren, Italian chipper in Ballybough
Posted on Wednesday, 1 June 2005

Ramadanmalent

Two guys working behind the counter in Spar,
one Dub, and one Asian. The Asian guy,
apparently a Muslim, was explaining to his
colleague about fasting during the holy month
of Ramadan.

After hearing about this, the Dub declares, 'Yeah,
sure we have that here too, only it's called Lent.'

Overheard by MP, Spar beside Pearse Street Station
Posted on Monday, 30 May 2005

Just a normal day in Dublin so?

I was walking by the Ambassador on Parnell
Street. Some old bloke was outside having a
smoke and just shouts out,

'F**king Sunday bloody Sunday and it's a
f**king Tuesday!'

Overheard by talkinghead, Parnell Street
Posted on Friday, 27 May 2005

Queue for the no. 39 bus

There was a fire drill today at the Department of
Health. There were about 300 people spilling
out onto the street. One of the bus inspectors
standing there yells,

'I hope you're not all for the bleedin' 39!'

Overheard by Anon, Hawkins Street
Posted on Wednesday, 25 May 2005

Magic

Working in a very nice Dublin hotel in the
carvery, when a little old dear comes up to the

carvery chef and asks him if she can have the chicken soup but without too much chicken in it. Quick as a flash and totally straight faced he replies,

'Listen love, this is a chef's uniform not a magician's.'

Overheard by Dave, at work
Posted on Monday, 23 May 2005

Not all it's cracked up to be

Last week on the bus passing the old Dundrum Shopping Centre, these two skangers sitting across from me look out the window and exclaim,

'Wouja lookit de new Dundrum Shoppin' Centre, bleedin' state of it already.'

Overheard by gdog, no. 63 bus
Posted on Saturday, 21 May 2005

Dangers of running with child

I was strolling through Stephen's Green three weeks ago. Nice sunny day and everyone was in good form. Even the down and outs with their cans were smiling. Then this heavily pregnant woman came dashing by in a mad hurry. One of the beer-can wielding lads shouted,

'Don't run missus. You'll boil yer waters.'

Even the ducks were laughing.

Overheard by Paul Quinlan, St Stephen's Green
Posted on Friday, 20 May 2005

Charity begins at home

In a charity shop a black man was buying a few items of clothing and a pair of flip-floppy type shoes. I don't know whether he didn't have enough to pay for everything or he was just chancing his arm, but he was asking for a discount on his combined purchases. The little old dear behind the counter was politely trying to explain to him that it's a bit cheeky to ask for discounts in a charity shop as the money goes to a good cause.

'I'm sorry dear, I can't give them to you for less, it's for charity, we're Gorta, the money goes to the third world, we help them out over there.'

To which he replied, 'The third world? Africa?!? That's me, help ME out over HERE!'

Overheard by Fenster, Gorta shop on Liffey Street
Posted on Friday, 20 May 2005

Sounds a bit fishy?

I was walking down Moore Street a few years ago, past all the traders with their stalls of haddock, potatoes and bananas, when I heard a loud female voice calling in pure Dublinese:

'Maria, get that young wan off deh fish, she's no knickers on!'

Overheard by Alonzo, Moore Street
Posted on Thursday, 19 May 2005

Urgent need of graffiti school

More overseen than overheard. Scribbled on the wall of the Four Courts some years back:

House of Diseption

Overheard by Ug, Four Courts
Posted on Thursday, 19 May 2005

Like he meant it!

Was walking down Grafton Street on my way to my exam the other morning. Little girl of about five was skipping towards me with her father behind her. She was generally laughing and giggling until she stopped in front of the window of La Senza lingerie shop. She looked at the mannequins and turned to her dad saying,

'Eeeeuuuuuw! Gross! Dad, look! Women's bottoms!'

Her father turned around like a shot, mouth hanging open, then caught himself and said, 'Yeah, ugh, really gross!'

Overheard by Sally, Grafton Street
Posted on Wednesday, 18 May 2005

Elephants aren't what they used to be

Coming out of the UGC cinema on Parnell a while ago, and a group of guys who had just seen 'Alexander' were having the following conversation:

Guy #1: 'Did you see the way they had those elephants in the battle scenes, stomping on everyone?'

Guy #2: 'Yeah, it just goes to show you how strong elephants used to be.'

Overheard by gdog, UGC cinema, Parnell Street
Posted on Wednesday, 18 May 2005

Irish racism

My brother was in a bike shop when a Chinese man entered the shop and asked one of the assistants for a tyre tube for his bike. The assistant asked what size tube he needed. The Chinese man said that any size would do.

When the assistant insisted that he couldn't sell him a tube unless he knew what size was needed, the Chinese man got agitated and said, 'You're being racist!'

At this point, another assistant in the shop piped up, 'How is he being racist? Sure you're not even black!'

Overheard by David, in a bicycle shop in town
Posted on Wednesday, 18 May 2005

Outer magnolia

While shopping in Texas Homecare in Nutgrove, I overheard a woman ask her husband to reach up and pass her down a tin of MONGOLIA paint!

Call it a hunch but I think she may have meant Magnolia!

Overheard by John, Texas Homecare, Nutgrove
Posted on Tuesday, 17 May 2005

Monkey magic

I was taking part in a college video last year. One scene involved a classmate climbing to the top of a 30-foot-high lamppost. Back in the editing suite we were looking over the footage when suddenly unknown to us this oul fella walks into the background of the shot and says as clear as a bell,

'Jaysus, someone should giv' 'im a ban-nan-na.'

Overheard by Martin, Ballyfermot
Posted on Monday, 16 May 2005

Silly sausage

Was in the queue at a hot-food counter recently and the guy in front of me was asking the girl behind the counter for a sausage roll. The girl asked if he'd like a large sausage roll or a small sausage roll.

'No, a SAUSAGE ROLL,' says the guy.

'OK, a large one then is it?' the girl asks, pointing to the sausage rolls on display. To which she gets screamed back at her,

'Are ye f**kin' steupit, a ROLL wit some SAUSAGES in it …'

Overheard by Noxy, shop in Dublin
Posted on Monday, 16 May 2005

Whole finger …?

Overheard two blokes I work with in Swords one day in the locker room:

Bloke #1: 'Did ya hear about Danny's accident at the weekend?'

Bloke #2: 'No, wha happened?'

Bloke #1: 'Got his hand caught in one of the pressing machine rotors.'

Bloke #2: 'Jaaayyssisss, was he badly hurted?'

Bloke #1: 'Got one of his fingers really bad and ripped it off!'

Bloke #2: 'Jaaayyssisss ... the whole finger?'

Bloke #1 (deadly serious): 'No ... the one beside it.'

Overheard by Alan, work place in Swords
Posted on Monday, 16 May 2005

Jews and their smokes

Just around when the smoking ban came in there was a phone-in show on the radio about it, and this one guy (Anto) rings in giving out.

Anto: 'Aaah ya knoo I just think da smokin ban is ya kno simetic ...'

Radio Guy: 'Wha?'

Anto: 'Aaah no ya kno anti simetic.'

Radio Guy: 'The smokin ban is anti Jewish?'

Anto: 'Aah well ah ...'

Overheard by Tomo, FM 104
Posted on Monday, 16 May 2005

Tightrope act

While walking through St Stephen's Green I stopped to watch this lad walking the tightrope and playing the fiddle at the same time. There were two lads in front of me and one says to the other,

'Sure that's bleedin useless, he's not even blindfolded.'

Overheard by Anonymous, St Stephen's Green
Posted on Sunday, 15 May 2005

Good old northsiders

I was at the bar one day and I overheard two lads ordering their drinks:

'Here mister give us a pint of Bulmer and I'll ave a pint of Millers.'

Smart-arse barman says to a co-worker:

'John, go out there and take the 's' off the Bulmers and put it on the Miller!

Overheard by tom, pub on the northside
Posted on Saturday, 14 May 2005

Seals Rising from the Dead

A teacher was talking about the Irish Seal Sanctuary; he started telling us about an autopsy and what was involved in it. At this point one of the lads in the class put up his hand and said,

'Was he alright afterwards?"

Overheard by The Cheese, a classroom in Dublin
Posted on Saturday, 14 May 2005

Cakin'

Two girls are about to enter a classroom on a hot day. One turns to the other:

'Ah no, I'm goin' t' be bleedin' bakin' in here!'

The other laughs and retorts, 'What are yeh? A bleedin' cake?'

Overheard by Dave, Swords
Posted on Friday, 13 May 2005

Best chat up line ever

Was walking along the road the other night when a car drives by with a few lads in it and all I hear is,

'You're luvly ya are! I'd do 10 years in Mountjoy for ya!'

Overheard by Lisa, Stillorgan
Posted on Thursday, 12 May 2005

The Irish culinary appreciation society

I was working in the restaurant one day when two girls came in and ordered two sandwiches from the menu. It states on the menu that all of the hamburgers and sandwiches are served with side salad.

The two women got their food and after a few minutes one of them called me over. She was pointing at the salad:

'Scuse me, mister, we only wanted two chicken sambos. What's with the bleedin flower sh*te?'

Overheard by Daniel O'Connor, pub in Dublin
Posted on Thursday, 12 May 2005

3-year-olds know everything

Was playing with my 3-year-old niece a few weeks ago. She had a board with the letters of the alphabet and little pictures of objects for each of the letters such as A for apple etc.

Me: 'What is 'M' for?'

Her: 'Mummy.'

Me: 'Well yes, but here 'M' is for mouse.'

Her: 'NO! 'M' is for mummy.'

Me: 'But lots of words start with 'M', like mouse, man, milk. What does milk start with then?'

Her (angrily walking away): 'Milk starts with cows!'

Overheard by Viv, my bro's house
Posted on Thursday, 12 May 2005

Sweet smell of success

Was at Dublin Airport and my flight had been delayed so we had to wait several hours in the departure lounge. One young couple sitting near me had a little girl who, after waiting around for a few hours was becoming tired and emotional. She kept crying that she wanted sweets from the shop, while her mother refused to give in to the request and tried to calm her down.

Realising she wasn't going to win through complaining alone, the little girl began screaming, 'MUMMY DOES BIG SMELLY FARTS!' at the top of her voice.

She soon got her sweets.

Overheard by Jack Wade, Dublin Airport
Posted on Wednesday, 11 May 2005

The Luas countryside service is delayed ...

While awaiting the Luas outside Heuston Station, a rather trollied looking fellow approached the Dublin Bus man who was just hanging around. The tram pulled in, and the drunk fella asked the bus man,

'Is this the Sligo train?'

Overheard by MC, outside Heuston Station
Posted on Wednesday, 11 May 2005

The Hill's alive ...

Two Dublin football supporters passing comment on a rather portly member of the county team on Hill 16 a few years back:

Dub #1: 'Jayzis, yer man turns like the Titanic.'

Dub #2: 'Yeah, and he's got an arse like an iceberg as well!'

Overheard by Eamo, Hill 16
Posted on Wednesday, 11 May 2005

No wonder she crashed

D4 girl #1: 'I crashed my car yesterday.'

D4 girl #2: 'Where?'

D4 girl #1: 'On the road!'

Overheard by kicks, UCD
Posted on Wednesday, 11 May 2005

The nutty professor

Was in college studying computer maintenance.
The professor was from Sallynoggin, a real
Dublin aul fella. Anyways I asked him how to do
a certain thing on the PC and he shouts down,
'RTFM' and I said, 'What do you mean RTFM?'
and he replies in loud voice,

'READ THE F**KING MANUAL!'

Overheard by anon, FAS, Loughlinstown
Posted on Tuesday, 10 May 2005

The munchies

Chatting to one of my patients randomly one
day, the conversation turns to drug addicts, and
what a terrible affliction it is.

'I know,' says he, 'I was on the bus the other day
and there was this strung-out fella, eatin' a
Vienetta out of a bag like it was an ice-cream on
a stick.'

I stifle a laugh, and try to maintain my
professional facade. Contemplating the Vienetta
for a minute, he then says,

'I mean, a f**kin' Vienetta! That thing is for, like, six f**kin' people!'

Overheard by Donal, dental surgery D2
Posted on Tuesday, 10 May 2005

Office

At work recently a colleague rang the local Ink Cartridge Supplies called Mr Inky. When the person answered was female he got a little confused and said, 'Emmm, is that Mrs Inky?'

Overheard by Domanval, at work
Posted on Tuesday, 10 May 2005

Boob talk

A few weeks back I found myself on the no. 38 bus going out to Blanchardstown. I happened to be sitting upstairs midway down the bus and for the best part of the journey all I could hear from the back seat was:

'Where's Mammy's diddies, where's Mammy's diddies, no, no you don't have diddies yet, you're too young, where's Mammy's diddies, where's Mammy's diddies, that's right, there's Mammy's diddies.'

Overheard by Shuggy, no. 38 bus
Posted on Tuesday, 10 May 2005

Empty vessels

On the bus from Mullingar to Dublin driving down the quays at low tide:

Woman #1: 'The river is very low isn't it?'

Woman #2: 'Yeah I think they drain it every so often.'

Woman #1: 'Really? I wonder where they put it?'

The bloke sitting next to me looked at me in disbelief. I told him that, yes, I heard it too, which seemed to reassure him a bit.

Overheard by Val, Mullingar to Dublin bus
Posted on Tuesday, 10 May 2005

WMDs

Walking down Dame Street one skanger yells across the street to another, 'Anto! Yer ma's a f**king weapon!' . . . great stuff.

Overheard by Debo, Dame Street
Posted on Tuesday, 10 May 2005

Mood swings

Walking along Sean McDermott Street on the way to work one sunny morning. Homeless guy looks up from reading his paper, smiles at me and practically shouts out, 'You're young, life is good, enjoy your youth!'

I replied, 'Thanks, I will.'

Very next morning the same guy, same place, looks up from his paper as I pass and says, 'F**k off, you're only a b*ll*x, you're all the same ye f**kin parasites.'

What can you say to that?

Overheard by Shwillo, corner of Sean McDermott and
Buckingham Streets
Posted on Tuesday, 10 May 2005

The potential dangers of the Irish Sea

On the DART home and a Dublin fella who could fairly be described as being hammered gets on. He starts talking to everyone and no one in particular and giving all manner of amusement to all.

In between offering advice to any celebrities on the train about giving autographs, and lamenting about local politicians not caring about recycling — 'Sure that's only a money-making scam anyway' — he stops to watch some windsurfers near Dun Laoghaire.

'Jaysus,' says he, 'it's a mad day for sorfin'. Imagine a big shark came along and ate them all.'

Pondering this for a while he concludes, 'That'd be f**kin' great!'

Overheard by Big T, on the DART on the way home
Posted on Monday, 9 May 2005

Cheeky train fella

I was getting the DART from Greystones. I went to the counter and asked the uniformed guy for a 'ticket to Sandycove, please'. Hands me the ticket. I then asked politely, 'How long will the train be, do you know?'

He sits back on his chair and with a dead straight face said, 'About four or five carriages.'

I had to walk away!

Overheard by JH, Greystones
Posted on Monday, 9 May 2005

Turd salad

While queuing in Avoca Handweavers at the weekend, I was shocked to learn that the enterprising folks in Avoca have in fact managed to manufacture and sell Turd Salad.

Lady in queue: 'I'll have shepherds pie, pasta salad and green salad.'

Assistant: 'Ma'am would you like a turd salad wit dat ... ?'

At which point at least 10 fellow onlookers buckled over with laughter.

Overheard by Tom, Avoca Handweavers
Posted on Monday, 9 May 2005

Funny cos it's true

One night in a nightclub in Dublin, as the lights came on one guy screams,

'Oh my god, everyone's so ugly!'

The looks he got from the women!

Overheard by Anonymous, Spirit Nightclub
Posted on Sunday, 8 May 2005

He does have a point

My girlfriend and I were waiting for the bus in town. She was leafing through a magazine that she bought. Then this old man came up to her, stared at her and said,

'You like looking through people's lives don't you?' and just stood in front of her staring at her.

Overheard by Andy, Nassau Street, waiting for no. 7 bus
Posted on Saturday, 7 May 2005

Tastes like chicken

Bloke asks foreign chef in the canteen, 'What's that?' pointing to the food.

Foreign chef says: 'Churkey'.

Bloke says: 'Churkey? What's churkey?'

Foreign chef says: 'It's like chicken.'

Bloke then thought it was some weird turkey/chicken hybrid — when it was just turkey.

Overheard by mbv, canteen in work
Posted on Friday, 6 May 2005

Dublin in the rare old days

Was walking home from school one day with a few friends and there was this old guy just sitting on the pavement reading the *Irish Times*. As we were going past he loudly remarked, 'Ah yes! Dublin in the rare old days, in the rare old days!'

Then presently went back to his paper.

Overheard by Clare, Griffith Avenue
Posted on Friday, 6 May 2005

Up Cork, Up Meath and Up ...

All Ireland final day in 1999 and we were all dressed in red and white (obviously supporting Cork). Lovely day so we were outside the Hogan Stand Bar enjoying the craic and all that when a typical head-the-ball 'sales man' approached us.

Head-the-ball: 'Ye's from Cork' (obviously educated to associate red jerseys with Cork).

Us: 'We are.'

Next thing, a car load of Meath supporters drives past and one of them roars out, 'UP MEATH'.

Before any of us could think of anything to say back, Head-the-ball (roars), 'UP YOURS!'

Had everyone outside the pub rolling around laughing.

Overheard by Pat, Hogan Stand Bar
Posted on Friday, 6 May 2005

The thin yellow line!

I was getting off the DART in Connolly when I heard the following announcement:

'Could all passengers on platform three please stand behind the yellow line,' to which no one moved, so the guy makes the announcement again, this time sounding a bit more irate. After no one moves, he decides to ditch the fake posh accent and yells,

'Could youse lot move behind the bleedin' line, I won't tell yis again!'

Overheard by K, Connolly Station
Posted on Thursday, 5 May 2005

Some might say that son!

I'm living in Clonakilty nearly six years now and on a visit to Dublin a few years back decided to 'treat' my two kids to a bus run from Rialto into the city centre. Naturally, it being a novelty, it was up the stairs and to the front seats.

As we crossed O'Connell Bridge my little lad Sean, who was just a babe in arms when we left Dublin, saw the Daniel O'Connell monument.

'Look Dad,' he said, 'Superman!'

Overheard by Hugh, no. 19A bus from Rialto
Posted on Thursday, 5 May 2005

Don't whistle while you work

Working on a building site on the quays, dossing around one day with the other builders. There was a crane banksman standing there with his walkie-talkie, a real Dub this guy was, and seeing as it was nearing the weekend I was in a good mood. So I started to sing to no one in particular,

'He's a crane op-er-ator, craaaaaane oper-atorrrr,'

(to the tune of smooth operator) and the banksman shouted,

'Are yew foookin BENT or wha?'

Overheard by Jiggers, the quays
Posted on Thursday, 5 May 2005

Sri Lanka

Students: 'We're collecting money for Sri Lanka, for charity.'

Student 1: 'Who is Sri Lanka?'

Student 2: 'I'm not sure, I think she's famous.'

Student 1: 'Yeah I've heard the name somewhere before. Is she a singer?'

Overheard by Michelle, St Mary's Holy Faith, Killester
Posted on Tuesday, 3 May 2005

Help the aged

My uncle is a landlord, and he has some elderly tenants. When the euro came in, an elderly lady was complaining about it to him because she couldn't get her head around the conversion:

'Why can't they wait 'til the old people die before they bring it in?' she asked.

Overheard by Anthony, Terenure
Posted on Tuesday, 3 May 2005

Eaten alive

While walking behind a funeral cortège in a Dublin graveyard, a rat scurried across the grass. One old lady said to another,

'I wouldn't like to be buried in this place, you'd be eaten alive.'

Overheard by Mick, Mount Jerome
Posted on Tuesday, 3 May 2005

It's a miracle!

My brother arrives into Dublin Airport and is dying for a pee. He makes it to the Gents but there's a huge queue. He sees that the disabled toilet is free so he decides to leg it in before he wets himself. After relieving himself he's coming out the door when an auld lad still waiting in the queue for the Gents sarcastically declares,

'JAYSUS, it's a f**king miracle!'

Good 'old style' Irish humour! My brother knew he was home!

Overheard by Grainne, Dublin Airport
Posted on Monday, 2 May 2005

'Just ignore him'

Two girls in a cinema in Dublin in the 60s:

'Oh Jaysus, the guy beside me is playin wit himself.'

Friend: 'Just ignore him.'

'I can't, he's usin my hand!'

Overheard by Joe, my aunt heard this in the
Metropole in Dublin in the 60s
Posted on Monday, 2 May 2005

Parental problems

Two aul dears queuing for the no. 27 bus. Just
caught the end of the conversation:

Old dear #1: 'Sure whoaya tellin. De kids dees
days is terrible bold.'

Old dear #2: 'And ye know it's not de parents I
blame, it's de mudders an fadders.'

Overheard by Anna, town
Posted on Sunday, 1 May 2005

Sausage discrimination

Myself and my flat mate decided to pay a visit to
the new shopping centre in Dundrum on the
opening day. In Tesco we decide to get one of
those sample tasters (Tesco sausages) from the
stall that they have for promotion of the food.
Obviously being students we approached the
woman at the stall:

Woman: 'Are yeee stoodens, lads?'

Me: 'Students? Yes we are.'

Woman: 'Sorry we can't serve stoodens, talk to
head awffice if you have a problem.'

They refused to serve us a piece of Tesco finest
sausages!

Overheard by a.m, Tesco, Dundrum
Posted on Friday, 29 April 2005

$x = crazy, y = old\ guy, z = 13a,$
$x+y+z=?$

So I'm sat on the no. 13A bus on my way into town when this old guy in his 80s sits down next to me.

Old guy: 'Alright?'

Me (nod politely not really wanting to get into a conversation).

Old guy: 'Do you know any algebra?'

Me (feeling confused and positive I've misheard him): 'Sorry?'

Old guy: 'ALGEBRA! You know x's y's that kind of thing?'

Me: 'Well I did a bit in school but that's a good while ago.'

Old guy: 'Jesus it's fierce handy stuff. Fierce handy stuff.'

And with that he turns away and doesn't say another word.

Overheard by Mic, no. 13A bus
Posted on Friday, 29 April 2005

Stupid computers

Student: 'Computers can be so stupid sometimes!'

Computer programming lecturer: 'Computers are only as stupid as the people who put the information in!'

Student (correcting himself): 'Yeah ... suppose!
Computer programmers are so stupid.'

Overheard by Locks, computer lab, DIT, Aungier Street
Posted on Friday, 29 April 2005

Did you make it yourself?

While bringing my dog (a Kerry Blue terrier) for
a walk in the local park, I encountered the
following from a passer-by:

Passer-by: 'That's a gorgeous dog! Is it a he or a
she?'

Me: 'Thanks, it's a he.'

Passer-by: 'It's very unique, what make is it?'

Me: 'Eh ... a Kerry Blue terrier.'

Overheard by Pete, Bushy Park, Rathfarnham
Posted on Friday, 29 April 2005

Putting the vegetarian argument to rest

Mother with her young son and teenage
daughter on the bus into town for a day out. An
argument ensues:

Young Boy: 'Mam, can we go to McDonald's
later?'

Mam: 'We'll see, don't forget that Cliona's a
vegetarian so she may not want to eat there.'

Teenage Girl: 'There's no way we're going to
McDonald's.'

Young Boy: 'That's not fair, anyway what's wrong
with eating meat?'

Teenage Girl: 'It's cruelty to animals.'

Young Boy: 'If we aren't supposed to eat animals, then why are they made out of meat?'

Teenage Girl — eyes to heaven.

Overheard by Rob, no. 15B bus
Posted on Friday, 29 April 2005

Stones

A few months ago I overheard two auld fellas in a city pub talking about an African woman who was to be deported. She did not wish to leave Ireland, claiming that she would be stoned to death in her own country after being found guilty of committing adultery. One auld fella says,

'I hope they don't bring that in here or they'll run out of stones.'

Overheard by DW, Foggy Dew pub
Posted on Friday, 29 April 2005

Garda exaggeration

Sitting in Tallaght District Court as you do, awaiting my own wrist slapping, a young fellah was up before the court on possession of cannabis resin.

Garda: 'The defendant was found in possession of approximately 20 grams of cannabis resin.'

Judge: 'In layman's terms about how much is that?'

Garda: 'It's enough for about 70 cannabis cigarettes, your honour.'

Defendant (in absolute shock): 'What the f**k are you smoking, you must be doing serious top loadin?'

Court and congregated skangers: — Hysterics

Judge: — Not impressed

Overheard by cormdogg, Tallaght District Court
Posted on Thursday, 28 April 2005

Higher de musik down

On the no. 27 bus a bunch of young skangers are sitting down the back annoying everyone with the hard house blaring out of their tinny stereo. One of their phones starts ringing and the owner takes a look at the caller ID screen and says:

'Jaysus, it's me ma, higher de musik down, willya!'

Overheard by Fenster, no. 27 bus from Coolock
Posted on Thursday, 28 April 2005

Free lift

Having snuck into the Trinity Ball and decided it wasn't worth it after all, me and a friend were heading for the exit behind a couple of posh gals, with their sandals in their hands.

We pass by a girl with vomit stains down her swanky dress and still with a beer in one hand, being loaded into a wheelchair by the bored looking ambulance fellas. One of the girls in front of us says,

'Jesus look at her. Lucky cow, she'll get a lift home in the ambulance.'

Overheard by Ruffy, by the Rubrics in Trinners
Posted on Thursday, 28 April 2005

Never a truer word was spoken

One strung-out skanger passing another strung-out skanger at a bus stop in Irishtown.

Skanger 1: 'Where ya goin?'

Skanger 2: 'Nowhere.'

Overheard by Katie, Irishtown
Posted on Thursday, 28 April 2005

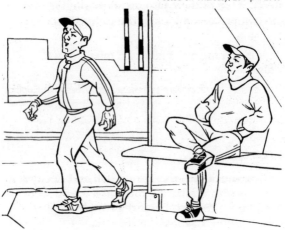

Colour dilemma

'I don't want cream. Cream is for girls. Girls are gay. I'm not gay. I want black. Black is deadly.'

Overheard by Giggler, 7-year-old telling his ma his choice of Holy Communion suit colours on the no. 51B bus, Clondalkin
Posted on Thursday, 28 April 2005

A glass of Dun Laoghaire

Two middle-aged English couples came into a bar and asked the barman did he know any good ports, to which the barman replied, 'Yes, Dun Laoghaire.'

Tourist: 'Ok, we'll have two of those and two Guinness, please.'

Overheard by katy, The Auld Dubliner, Temple Bar
Posted on Thursday, 28 April 2005

Breadless sandwich

Me: 'Can I have a brown bread sandwich?'

Girl serving: 'We have no brown bread.'

Me: 'Can I have a roll then?'

Girl serving: 'We have no rolls.'

Me: 'Can I have a white bread sandwich or a bap or something?'

Girl serving: 'We have no white bread or baps.'

Me: 'What have you?'

Girl serving: 'Wraps.'

Overheard by Stephen, sandwich bar in Fare Play shop in Esso
garage at Loughlinstown
Posted on Wednesday, 27 April 2005

Tarantula rain

Was sitting in my sister's car coming to work one morning, when she starts complaining about the dirt of the car. I asked her how it got so dirty. Her reply:

'I drove to Ashbourne last night in the tarantula rain.'

As opposed to torrential!

Overheard by Anonymous, on way to work!
Posted on Wednesday, 27 April 2005

Some people have it tough

Two Dublin 4 women in conversation on bus:

D4 #1: 'Have you been away at all?'

D4 #2: 'No just a few short breaks, nothing major.'

D4 #1: 'Where did you go?'

D4 #2: 'We were in New York for a weekend at Christmas then for Valentine's we went to Paris and at Easter we had a week in West Cork.'

D4 #1: 'I bet you can't wait to get away again?'

D4 #2: 'Oh yeah, like a real holiday abroad.'

Overheard by anonymous, no. 46A bus
Posted on Wednesday, 27 April 2005

The weathermen

In college I overheard two lads from Galway talking about a holiday one of them had just come back from:

Lad #1: 'So, how did you find the heat?'

Lad #2: 'Ah, shur it wasn't the heat, it was the humanity that would kill ya!'

TV3 Weather might have some competition on their hands!

Overheard by Anonymous, DIT, Aungier Street
Posted on Tuesday, 26 April 2005

Geographically in limbo

Sitting in one of the larger lecture theatres in Bolton Street at the information sessions they do for Leaving Cert students. After a gruelling two hour talk about the relative merits of studying engineering in the DIT, the chairman asks anyone with any questions to submit them to the panel by writing them down on a piece of paper and passing them down to the front.

My mate starts writing frantically, and passes his question forward. The chairman collects it and reads it out:

'Is there any relationship between geography and engineering?'

To which the same chairman replied, with the sternest of looks in the direction of my mate,

'Well you found your way here to the lecture didn't you?'

Overheard by RonnieDrewsDublin, DIT, Bolton Street
Posted on Tuesday, 26 April 2005

Where's a revolving door when you need one?

While walking out of a hotel lobby with a friend and her mother, her mother was having a hard time trying to pull open the door. So my friend says to her mother,

'Mam, it says PUSH on the door!'

To which her mother replies,

'I know it says PUSH but it doesn't say which way!'

Overheard by Barry, Bewley's Hotel
Posted on Tuesday, 26 April 2005

Never assume a Dublin bus driver knows the way!

I was getting a replacement bus from Portmarnock DART Station to the city centre as there are no DART services at the weekends on the northside. It was a Sunday afternoon and I was the only passenger on the bus. There was the inspector/supervisor guy talking to the bus driver who was obviously foreign. I listened more carefully and realised the inspector guy was giving the bus driver directions! I immediately thought … feck!

Then, to my great amusement, the inspector turned to me and asked me, 'Young man, do you know where you're goin?' To which I replied, 'Yeah.'

He then said, 'You wuddin mind keepin an eye on this lad and showing him the way, wud ya?'

!?

Turned out the bus driver was from Guatemala and I had a great chat with him and we ended up going a little bit out of the way, but it was one of my more enjoyable Dublin Bus experiences!

Overheard by Anonymous, Portmarnock
Posted on Tuesday, 26 April 2005

Rugby goys

Was on a packed Luas on the way into work the other day, and we pull up to Ranelagh. This jock in a suit and tie is trying to get on, but there was no room, so next thing he says, 'Roysh goys rugby squeeze' and he forces himself onto the

Luas. He spent the rest of the journey into Stephen's Green muttering to himself.

Extraordinary!

Overheard by Chris, on the Luas (Ranelagh)
Posted on Tuesday, 26 April 2005

The wristband inspector

A curious 'head-the-ball' impatiently waiting for a bus decides to question a young student (who knows it's probably in his best interests to answer) about his array of wristbands.

Head-the-ball: 'What are they about bud?'

Student: 'Em just different charities.'

Head-the-ball: 'Yeah? What's the yellow one for?'

Student: 'It's for a cancer charity.'

Head-the-ball: 'What's the white one for?'

Student: 'It's an anti-racism bracelet.'

Head-the-ball: 'What's the black one for?'

Student: 'It comes with the white one.'

Head-the-ball: 'What's the blue one for?'

Student: 'The blue one's for anti-bullying and the red one's for Childline.'

Head-the-ball: 'Do you have any more?'

Student: 'No, that's it.'

Head-the-ball: 'Good man.'

Overheard by Jimmy, bus stop outside IT, Tallaght
Posted on Monday, 25 April 2005

Have a seat

Imagine a nice night out with friends in town in a bar I won't mention. You go to the loo and notice a girl sitting on the sink and think, oh there's loads of seats outside, then you realise she is sitting there for a reason. All the loos are full and she happily tells you, 'Jesus I was dying.'

Disturbed? I think so!

Overheard by saoirse, pub in Dublin
Posted on Monday, 25 April 2005

Only trying to help

Sitting on NiteLink at 2 a.m. trying to keep myself to myself. When approached by a young Dublin lad on his way home, suitably refreshed after a night on the Beer.

Dub: 'Does dis bus stop in Palmerstown?'

Me: 'I dunno, why don't you ask the driver?'

Dub: 'Ahh why don't you ask me bollix!'

Me: ?

Overheard by Niall, NiteLink to Lucan
Posted on Monday, 25 April 2005

Dog story

'Rover! Cameer ya bollix!'

Overheard by Barbara Woodhouse, street
Posted on Friday, 22 April 2005

Decent bloke

Girl: 'Giz a kiss.'

Bloke: 'Let me swally me phlegm first.'

Overheard by Trixibell, Talbot Street
Posted on Friday, 22 April 2005

Ireland of the welcomes!

In Roddy Boland's in Rathmines one night I overheard a group of Italian guys (tourists) trying to chat up two Irish girls and not getting very far. One of the Italians started waxing lyrical about one of the girls and her 'beautiful pale skin' and said,

'In my country, you would be a princess.'

To which the Irish girl replied,

'And in my country, you'd work in a chipper, now f**k off.'

Overheard by Kaz, Roddy Boland's
Posted on Friday, 22 April 2005

Handbags

At a well-known tourist bar in Temple Bar the musicians are trying to get the crowd going:

MC: 'Is there anyone here from Germany?'

Germans: 'Yeahhhhh!'

MC: 'Is there anyone here from England?'

English: 'Yeahhhhh!'

Irish: 'Boooo!'

MC: 'Is there anyone here from Cork?'

Cork People: 'Yeahhhhh!' etc. etc.

MC: 'Is there anyone here from Limerick?'

Limerick People: 'Yeahhhh!'

MC: 'Well the rest of yiz, mind your bleedin' handbags!'

Overheard by Mick, Oliver St John Gogarty's

Posted on Friday, 22 April 2005

Irish law is never black and white

In one of the Dublin district courts during a hearing the injured party is being questioned by the defence barrister. The barrister is really trying to put pressure on the man and questions whether he can identify his client who allegedly assaulted him. The injured party is sitting in the witness box and without flinching points across the room and says loudly,

'Yer man there, the black fella.'

The defence barrister loses the rag and begins ranting about being prejudicial to his client's skin colour and so forth. The barrister continues along this line of attack and says indignantly to the injured party who is still in the witness box,

'Can you identify the man in this courtroom who you allege assaulted you, without referring to his skin colour?'

The injured party looks up at the judge and then at the barrister, shrugs and says, 'Yeah.'

The barrister asks him to do so. The injured party points again across the courtroom and says,

'Yer man sitting over there between the two white blokes.'

Overheard by Anonymous, Dublin District Court

Posted on Thursday, 21 April 2005

I don't give a Ratzinger

I was in a queue in Tesco in town the other day after work when I heard two lads talking about the new Pope:

'What do you think about the new Pope?' said one to the other.

The reply: 'I don't give a Ratzinger ...'

Boom boom!

Overheard by John, Tesco
Posted on Thursday, 21 April 2005

Good news for Robbie Keane then

Overheard two lads talking about football:

Lad #1: 'I think Robbie Keane has lost his impotence' (meant to say *impetus*).

Lad #2: 'Impotence!? Will you stop using big words for feck sake' (failing to pick up on his mate's error).

Overheard by Sean, Hanlon's pub
Posted on Thursday, 21 April 2005

Grand opening

Was at my grandmother's funeral when during a quiet part of the mass my daughter (three years old) asked,

'Daddy, when are they opening the box?'

Overheard by Roy, church in Raheny
Posted on Wednesday, 20 April 2005

Country girl in the big smoke

Country girl gets on no. 16 bus and asks driver how much is the fare.

Driver replies, 'Where are you going?'

Country girl says, 'To get my hair done!'

Overheard by Helen, no. 16 bus
Posted on Wednesday, 20 April 2005

Red sky at night ...

In the back of a cab on a summer's night going up the quays, it was a beautiful evening with a red sky.

'Red sky at night ...' said my friend Neil, waiting for one of us to finish the well-known phrase.

'... Tallaght's on fire,' intercepted the cab driver.

Hearty laughs all round.

Overheard by Ems, back of a cab
Posted on Wednesday, 20 April 2005

A real breakfast roll

While in a Spar shop a young shop assistant was serving me at the deli counter. I asked her for a breakfast roll; she was obviously new to the job and went to her boss. I missed some of the conversation but I did hear her ask the boss,

'So will I give yer wan cornflakes or rice krispies in a bread roll or somtin, I haven't a clue wah she's on abou?'

She had failed to notice the hot counter …

Overheard by squeegie, Spar shop
Posted on Wednesday, 20 April 2005

Alternative history

Was walking past the GPO and an English bloke was showing off his knowledge of Irish history to a couple of English girls.

'That building is the GPO, it was where the Irish had their revolution in 1910!'

Well, he wasn't that far off!

Overheard by penny, GPO
Posted on Wednesday, 20 April 2005

Chugger excuse

For those of you who don't know, a 'Chugger' is an in-your-face 'Charity Mugger'. One of those over-confident, dreadlocked, hoody-wearing, studenty-type, 'out-of-work actor type' people who stands in the street with a clipboard soliciting donations to the Feline Liberation Army or some other worthy cause.

Scene: A chugger approaches two lads strolling through Temple Bar:

Chugger: 'Hi goys! Do you have a moment?'

Guy #1: 'Eh ...'

Chugger: 'Roysh, what we do is ...'

Guy #2: 'I already have an account with this charity.'

Chugger: 'Oh, well done.' (Then turning his attention to guy #2) 'How about yourself?'

Guy #2 (sheepishly): 'So do I.'

Overheard by Pete, Temple Bar (where else?)
Posted on Wednesday, 20 April 2005

The real Gaelic football?

On the Aircoach heading over the Royal Canal with a vista of Croke Park in the distance, one Spanish guy — appearing all-knowledgeable about Dublin — turns to his newcomer friend and, pointing, says,

'That's where Celtic play ...'

Overheard by Nicola, Aircoach
Posted on Wednesday, 20 April 2005

De BIG leeher o' milk

Girl at petrol station to shop assistant who has brought her order of a 'leeher o' milk' to the hatch:

'Are ya f**kin' deaf or wha? I wanted de BIG leeher.'

And off she went a moment later as happy as Larry with her 2-litre carton!

Overheard by Mary, Clondalkin petrol station
Posted on Tuesday, 19 April 2005

Seen through a child's eyes!

A young boy was in mass with his granny the other day and he insisted on sitting in the middle of the aisle directly in front of the altar. When his granny tried to drag him in to sit beside her, the little boy turned around and told her that he was sitting in the middle,

'So God could get a better view of him!'

Overheard by Emma, mass in Blackrock
Posted on Tuesday, 19 April 2005

Trivial Pursuit

Our friends were staying with us for a weekend. We were pretty broke so we decided we'd stay in and have a few drinks AND buy Trivial Pursuit ... how exciting! We visited Argos for our purchase. While paying for it at the till, the cashier verified my purchase ... 'Trivall Pursue'.

Overheard by Brenda, Argos, Blanchardstown
Posted on Tuesday, 19 April 2005

Fingers for toes

Working in Simon Harts shoe shop on Henry Street I had a foreign lady come up to me and say,

'I think I need another size, my fingers are too tight in this one.'

Overheard by Gillian, Simon Harts, Henry Street
Posted on Tuesday, 19 April 2005

Geography and History lessons needed

As I was crossing College Green last Saturday, I overheard a young Dubliner say to her friend, 'Do you know where you are now?' to which the friend, presumably from outside Dublin, replied 'Nope.' So the Dub said, sweeping her arm in the direction of the Bank of Ireland and Trinity,

'The Four Courts!'

Overheard by Aoife, College Green
Posted on Tuesday, 19 April 2005

Sixteen Chapel, Rome

Asked my 6-year-old son what he learned at school today. He replied,

'They were picking the new Pope in the "sixteen chapel"!'

Overheard by Larry, at the school gate
Posted on Tuesday, 19 April 2005

Irish queen

Walking down Pearse Street the other day and to my utter annoyance I heard one American tourist say to the other,

'Does the Queen rule here?'

Overheard by taytos, Pearse Street
Posted on Tuesday, 19 April 2005

Good Friday Agreement

A friend of mine was explaining to an African work colleague in Ballyfermot the Christian calendar, and all the holidays and feast days. He was going over Shrove Tuesday, Ash Wednesday, Palm Sunday etc. When he reached Good Friday, the African colleague butted in,

'Yes, I know this holiday — this is the anniversary of peace in Northern Ireland, so we all get a holiday.'

[Good Friday Agreement!]

Overheard by Jason T. Flamingo, work in Ballyfermot
Posted on Tuesday, 19 April 2005

Point of no return

A true blue Dublin elderly couple walked up to the ticket window at the DART station. They looked a little confused — like maybe they don't use the DART that much — and whispered among themselves for a few seconds.

Eventually the man says to the ticket guy, 'I need two return tickets.'

Ticket guy: 'Where to?'

Old guy: 'Here!'

Overheard by Dermot, Kilbarrack DART Station
Posted on Tuesday, 19 April 2005

Ah Jaws'us!

Walking over the Ha'penny Bridge, a mum and her kid were in front of me … the kid is crying.

Mum: 'If you don' bleedin' shuddup I'll throw you to the sharks!'

Overheard by Jemima, Ha'penny Bridge

Posted on Monday, 18 April 2005

Loik!

D4 head (wearing a bright yellow shirt):

'Loik what is up with pink shirts lately! Loik do fellas not want to show their masculinity or something?'

Overheard by Denver, Grafton Street

Posted on Monday, 18 April 2005

Those PlayStations

A commonly heard comment from GAA people in conversations on the debate of Croke Park on the radio over the last few days:

GAA man: 'The GAA has done a lot for the children of this country. Our activities keep them away from drink, drugs and playstations …'

Overheard by Leo, Dublin Radio

Posted on Monday, 18 April 2005

One of the lad(ie)s

Dublin Airport, off on holidays to Portugal with the lads, when my mate was next in line for passport control.

'Ever been abroad before?' the passport controller asked.

'No, I've always been a man!' came the reply.

Kicked off the holiday! Absolute classic!

Overheard by BianoBoy, Dublin Airport

Posted on Monday, 18 April 2005

The leaning toxer of Eiffel

Sitting in Arnott's café and there is this fella there obviously taking his elderly mother out for some Sunday shopping. Over a cup of coffee he's showing her photos from a recent trip:

'Now ma, there's the Eiffel Tower,' he says as he passes over a photo.

After a quick look at the photo she replies, 'Oh they've stopped it leaning so, that's good.'

Overheard by Stephen, Arnott's café

Posted on Monday, 18 April 2005

Not so hard to get into college after all ...

Overheard two girls on the bus discussing college recently.

Girl #1: 'So are there more guys or girls on your course then?'

Girl #2: 'Definitely more girls ... I'd say it'd be 65:55 ...'

The correction never came.

Overheard by Fembot, no. 16A bus
Posted on Monday, 18 April 2005

'A test bus'

On the no. 45 bus, a route which takes in some of Dublin's leafier suburbs. Up the front of the top deck of the bus was an American family, taking it all in. Anyone who knows this route will be familiar with the sound of the branches from the overhanging trees brushing and thumping the side of the bus.

This sparked a vocal debate among the Americans about how the trees were cut. In the end they settled on the theory that a 'test bus' which had a kind of rotating saw on the top corner, must go out every morning to cut the branches back ...

Overheard by The Jackal, no. 45 bus
Posted on Monday, 18 April 2005

Wrong sport

Overheard on the way to a canoe water polo championship.

Woman to her friend: 'But I don't understand how they get the horses into the water ...'

Overheard by OI, in Dublin
Posted on Monday, 18 April 2005

Radio GAA GAA

I was at a GAA club football match and quite near me was a young man listening to the radio. He was listening to pop music on 2FM. That day there also happened to be quite a big inter-county match taking place in Croke Park. A middle-aged man sitting in front of me, obviously curious as to how the big game was panning out, turned to the young man and asked,

'Can you get Telefis Eireann on that yoke?'

Overheard by Finian Murray, local GAA club
Posted on Monday, 18 April 2005

Vindaloo and Guinness

On a packed train and there was somebody who obviously had been eating Vindaloo and had gallons of Guinness the night before — the stench was unreal! This old lady got so annoyed and screamed all over the carriage,

'Can the person who is farting please stop; you're turning my god damn stomach.'

At this the carriage of people fell around
laughing …

Overheard by Dearbhla, on the DART heading into work
Posted on Monday, 18 April 2005

Corrugation of kids

A neighbour of ours who lives in a corner house
was complaining about kids hanging around at
the side of her house. She asked my Ma why the
kids had to 'corrugate' outside her house all the
time.

Overheard by Jimmy, Finglas
Posted on Sunday, 17 April 2005

Didn't lick it off the stones

A friend of mine, teaching junior infants in
Tallaght, asked a mother to come and see her
because she was concerned about the bad
language being used by one particular child.
Every day at breaktime when she asked the
children to sit down so they could have some
milk and biscuits, the little girl would say,

'F**k you and your milk and biscuits, I'm
playing.'

She told the mother what was happening and
the mother paused for a moment.

'Diya know wha ti do,' said the mother, 'f**k
her, don't give 'er any, the ungrateful little get.'

Overheard by Anonymous, school in Tallaght
Posted on Sunday, 17 April 2005

Thrilled and dilated

Working as an EMT on a Dublin ambulance, I was bringing a 16-year-old girl to the Rotunda Hospital.

'Would you say you're dilated?' I asked her. To which she replied,

'Dy-lay-rah? I'm over the f**kin moon!'

Overheard, Dublin ambulance by Sheller
Posted on Sunday, 17 April 2005

Worldly mothers part III

Watching the Ireland v England Six Nations match with my family, the camera zooms in on Roy Keane in the crowd.

Dad goes, 'Wudja look who it is!'

Mum (sincerely) goes, 'What's Charlie Bird doing at a rugby match?'

Overheard by dani o'meara, sa bhaile
Posted on Sunday, 17 April 2005

Dairy-pod

I was walking through my bro's school with a stick of butter and this kid walked over to me and said, 'Oh deadly, how much songs does that hold?'

Overheard by Poj, Scoil Mobhi
Posted on Sunday, 17 April 2005

A reasonable threat

Mammy: 'If you're not good for your mammy, I'll put you in a black sack and leave you in the mountains.'

Overheard by Jenny, no. 3 Ballymun bus
Posted on Sunday, 17 April 2005

A '10 minute' '15 minute' break

Musician: 'I'm just taking a quick 10 minute break, I'll be back in about 15 minutes.'

Overheard by Brian, Three Rock pub
Posted on Sunday, 17 April 2005

Whodini?

I was buying a scratch card (classy!) in downtown newsagent. 'What type of card dja want love?' 'A winning one,' I reply wittily. 'Ahh come on now love — I'm not bleedin' Houdini!'

Overheard by Sunniva, Dame Street
Posted on Sunday, 17 April 2005

Just plain disgusting

A gang of oul fellas leaving the Black Sheep absolutely plastered. One stops and starts vomiting behind a car. 'Will ya hurry up for f**k sake, Deco, wor bleedin freezin.' Deco shouts back, 'Jaysus will yis wait til I get me teeth.'

With that he fishes his false teeth out of the pool of vomit and puts them straight back into his mouth and says, 'Are we gettin a burger or wha?'

Overheard by Anonymous, Black Sheep
Posted on Saturday, 16 April 2005

2 weeks in Pavarotti — priceless

I work with two oul lads and one comes in the other day delighted with himself, announces he's after getting two tickets for Pavarotti. To which the other replied,

'Jaysus, dat's great, are yis goin' for one week or two?'

Overheard by Dave, Tayto
Posted on Saturday, 16 April 2005

Meath Hospital

Worried about a series of nose bleeds, my friend went to see his local doctor in Inchicore. When the doctor suggested that he would probably need to go to Meath Hospital (in Dublin of course), he replied,

'Is there any chance I could go to one in Dublin?'

Overheard by Dave, Inchicore
Posted on Saturday, 16 April 2005

Brains from the 'Brack

My football team recently got a new manager from Ballybrack. At one of his first training sessions he was taking the warm-up, wanting us to increase the pace. He instructed, 'Right lads, up to three quarter pace … 87 per cent.'

We have lost our first five games this season …

Overheard by Blackadder, training in Ballybrack
Posted on Saturday, 16 April 2005

Cruel but funny

A couple of years ago I was waiting for a bus to Maynooth at the Abbey Street terminus. A very short guy walked by wearing a Dublin Bus uniform, when some bloke shouts out,

'Ere Mister, are you a mini-bus driver?'

Overheard by Mick, waiting in line for the bus to Maynooth
Posted on Saturday, 16 April 2005

Angina luv?

I'm a medical secretary and last week the doctor I work for was stunned when, while giving an examination to a woman who had complained of chest pains, he murmured to himself, 'Angina,' to which she replied,

'Enjoyin' it? I'm bleedin' lovin' it!'

Overheard by Anna, Mater Hospital
Posted on Saturday, 16 April 2005

Fussy

Two 'yaw roights', dolled up to the nines, admiring each other, drinking mudshakes and waiting to be asked to dance. Eventually an average looking guy approached one of them.

Guy: 'Grea' in here isn it, de ye wan ti dance?'

The girl looked at him scathingly from head to toe and replied as bitchily as she could, 'No thanks, I'm fussy about who I dance with,' and then smirked at her friend.

Quick as a flash the guy replied, 'I'm not love, that's why I asked you.'

Overheard by x, Turks Head
Posted on Saturday, 16 April 2005

Nice

Two culchie women choosing soft drinks — one has a Fanta, the other a Sprite Zero.

Sprite Zero Lady: 'Sure get this one, it's meant ta be good for ya.'

Fanta Lady: 'Ah but I like this one better.'

Sprite Zero Lady: 'But this one's got zero carolies!'

(misspelling intentional)

Overheard by S, Tesco in the Dundrum Town Centre
Posted on Saturday, 16 April 2005

Language barriers

I was working in Arnotts (Sports Shoes) last summer, when a young Chinese couple came up to me to enquire about a size of a pair of runners. The man seemed to be impatient and in a hurry. I asked him, 'Are you rushing?' to which the two of them looked at me in disgust and replied out loud,

'No, we are Chinese!'

Overheard by Sean, Arnotts
Posted on Friday, 15 April 2005

Em, water I guess

Group of Kerry lads walking in the Clonskeagh entrance of UCD, first day of college; one of the lads turns, looks up at the large tall structure and asks,

'Lads, what's stored in the water tower?'

1st Class Honours!

Overheard by J Perryman, UCD
Posted on Friday, 15 April 2005

Lookin great!

Went to the toilet in the Windjammer pub, Townsend Street. From the cubicle I overheard two women:

Younger woman: 'Jaysis, Margaret, you're lookin great! What age are you now?'

Older woman (proudly): 'I'm 74.'

Younger woman: 'Jaysis, that's the age Rob's mother was when she died!'

Overheard by Anonymous, Windjammer pub
Posted on Friday, 15 April 2005

Seven Letters — 12 Across

While listening to a couple of mates today doing a crossword at lunchtime:

Crossword guy: 'Capital city of Cyprus?'

Friend: 'How many letters?'

Crossword guy: 'Seven.'

Friend: 'Any letters?'

Crossword guy: 'Yep, third letter is "C".'

Friend: 'Any other info?'

Crossword guy: 'Yep, it's 12 Across.'

Friend: 'Oh, Nicosia!'

Overheard by Paddy, Hewlett Packard canteen
Posted on Friday, 15 April 2005

Croke Park (a heated debate)

Man #1: 'So do you hope the GAA vote yes to change Rule 42?'

Man #2: 'What? What the f**k you on about?'

Overheard by Macker, Boardwalk
Posted on Friday, 15 April 2005

No, we don't sell dictionaries

Customer: 'Is that sign going to be permanent?'

Cashier: 'For a little while.'

Overheard by Dec, Eason's
Posted on Friday, 15 April 2005

Jesus saves

Priest tells joke at mass: 'The devil and Jesus were both doing work on their computer, then there's a power cut. The devil loses all his work but Jesus doesn't, because Jesus never forgets to save!'

Overheard by Greg, mass in Coolock
Posted on Friday, 15 April 2005

Boy or girl?

Heard a girl answer her phone in the waiting room of Holles Street Maternity Hospital:

'Well, tell me, am I an Auntie or an Uncle?'

Overheard by Roy, Holles Street
Posted on Thursday, 14 April 2005

Engineering solutions

I was sitting on a plane in Dublin Airport recently, about to take off for Prague, when one of the air hostesses noticed a panel above my seat was hanging down. She said we couldn't take off until this was sorted by an engineer. Ten minutes later, the engineer comes on. He has a look at the panel while stroking his chin. He then walks off and comes back 15 minutes later with Sellotape and begins to tape the panel back in place.

Someone says sarcastically, 'Do you want a piece of chewing gum just to make doubly sure?'

The engineer laughs and says, 'You think this is bad! You should see the wing!'

Overheard by Yossarian, sitting on Aer Lingus flight on runway at
Dublin Airport
Posted on Thursday, 14 April 2005

No minerils!

I was in the Liffey Valley Shopping Centre during Christmas and decided to visit the 'Food Court'. The place was chock a block with queues of people. Unfortunately McDonald's had run out of soft drinks and instead of the expected 'McDonald's would like to apologise for the lack of soft drinks and encourage you to try our delicious shakes etc.' message, an employee was standing in front of the queue to deliver a special announcement:

'Dere's no point en' queuin', we've no minerils!'

Overheard by Anthony, Liffey Valley
Posted on Thursday, 14 April 2005

Smoking's bad for your feet

I was smoking on the upper deck of the no. 17A. The bus driver comes over the speaker and says, 'We would like to remind passengers that smoking is not allowed on the bus.'

I was just putting it out when he continued, 'Smoking causes blisters on your feet when you have to get out and walk.'

Overheard by Annmarie, no. 17A bus
Posted on Thursday, 14 April 2005

Taxi driver wisdom

Getting a taxi home from town after being at a gig in memory of Phil Lynott of Thin Lizzy. The driver was (of course) a Lizzy expert. His opinion of Phil Lynott was:

'Ah yeahhhh, Philo was the only really COOL Irish rock star, yenowadimean? Like, Bono ... he's just a f**kin social worker with a singin' career.'

Overheard by flish, taxi
Posted on Thursday, 14 April 2005

Tax the passengers

On the no. 41A bus heading for town, two guys got on in their 'nice' shell tracksuits and caps at 45 degree angles. One of the guys spies a poster on the bus for 'bustext' to which he loudly proclaims,

'BUS-TAXT? Look at that, the gov-dern-ment trying to rip us off again!'

Overheard by Anonymous, no. 41A bus
Posted on Thursday, 14 April 2005

Allegators

Working in Sheriff Street for An Post. We had a serious union meeting where the head of the branch was giving out that someone was making allegations about him ... he said,

'If I catch the allegators there's gonna be trouble!'

Enough said ...

Overheard by Fergus, Sheriff Street (An Post)
Posted on Wednesday, 13 April 2005

Visce?

A typical Trinity/D4 toff asking a lunch lady in the Buttery:

Toff: 'Sorry, is there anywhere I can get wawter?'

Lady: 'Sardy, love?'

Toff: 'I want wawter.'

Lady: 'WHA?'

Toff: 'WAWTER.'

This went on for an amazingly long time till she finally copped it and said, 'Ohhh … whaaaaaaaateh,' with a big smile on her face.

Overheard by Jemima, The Buttery, Trinity
Posted on Wednesday, 13 April 2005

Our Lady of Fatima Mansions

Religion teacher: 'Anyone ever hear about the story of an apparition of the Virgin Mary at Fatima?'

Girl: 'Fatima? Wha, ya mean Fatima where the Luas stops?' (referring to the Luas stop at Fatima Mansions)

Overheard by Stephen, Religion class in Dublin school (5th year class)
Posted on Wednesday, 13 April 2005

Bisexual patients

While visiting the Mater Hospital, hearing an old man complaining about the current conditions in hospital and being kept in a unisex environment:

Old Man (to his daughter): 'I'm 92 years old and here I am being left on a bed in a corridor with all these other patients, and to make it worst it's bisexual!'

Overheard by Bill, Mater Hospital
Posted on Wednesday, 13 April 2005

Blind ignorance

At the cinema waiting for a friend I began listening to these two lads having a chat about what films they wanted to see.

Lad 1: 'I'd like to see this Ray movie everyone iz on about.'

Lad 2: 'Heard abou that. What's that abou?'

Lad 1: 'Dunno man, think it's about Stevie Wonder or somethin!'

Overheard by nuno, UCI Cinema, Tallaght
Posted on Wednesday, 13 April 2005

Isaac's index of Irish shares

Heard on the no. 46A into Dublin. Two D4 type girls sitting in front of me.

Girl #1: 'If I wanted to learn about shares, loike, what should I do?'

Girl #2: 'Dunno, maybe find that Isaac guy, my dad is always talking about him and his index of Irish shares.'

Overheard by Pamela, no. 46A bus
Posted on Wednesday, 13 April 2005

Brother or sister?

I was on the no. 33 bus when I overheard a mother and her son talking about how she was pregnant. The mother turns to her son who was about four and says, 'So, what would you prefer, a sister or a brother?'

And the son replies, 'No, I want a hedgehog.'

Overheard by Lisa, no. 33 bus
Posted on Wednesday, 13 April 2005

Real rugger bugger

There would often be a question as to whether Leinster rugby fans are REAL rugby supporters. This question was answered at a Leinster home match in Donnybrook when a D4 type standing behind us shouted, 'Come on Orland!'

'Nuff said!

Overheard by partygirl, Donnybrook
Posted on Wednesday, 13 April 2005

A shed full o' laughs

I was catching an early flight from Dublin
Airport and parked in the long term car park.
The Aer Rianta bus driver warned us to remove
all our personal items. We all listened intently.
He finished by saying,

'I'm only tellin' ya dis because I can't fit an'tin
more into my shed at home.'

Oh how we laughed!

Overheard by Ronan, Dublin Airport
Posted on Wednesday, 13 April 2005

Theoretical universe of love

In work a few months back, two lads started
talking about the world-famous, wheelchair-
bound physicist Stephen Hawkins.

Dude 1: 'Yeah, he's a genius alright and he's
really rich, but I read in the paper that his wife
beats him stiff.'

Dude 2: 'No way, that's disgraceful!'

Dude 1: 'Yeah, she's really mean to him. I mean
why would you want to marry someone just to
be horrible to them?'

Dude 2: 'Well if some super-rich dude in a
wheelchair wanted to marry me, I'd totally do it!
Just call me Mrs Wheelchair.'

Silence ...

Overheard by Jim, in work
Posted on Wednesday, 13 April 2005

Dublin bus drivers are legends

Some heavy rain during the winter caused floods on roads north out of Dublin. At evening rush hour it took almost three hours to get from the city centre to Santry. The driver of the no. 33 bus kept everybody in good humour by singing songs and cracking jokes. But an impatient Russian builder (obviously not familiar with joviality!) proceeded to give the driver a tongue lashing as he was getting off the bus for causing him to be very late for work (seemingly Dublin Bus controls the weather, which is handy if you don't want to start your route till you've had another cuppa).

The bus driver responds, 'Sure why didn't ye say anything before, if I had a known I would a let ye out to swim.'

Overheard by Anonymous, no. 33 bus
Posted on Tuesday, 12 April 2005

Flight stimulator

Was watching RTE news at six today. The presenter was talking about the security scare at Dublin Airport. He then turned to this young one 'security expert' in the studio. She explained that some knives and a fake bomb were smuggled through security, before reassuring viewers that it was just a 'stimulated exercise'.

Overheard by Jack, on RTE
Posted on Tuesday, 12 April 2005

Great mind never bores

At a rather prestigious award ceremony at UCD they had an old alumnus come to talk to a fairly well-to-do audience of Ireland's foremost academic minds. The former student was getting on a bit and despite his respect as a great mind in his field, he was Dublin through and through. As a host for the event I was to walk him on and off stage.

As he was introduced to rapturous applause he turned to me and said in a thick Dublin accent,

'Jaysis, they spent six years trying to kick me out for drinking, fornicating and drinking more and they invite me back 50 years later to say thanks! … Gobshites the lot of them.'

Not sure what he talked about after that but needless to say he stole the show for me with that line.

Overheard by Sarah, UCD presentation
Posted on Tuesday, 12 April 2005

Tres witty

I work for a funeral directors firm in Dublin. We assisted an archaeology team at an old inner city church which was clearing the contents of several medieval crypts. The material found was examined and then taken to Glasnevin for cremation. The church is beside Wolfe Tone Park, a well known spot for winos and longterm homeless to spend the day.

As I was carrying one of the containers to our ambulance, one of the drunk lads shouts out,

'Oy, comeer mister, I've a bleedin' bone to pick with you!'

Overheard by Michael, Wolfe Tone Park
Posted on Tuesday, 12 April 2005

Loose grasp of Geography

In a taxi on the way to the airport, the honest-to-goodness Dublin cabbie engages me in conversation:

Cabbie: 'So off on yer holiers?'

Me: 'Going to a wedding.'

Cabbie: 'Oh yeah? Whereabouts?'

Me: 'Prague.'

Cabbie: 'Prague? Dat's eh ... Budapest, innit?'

Conversation became stilted thereafter ...

Overheard by The Owl, taxi to the Airport
Posted on Tuesday, 12 April 2005

Give that man a job

Interviewing a few lads for floor staff in wholesalers:

Me: 'What are your main strengths?'

Man: 'I'm very hardworking, brave and above all modest' (I think he meant honest).

Me: 'OK, what are your main weaknesses?'

Man: 'Cryptonite.'

Had to give him the job after that!

Overheard by Batistuta, wholesaler in Fairview
Posted on Tuesday, 12 April 2005

Young Logic

My 5-year-old sister comes out of Christmas mass and says to my mam, 'How can he be born at Christmas if they hanged him at Easter?'

Overheard by Gerry, Clougherhead chapel
Posted on Monday, 11 April 2005

Weight Watchers

Woman in chipper says to person taking orders, 'Hav ya anythin Low Fat? I'm on a diet.'

Overheard by Shel, Macari's chipper, Dublin
Posted on Monday, 11 April 2005

People that never died before ...

Two women were talking the other day about a well-known local who had just died. Visibly moved and taken aback by the event, the first woman says, 'Jaysus, it's shocking, the amount of people dead in the last while.'

And the second says, 'Shocking alright, there's an awful amount of people dying nowadays that never died before.'

Overheard by Gaby, Pearse Street
Posted on Monday, 11 April 2005

Eurovision

I was in the shopping centre the following morning after the Eurovision, exchanging the usual banalities with customers, when someone asks if we saw the Eurovision last night, to which the auld fool says,

'Yeah, same old story, them Latin American countries voting for each other!'

Overheard by Anonymous, Donaghmede Shopping Centre
Posted on Monday, 11 April 2005

More taxi driver wisdom

I am having a bizarre meandering conversation with your usual header of a taxi driver when he asks me what I study. I tell him Arts in UCD to which he replies, 'Jaysus, sure you artists only earn money after you die!'

Overheard by Mark, Dublin taxi
Posted on Monday, 11 April 2005

Velcroman

On our way to a Shels match myself and my mates were running for a DART but just missed it (in the typical painful way — doors close just before we got down to the platform). One of my mates (let's call him Velcroman for legal reasons) said:

'Wouldn't it be great if the DART was covered in velcro so when it's pulling out of the station you could jump on and attach yourself' (assuming everyone wears some kind of velcro suit!).

We just couldn't stop taking the mick and then he dug himself even deeper when another of my mates asked how you'd get off. Velcroman's reply was,

'They could employ some guys to stand at each station with big sticks to pry people off.' We couldn't believe it, he was actually serious!

Later, after the match, we again just missed a DART. Velcroman comes up with another ingenious plan:

'OK if you don't like my velcro idea how about one big long DART stretching from Howth to Greystones so you'd never miss one!'

Priceless conversation!

Overheard by Not tonight son, on the way to
and from a Shels match

Posted on Monday, 11 April 2005

Weeta-thicks!

One morning I was after staying in a hotel and I was eating my breakfast and I see an American couple eating weetabix with marmalade on it. Then I hear the couple say to a waitress,

'Your brown bread is very dry. I've heard a lot about your brown bread in America.'

Overheard by anon, a hotel in Dublin

Posted on Monday, 11 April 2005

Questioning one's omelette management abilities

In Argos one day I overheard a man shouting at the girl behind the counter, saying that he wants a refund. The girl tells him that the manager has already told him that he's not getting his money back. The man replies,

'Your manager? She couldn't manage a f**kin omelette!'

Overheard by Kate, Argos
Posted on Monday, 11 April 2005

More snob 'location confusion'

One day I was in the dressing rooms in Penneys. I heard someone's phone ringing. A woman with a posh accent answers and starts yappin away! The person on the phone must have asked her where she was:

'Oh, I'm in Atmosphere! It's a store near Debenhams and Morks!'

Overheard by anon, Penneys, Mary Street
Posted on Monday, 11 April 2005

You've gotta make sure

Was working in a music store and an old enough woman came in and asked, 'Do you sell CDs?'

I pointed her in the direction of ... well ... the whole shop.

Overheard by Edwina, music store
Posted on Monday, 11 April 2005

Pronunciation is Key

Having a pint one Sunday evening, and the conversation at the table next to us gets round to holidays and who's going where. One of the men at the table turns and says,

'I'm going to Majorca (pronouncing it with a J instead of a Y).'

He is immediately corrected by a 'well educated' female friend who is delighted to inform him that it's not madge-orka, but may-orka.

She continues, 'Anyways when are you going?'

To which the guy replies, 'Last week in Yune, first week of Yuly!'

Overheard by Bomber, Kielys, Donnybrook
Posted on Monday, 11 April 2005

I want a munchkin now, Daddy!

Two girls sitting behind me on the no. 48A bus were reminiscing about the old Willy Wonka film and one of them says,

'What was the name of de little fellas again? Yeh know, de ones dat went Oompa Loompa?'

'Munchkins ya tick!' replied the smart one …

Overheard by Batterburger, no. 48A bus
Posted on Monday, 11 April 2005

Spelling it out

In Ireland we have this weird habit of spelling
words out loud when children are present, so
that they don't understand us, you know, like,
'I'll call ya later when the child is in B-E-D.'

Well, I was in McDonald's a couple of weeks ago
and a couple and their daughter were at the
counter ordering. The husband orders
something, and when told they didn't have it, he
says 'F**k'. Then the wife turns to him and
shouts,

'How many times do I have to tell you not to say
fuck in front of the C-H-I-L-D?'

Overheard by PONCHO, Micky D's
Posted on Friday, 16 March 2007

How much is the bus?

A friend of mine had an accident years ago with
a chainsaw in which he lost one finger and part
of another. We were in a bar one night, about to
get a bus to another disco, and a guy shouts

across the bar to him enquiring how much the bus would cost. He put up his hands to signify €10 and the guy shouts back at him, 'What, €8.50?!'

Overheard by Anonymous, pub
Posted on Friday, 16 March 2007

Rough justice

In court a few years back the usual traffic violations were being called up. A man wearing a Dublin Bus uniform and carrying a Dublin Bus bag gets called. The judge asks the prosecuting Garda what he has him here for. 'Driving in a bus lane, your honour,' explains the Garda.

After the courtroom stops laughing the judge says to him, 'You should know better than most as you're a bus driver.'

The accused replies, 'I'm sorry, your honour, but I taut I was in me bus.'

Overheard by Phil, the Four Courts
Posted on Thursday, 15 March 2007

Bono speaks

At the U2 concert in Croke Park, Bono asks the audience for some quiet. Then in the silence, he starts to slowly clap his hands. Holding the audience in total silence, he says into the microphone, 'Every time I clap my hands, a child in Africa dies.'

A voice from near the front of the audience pierces the silence:

'Fookin' stop doin' it, then!'

Overheard by Anonymous, Croke Park, 2005
Posted on Wednesday, 14 March 2007

Sex education gone wrong

While travelling home on the Luas recently, I heard a group of four young girls speak about a class they had that day in school. One announces to the group,

'Oh my God, that was terrifying wasn't it? Who do you think has one, I'd say it's you Amanda, like you were with your man and everyone knows he's been with everyone.'

Amanda: 'The cheek of you, it's not me. Ya heard what Miss said, one in four of your age group have an STI. It could be anyone.'

I think they may have needed less sex education and more Mathematics!

Overheard by Anonymous, on the Luas
Posted on Tuesday, 13 March 2007

8 December

Getting on to a bus on O'Connell Street one day, and there were a few other people getting on. Just before it was my turn, the guy before me shouted, '1.20 please' to the driver, in a country accent. The bus driver nodded with his head towards the box where you throw the money in. The young lad from the country then leaned over and shouted into the box, '1.20 please!'

Overheard by Anonymous, O'Connell Street
Posted on Tuesday, 13 March 2007

The trouble with neighbours

My cranky no-kids neighbour had a major problem with us unruly brats when we were young (I'm the youngest of seven). After years of listening to her complaints, my older brother had had enough. Calling one day to complain about the family dog she says to my brother, 'My husband is going mad, your dog is always chasing him in the car,' to which my brother replies,

'I'm sorry, Mrs Quinn, my dog doesn't have a car.'

Overheard by Anonymous, at home on the doorstep
Posted on Saturday, 10 March 2007

At the cleaners

Waiting for my turn in a dry-cleaners recently, a man was having difficulty in getting his suit back.

'It's a Giorgio Armani,' said the customer patiently.

'A wha'?' said the assistant.

'A Giorgio Armani!' he replied rather haughtily.

'Hey, Monica, can you find a George O'Malley suit down there?'

Overheard by Anonymous, south Dublin dry-cleaners
Posted on Wednesday, 7 March 2007

Horse on bus

Got on the no. 27 bus into town one morning, and the bus driver was in such a state of convulsive laughter at something he was hearing over the bus radio that he couldn't take my fare. When he eventually calmed down he said,

'There's a horse after getting on the bus in Darndale and they can't get him off!'

Overheard by Anonymous, on the no. 27 bus
Posted on Tuesday, 6 March 2007

One is not amused

On the bus, couldn't help overhearing two old dears …

Old Dear #1: 'So have ya the place ready for the christening?'

Old Dear #2: 'I have. I was scrubbing all week. It's fit for the Queen now.'

Old Dear #1: 'I hear she's a fussy bitch alright.'

Overheard by Cabra Joe, on the no. 121 bus into town
Posted on Monday, 5 March 2007

Haircut?

Girl: 'Hey, how are you? Did you get a haircut?'

Boy: 'What? Are you serious!? Of course I did!'

Girl: 'Jeez, calm down, I wasn't sure.'

Boy: 'What do you mean you're not sure!? I used to have an afro!'

Overheard by Anonymous, Grafton Street
Posted on Saturday, 3 March 2007

Lunatic!

A crowd of us outside Café en Seine on Dawson Street on Saturday night, watching the lunar eclipse, when I overheard a D4 girl answering her mobile phone and exclaiming excitedly,

'Hi Nicola! We're outside watching the moon orbit the sun!'

Nobody bothered correcting her!

Overheard by Pete, Café en Seine on Dawson Street
Posted on Monday, 5 March 2007

Who knew Dublin Bus drivers had chauffeur training?

On the bus home from work before Christmas, absolutely lashing rain. The bus pulls up at a stop, obviously a few feet from the footpath. Doors open but no one gets on, then I hear a roar from outside,

'Can ya move da bus in closer, I'm wearin' sandals!'

… and the driver did!

Overheard by Ali, on the no. 65B bus
Posted on Tuesday, 6 March 2007

Save the moles!

I was in Dublin Airport and I was buying a pack of notebooks for my daughter. They were really thin and bound in cardboard, but it said 'moleskin', so up at the till the lady said, 'Dat'll be €17 there now, love, dat's very spensive isn't it?'

'I know … it's because they are moleskin,' I replied.

Then she said under her breath — not even to me, 'Ah, de poo-ur moles!'

Overheard by Lorcan, Dublin Airport
Posted on Wednesday, 7 March 2007

Fraddles

A friend of my Dad's was going on holiday and wanted to buy some clip-on sunglasses to attach to his specs. He went into a chemist and asked the girl behind the counter if they sold any.

'Fraddles?' asked the shop assistant.

'Yeah, Fraddles, is that what they're called? I'll have a pair of Fraddles, please.'

'No,' said the shop assistant, 'Do you want them FOR ADULTS or children?!'

Overheard by Anonymous, in an unnamed Dublin chemist
Posted on Wednesday, 21 March 2007

Child running for bus

As I am a bus driver for many years with Dublin Bus, I come across some very funny incidents. A woman with two small children was running for the no. 3 bus at Westland Row, so I waited for them. The youngest of the small kids was called (I can only guess) Chantelle. As the mother was calling the child to hurry up, she mouthed,

'Chanfuckintelle, will you hurry up!'

I'm still laughing about it ten years on.

Overheard by Dave, on the no. 3 bus at Westland Row
Posted on Thursday, 8 March 2007

Taxing the lion ...

On O'Connell Street, a charity worker had stopped a pedestrian.

Charity worker: 'Would you like to buy a line, sir?'

Guy: 'I'm from the country, why would I want to buy a lion, sure he'd eat all the sheep ...'

Overheard by Michael, O'Connell Street
Posted on Thursday, 8 March 2007

Happy talk

This is probably one of those 'ya had to be there' things but it still makes me laugh.

Happened about seven years ago, was working in a hotel in the city centre as night manager. I had a night porter on with me who was a lovely fella but had a dreadful stammer. I ordered a taxi for some people leaving a function and this taxi driver comes in and roars, 'Did y-y-youse order a Teh-teh-teh-TAXI?'

With that the night porter appears from the back office with this big, angry head on him and says,

'Are you tay-tay-tay-takin' de p-p-p-piss owra m-m-m-me?'

Overheard by Snow White, hotel in city centre
Posted on Friday, 9 March 2007

Tony O'Toole's fault!

While waiting for my luggage at carousel no. 3 at Dublin Airport, a voice over the intercom:

'Whoever's waiting at carousel no. 3, move to no. 5, 'cos Tony O'Toole broke it!'

Overheard by Anonymous, baggage at Dublin Airport
Posted on Wednesday, 7 March 2007

Safe as houses

My slightly superior neighbour was boasting to my Mam about how fantastic her precious youngest son was doing since emigrating to New York. She said, 'Oh he's doing brilliant, he's living in one of the condoms that they're all living in over there.'

My mother just smiled smugly.

Maybe I'm out of touch but I think she meant condominium …

Overheard by my Mam, Finglas
Posted on Monday, 5 March 2007

Kids can sometimes be too honest!

I used to work in a well-known 5-star D4 hotel. I took a fancy to their lovely china cups with the hotel's initials printed on them. I didn't think a couple would be missed.

One day I treated my Mam and eight-year-old sister to afternoon tea there. As my colleague served them, my little sister says in a loud voice to my Mam,

'Hey Mam, they have the same cups as us!'

Overheard by Anonymous, D4 hotel
Posted on Saturday, 3 March 2007

I hit a Pole

Last week I was walking in Sandyford near the Mint. A woman driver had her car parked on the path with the hazard lights on. Coming closer it was clear that she had hit a Yield sign when going through a left slip road. She was on the phone telling someone about her accident.

'I hit a pole, luckily there's not much damage to the car …'

'No! A Yield sign, not a Polish person!'

Overheard by Southsider, Sandyford
Posted on Thursday, 1 March 2007

Bring on the harassment lawsuit …

Coming up to the counter in McDonald's, I heard the middle-aged manager say to the tired-looking girl sweeping the floor, 'Go on, sweep me off my feet.'

I had to bite my lip …

Overheard by Anonymous, McDonald's, Blackrock
Posted on Monday, 26 February 2007

Huh?

Standing waiting with five others for the no. 18 bus in Rathmines. A guy walks by, recognises a familiar face amongst the group and says,

'Ah there yeh are again, Charlie. I saw yeh the other day on O'Connell Street, but by the time I caught up with yeh, you were gone.'

Overheard by Seamus, Rathmines
Posted on Sunday, 25 February 2007

Inspiration for the day

After a long slog all the way from Tallafornia into town on the no. 65 bus, the bus driver pulled up on Dame Street where the majority of people got out, and the bus driver yelled at everybody, 'Fly my pretties, FLY!'

Overheard by Twister, on the no. 65 bus
Posted on Thursday, 22 February 2007

Always in the last place you look

On the no. 111 bus (single decker), we were travelling along behind a no. 7 bus (double decker). They both follow the exact route for 20 minutes or so.

Both buses were pulling up towards a bus stop. The no. 7 lets people off and a fairly scum-baggish looking chap is one of them. He goes to his jeans pocket and it seems like he has lost something.

In the meantime he hasn't noticed the no. 7 leave and the no. 111 pull into the stop to let people off.

He pushes through the people getting off, has a sudden realisation halfway down the bus and says,

'What happened to the f**kin' stairs?'

Overheard by Anonymous, on the no. 111 bus
Posted on Thursday, 22 February 2007

Law abidin'

On a train from Dublin to Galway, August 2006.
One very drunk man was causing no end of
trouble, to the extent that the train had to be
stopped so he could be thrown off. His very
embarrassed friend was trying to calm him
down, so Mr Drunk roars at him, in a very
strong Dub-el-in accent,

'Wha' are yous getting law abidin' on me for? I'll
law abide you in a min-a!'

If only …

Overheard by Sweary, train, Dublin to Galway
Posted on Wednesday, 21 February 2007

All 'Fore' Americans

Coming into Dublin, cabin crew distribute cards
to non-EU passengers, which for many provides
some good entertainment. On one such
occasion an American lady proclaimed, 'Excuse
me, Mam, this card is looking for four names
and I've only got three.'

Rather than getting into the technicalities of the
word 'forename', I smiled and told her three
names would do nicely.

Overheard by Karen, Aer Lingus flight
Posted on Wednesday, 21 February 2007

Young at heart

Not so much heard as seen.

Was standing in a queue for a bank machine on
O'Connell Street beside one of the Londis shops

when out bursts this young lad, with a security guard chasing after him. The guard catches up with him and pins him on the ground, and the young lad throws away about six dirty mags that he had stolen.

The security guard proceeds to beat him and this old man on a walking stick walks over and picks up the mags, like he's helping the security guard. Then he abandons his walking stick and runs down the road with one leg trailing behind him.

Some smart-arse shouts after him, 'Run, Forrest, run!' leaving myself in hysterics and a much bemused Asian tourist!

Overheard by Anonymous, O'Connell Street
Posted on Friday, 2 February 2007

Spit

Was in Ballyfermot a few years ago and was waiting to cross at the traffic lights. A young mother was standing beside me and was holding her young son's hand. The boy spat into the pedestrian crossing button, looked up at his mother and exclaimed, 'Mah! Sumwuns goin' teh press dah!'

Overheard by James, traffic lights near Ballyfermot church
Posted on Thursday, 1 February 2007

Late-night Luas

Whilst standing on a late-night Luas to Tallaght, a drunken couple were having a row. The husband, who was crippled, seemed unfazed at the distress he was causing the other passengers. At St James's Hospital, another drunken man stepped on and began accosting the drunken husband for the way he was treating his wife. A verbal row ensued between the drunken trio.

The husband, clearly frustrated, claimed he was going to beat the man up and suggested they should take it outside at the next stop. At this point the wife leans in and whispers some words of advice that nobody in the carriage can hear. The husband responds,

'What do you mean I'm in a f**king wheelchair!?'

Overheard by Kevin, on the bleedin' Daniel Day
Posted on Wednesday, 31 January 2007

Early planning

26 January in Milosky's Woodworkers supply centre in Terenure. One of the staff was making some polite conversation with my father:

'You know, it's only 11 months until St Stephen's Day!'

Overheard by Leo, Milosky's in Terenure
Posted on Tuesday, 30 January 2007

Too much information

After asking the young assistant at the ice-cream stand in the Omni Centre for two ice-cream cones, she says, 'I'll be back in a minute, love, right?'

A lifetime later she comes back, hands me the

ice-creams and says, 'Sorrrreee bout dat, luv, I had te go to de toilet!'

Lovely!

Overheard by Philip, Omni Centre, Santry
Posted on Saturday, 27 January 2007

Final resting place

Some time ago a friend and I were at a funeral. It was cold and raining. On the way from the burial we pass an open grave: very mucky with water puddled at bottom. My friend looks in and says,

'Wouldn't you die if you had to go in there!'

Overheard by Bubbles, Glasnevin Cemetery
Posted on Friday, 26 January 2007

I don't know where she gets it

Heard on the no. 78A bus:

Woman #1: 'Yer little wan's getting awful big, how old is she now?'

Woman #2: 'Oh, Britney's going on four, oh, and you should hear the f**king language out of her. Tell Anto to f**k off, Britney!'

Britney: 'F**k off!'

Woman #2: 'Jaysus, I don't know where she gets the language outta.'

Overheard by Chuck, on the no. 78A bus
Posted on Friday, 26 January 2007

Ahh, Ma!

In a checkout queue behind mother and son (11+) with earphones in and he pipes up in a really loud voice,

'Ahhh, Ma, did you put this Barry Manilow co-pack-arama shite on my iPod?!?!?'

Overheard by Anonymous, Tesco, Clearwater
Posted on Friday, 26 January 2007

Take-away

Late Saturday in Burger King, O'Connell Street, I overheard a young fella ask for a 'BIG MAC', to which the assistant replies, 'Sorry, but that's a McDonald's burger.'

The young fella replies, 'I know, Bud, don't be long!'

Overheard by Frozenthumbs, Burger King
Posted on Thursday, 25 January 2007

Cup of tea

A guy from the inner city works for my uncle in a trophy shop on Marlborough Street. He was making tea for my uncle and a sales rep who had called in. He brings in the two cups of tea and forgets which cup he had put the sugar in, so he takes a slug out of one of the cups and says to the sales rep, 'Yep, that's yours.'

Overheard by Anand, Marlborough Street
Posted on Thursday, 25 January 2007

Extra vanganza!

On the bus coming home from town the other day, just going past Parkgate Motors. Two girls were sitting behind me. One of them turns to the other and asks, 'What is a vangaza?' The other says, 'Wat, why?' 'Well,' she says, 'that garage's cars have extra vangaza!' The other just goes, 'Don't know?'

I looked at the garage, and in big letters it said,

'Car Extravaganza'!

Overheard by Sam, on the no. 25A bus
Posted on Thursday, 25 January 2007

She was clearly confused!

I was walking along the canal beside Portobello College when a swan began to get out of the

174

canal. A young girl with her boyfriend notices
this and says to him excitedly,

'Oh look, the big duck is gettin' out of the sea!'

Overheard by Lou, canal at Portobello
Posted on Thursday, 25 January 2007

National Development Plan me arse!

Overheard an old man in the Cherry Tree pub
criticising the government's newly published
National Development Plan in which €184
billion will be invested over the next seven
years.

He moans, 'For jaysus sake, how am I gonna
benefit from dat! Why don't dey just divide the
€184 billion by four million people! Dat way
we'd all get €46,000 each!?

How did he work that out in his head?

Overheard by Anonymous, Cherry Tree pub, Walkinstown
Posted on Thursday, 25 January 2007

Carnival time in Gort

Passenger #1: 'Did you see your woman from
"Coronation Street" is on tonight, trying to trace
her ancestors in Gort?'

Passenger #2: 'She'll have a job, the place is full
of bleeding Brazilians.'

Overheard by Paddy, on the no. 19 bus to Rialto
Posted on Wednesday, 24 January 2007

A good catch

In Tamango's niteclub several years ago a guy kept asking my friend up to dance and she kept turning him down. After about an hour of him pestering her, we left the club.

As we were leaving, he turned and shouted, 'I didn't catch your name.'

To which my friend replied, 'I didn't f**king throw it at you!'

Overheard by Amanda, Tamango's at the
White Sands Hotel, Portmarnock
Posted on Wednesday, 24 January 2007

Drunk as a skunk

Drunk girl: 'You are locked!'

Drunk man (practically being carried by the girl): 'I amn't!'

Drunk girl: 'Fifty euro says you wet the bed!'

Overheard by Anonymous, outside the
Foggy Dew on Dame Street
Posted on Tuesday, 23 January 2007

Toilet break

Getting off the no. 16 bus in Terenure, I wonder why the driver is turning off the bus engine. As I'm stepping off the bus, the driver gets out of the driver's cab and I hear him say loudly to all the people on the bus,

'I'm running into the Spar to use the toilet, I'll

be back in a minute, but don't worry I'll get yous all ice-creams!'

I giggled all the way down the road!

Overheard by Clare, Terenure village
Posted on Sunday, 21 January 2007

Kids in pubs, what do you expect?

In the pub over Christmas one afternoon. There's a gang of lads in the corner, and one of them had his son with him. This kid, about four or five, suddenly gets up and grabs his coat.

'Where you going?' his dad asks.

'Out for a smoke,' the little fella answers.

Overheard by AG, Skerries
Posted on Thursday, 18 January 2007

Whiskey in the bar

A friend of mine was in a bar in Malahide and he asked the (Polish) girl behind the counter for a 'Paddy'. She went and filled him a glass of 'Powers'.

He said nothing the first time, but the second time, as she was heading for the 'Powers' again, he said, 'There's a bottle of Paddy on the shelf there.'

'Oh' she said, 'I thought they were the same. Everywhere I go I see "Paddy Powers"!'

Overheard by Stephen, Malahide
Posted on Wednesday, 17 January 2007

Oh dear

At the Zoo during the weekend, I was looking at the penguins, when I overheard a woman telling her son, 'Ah, look at the ducks!'

Overheard by Jane, Dublin Zoo

Posted on Wednesday, 17 January 2007

Nick-Nack-Paddy-Wack-in-the-Ilac

In the Ilac Centre on Saturday, waiting at the ground floor for the lift to the car park. A large group of people were also waiting. As the lift doors open, we all wait for the lift to empty before piling on. Standing at the back of the lift that quickly became full, leaving a group of six or seven unable to fit on.

One woman about 50 years old, bloke's haircut, bleach blond/yellow, about 5 foot, typical wife-swap head on her, starts telling everyone to push back so she could fit on. Everyone looks around and sees there is no room. A man at the front tells the woman, 'There is no room.'

She says, 'Push back!'

He says, 'There is no room, just wait.'

Furiously, she says, 'Diya want me to drag ya out of da lift and ya can bleedin' wait?'

Everyone just sniggered at her muppet mentality and the lift doors closed in her face.

Classic.

Overheard by Stephen, Ilac Centre

Posted on Monday, 15 January 2007

Never wear a short skirt ...

I was out on Friday night with a couple of girls I used to work with. One of them, who shall remain nameless to spare her blushes, was wearing high heels and an incredibly short skirt. We were walking from one pub to another when a group of four lads, about fifteen years old, passed us and quick as a flash one pipes up,

'Jaysus, if I'd legs like that I'd walk on me hands!'

Overheard by Anonymous, Wexford Street
Posted on Monday, 15 January 2007

Anybody there?

I was in a pub toilet the other night and an obviously drunk woman stumbled in.

'Mary!' she called.

'Yeah?'

'Are you in here?'

A pause, as 'Mary' thought about this: 'Yeah.'

The rest of the queue was in stitches!

Overheard by Tina, ladies' toilets, Frazers
Posted on Sunday, 14 January 2007

Free green thingies

While shopping in Tesco, my girlfriend's mother is packing her bags while the girl behind the till is scanning her shopping. She picks up one of the items and holding it up says,

'Wha's dat?'

'It's an avocado.'

'Av-a-wha?'

'Avocado.'

'Ah f**k it,' she says and throws it into one of the bags — without scanning it.

Overheard by Anonymous, Tesco, Finglas
Posted on Saturday, 13 January 2007

Monkey magic

On entering Dublin Zoo not so long ago, there was a monkey swinging from his treehouse to a tree via rope and making — well — monkey sounds! Then I overhear a little girl about seven ask her mother, 'Maa, is that monkey real?'

Her bigger brother then interrupts: 'Nooo! It's a bleeding man in a monkey suit, ya thick ya!'

Then the mother clips the lad on the head and says, 'Don't f**king ruin it for her, ya little b*ll*x!'

Ahh, ignorance is bliss!

Overheard by Pips, Dublin Zoo
Posted on Friday, 12 January 2007

I'm on the night train — bottoms up!

The Sunday Waterford-to-Dublin rail service had recently banned alcohol on the service, prohibiting all alcohol on board, in addition to roving security patrols up and down the train. The reason for the Elliot Ness style clamp-down was gregarious hoards of anti-social commuters clambering aboard after a heavy weekend in Kilkenny, still pissed, smoking pot, drinking their voddy and fouling the air with their nasal tones and mangled grammar, not to mention their booze-infused flatus.

To copperfasten Irish Rail's no-nonsense intent, the announcer on the PA announced the following one evening:

'This is the five o'clock service from Plunkett Station Waterford to Heuston Station Dublin. THERE IS NO ALCOHOL PERMITTED ANYWHERE ON THIS TRAIN, there is no baggage permitted on seats, there is no smoking permitted anywhere on this service including toilets. Anybody found contravening this will be removed from the train by the Gardaí at the next station.'

There was a pause and then the mic was keyed again:

'Just stay quiet and you'll get there.'

Overheard by Jack, Waterford to Dublin train

Posted on Friday, 12 January 2007

Talk isn't cheap

Was standing outside the post office on Cork Street, waiting for it to open, when this auld one started chatting to me.

The conversation got around to the ever-increasing house prices. She told me that because it is so expensive to buy in Dublin, her daughter and her daughter's husband had to buy a house in Co. Meath but, 'Dey don't like it

ar all 'cos dey hafta commUUN-icate for two
hours a day.'

Overheard by Danixx, Cork Street

Posted on Friday, 12 January 2007

Bad manners

I was sitting on a bench in Malahide Castle when
a couple with a young girl came and sat on the
bench opposite me. The mother gave the little
girl an orange to keep her quiet.

The parents were in the middle of a
conversation when the child began to sob
loudly. Juice from the orange had squirted into
her face. When asked what was wrong, the little
girl tearfully stated,

'The orange spat at me!'

Overheard by Amy, Malahide Castle

Posted on Friday, 12 January 2007

Can you bring me the bill, please?

I was sitting in a coffee shop having lunch and a
mother and her young daughter were sitting at
the table next to me. On finishing their lunch,
the young girl went into the bathroom.

A few minutes later, obviously having had a bout
of diarrhoea, she came out and announced
loudly to her mother,

'Mommy, Mommy, my poo has melted!'

Overheard by Ann, coffee shop in Malahide

Posted on Friday, 12 January 2007

Chivalry me arse

I was out driving the car along Kevin Street when it broke down. Got out of the car and was looking at it when a young fella passing by shouted,

'Hey missus, do you wanta push?'

I said, 'Yes please.'

He said, 'Go ahead!'

Overheard by Ann, Kevin Street
Posted on Friday, 12 January 2007

Teddy bear's bum

Donegal teacher teaching in a Dublin school. She shows the children a map of Ireland and shows them where Donegal is. She tells them that Ireland is shaped like a teddy bear, so Donegal is the head i.e. the brains of the country.

A week later, Co. Wexford came up in conversation. A child asked where on the teddy bear was Wexford. When they were shown, one wee fella said,

'Ah jaysus, Miss, I wouldn't go there on me holidays!'

Overheard by Anne (I was the teacher), in a Dublin school
Posted on Friday, 12 January 2007

The science of alcohol

In Pravda, Thursday night, outside having a smoke. This couple are on their way inside. She turns around and says to him, 'It's not as cold as it was earlier.'

Guy behind them: 'That's 'cos you're locked.'

Thought it was classic.

Overheard by Big Al, outside Pravda pub
Posted on Friday, 12 January 2007

A youthful imagination

On the bus last Thursday and this mother gets on with her four-year-old daughter. The daughter sits down first and then the mother beside her. Immediately the child starts crying.

When her mother asks her what the problem is, she replies, tearfully, 'You sat on Jalu!'

I can only assume 'Jalu' was an imaginary friend …

Overheard by Sean, on the no. 16 bus, Rathfarnham
Posted on Thursday, 11 January 2007

Nothing in life is free, not even the Herald!

Walking past the start of the Luas line at St Stephen's Green. A man is selling the *Evening Herald*. A young woman walks past and takes a newspaper from him. She then proceeds to walk away. He looks at her, puzzled and says, 'Eh, one euro please.'

She hands it back to him: 'Sorry I thought it was free.'

Overheard by Ciara-Ann, outside St Stephen's Green
at the Luas stop
Posted on Thursday, 11 January 2007

Inflation nation

A New York friend of mine was in Dublin over the Christmas and New Year period. He had finally got to grips with Dublin's confusing transport system and had even got the hang of the exact change fare on the buses (having been stung with getting no change on more than one occasion).

On New Year's Day he got on a bus with his exact change, only to discover the fare had gone up by 5c. He says to the driver,

'Geez man, it was €1.35 yesterday, what the hell is goin' on?'

To which the driver replies, dead pan, 'Happy New Year!'

Overheard by Anna, on Dublin bus
Posted on Thursday, 11 January 2007

Do It Yourself

I used to work in a B&Q hardware store. A woman walked in one day and I overheard her ask,

'Do you know anywhere around here where I can get nailed?'

Overheard by Miley, B&Q, Airside Retail Park, Swords
Posted on Thursday, 11 January 2007

Painful passing experience

In the local pub one evening, decided to use the toilets (once the seal is broken, have to go every half hour).

Picture the scene: three urinals and the one in the middle is the only one free. I tend to suffer from stage fright and the fact that two guys were standing on either side of me didn't help matters. The guy on my left said,

'Jaysus, I'll have to pay a visit to the doctor, this is now beyond a joke.'

I asked was everything ok, to which came the reply,

'I don't think so … I keep pissing these Blue Lumps.' (Channel Blocks)

Needless to say, I almost wet myself!

Overheard by Keith, Tolka House
Posted on Wednesday, 10 January 2007

Real Dublin poetry

At the Dublin versus Mayo match last autumn, a mate of mine on the Cusack Stand overheard another supporter say,

'Ah jaysus, dere's a great sight … the hill wavin' like a showal a' mackerill!'

A truly beautiful simile!

Overheard by Rob, Croke Park
Posted on Wednesday, 10 January 2007

Sarky security

Standing in Arnotts a few weeks back, I overheard some 'chung wan' ask the security man where the bargain basement was.

He was on the ball and replied, 'First floor.'

Overheard by Biffo, Arnotts
Posted on Wednesday, 10 January 2007

A hard pill to swallow

Years ago, a group of us, while returning from college on the DART, were yapping away as students are wont to do. One member of the group was going on a bit much about some academic nonsense — in fact we had all tuned out with boredom — when an auld fella on the seat beside us turned to him and said,

'Hav yez got a Disprin or a Anadin?'

We shrugged and the auld fella pointed at our boring friend and said,

'Cos I have a pain in me b*llix listenin' to tha' shite!'

Overheard by Rob, on the DART
Posted on Wednesday, 10 January 2007

All you need is love

Waiting for the train yesterday at Pearse Station, when I overheard a girl beside me (a real Howaya) trying to get her boyfriend to stop grabbing her.

Or, as she put it, 'Stop feelin' me bleeedin' hole!'

Overheard by Count Dooku, Pearse Station
Posted on Wednesday, 10 January 2007

Terminology crisis

In a training class today in the office, the trainer apologised in advance, explaining that the course material was new and that we were the first class she was going to train on it, so we would be her …

Before she could say it, the loo-la Spanish bird in the office that has not been able to manage English pronunciation despite four years in Dublin, shouts out …

'We will be Guinness Pigs!'

Priceless, never a truer word said, I pondered.

Overheard by Swissoff, in the office
Posted on Wednesday, 10 January 2007

Lift of sardines ... and one tomato

In a lift at Arnotts in town a few weeks ago. Quite squashed. The lift stops on the first floor and this couple are waiting to get in, but nobody gets out. This guy gets in and says, 'Ah, come on, Mary, there's enough room here, these people will shift!'

When she still shows reluctance, and obvious embarrassment, some guy shouts from the back, 'C'mon, Mary!'

Soon everyone's saying, 'C'mon, Mary!'

She gets on with a face like a tomato!

Overheard by Sean, Arnotts in town
Posted on Tuesday, 9 January 2007

Olden days

I was walking through town the other day and an old gent in front of me tripped and fell. Naturally, I helped him up, and in doing so he said,

'Jaysus, they don't make paths like they use to, that wouldn't have happened in my day, damn foreigners.'

Of course, I agreed with the aul' racist!

Overheard by Mike, city centre
Posted on Tuesday, 9 January 2007

He ain't heavy ...

Guy#1: 'How's that brother of yours?'

Guy#2: 'He is still a miserable f**ker.'

Guy#1: 'Ah c'mon, he's not dat bad.'

Guy#2: 'I only talk to him in case I need a transplant, or bone marrow.'

Overheard by P, McDonald's, Dublin Airport
Posted on Tuesday, 9 January 2007

He actually had to think about that

Hanging around the old Dundrum Shopping Centre last Sunday, I overheard these guys talking:

Guy#1: 'Yeah, I had salmonella dere a few years ago.'

Guy#2: 'Did yeh die?'

Silence for a few seconds.

Guy#1: 'Nope.'

Overheard by Sean, the old Dundrum Shopping Centre
Posted on Monday, 8 January 2007

The sandwich maker

In O'Brien's Sandwich bar the other day and the girl who was about to make my sandwich turns to her work mate and says,

'I f**kin' hate makin' sandwiches.'

Overheard by Janine, O'Brien's, Blanchardstown
Posted on Monday, 8 January 2007

The common language

Bus from Phoenix Park to town, heading up the quays. Two Dublin girls sitting behind me.

Dublin Girl: 'Why do all deese forddinerts come over heeor?'

To which her friend replied, 'Dey learn de English langwitch.'

Dublin Girl: 'Why do dey wan teh learn deh English langwitch?'

Response: 'Cos it's deh most comminist langwitch in da world.'

With that, the younger of the two young women responds, at the top of her voice for the whole bus to hear (you know the type) …

'I speak English and I don't go arowind braginn dah im BALEEEDIN' COMMIN!'

The looks she got from tourists was priceless and of course, the rest of us Irish on the bus were nearly in tears.

Overheard by Magillycuddyreeks, bus from Phoenix Park
Posted on Monday, 8 January 2007

D4

This was in a lecture in UCD and the lecturer was trying to determine how many D4 heads were in the class (for some reason).

Lecturer: 'So, hands up who thinks they might be considered a D4 type.'

No response until after five minutes of silence.

Some student: 'Well, it's not very D4 to say you're a D4.'

Overheard by Stephen, lecture in UCD
Posted on Sunday, 7 January 2007

Mistaken identity

A few weeks ago walking past the statue of Phil Lynott I noticed an American couple. The wife (I presume) said,

'Quick, George, take a photo of me beside Michael Jackson!'

Overheard by Higgs, Grafton Street
Posted on Friday, 5 January 2007

Late buses

Several years ago, I was on the no. 123 Imp bus in Dublin. It was a dark and rainy day and the traffic was mad. The buses were all running late. The crowded bus I was on stopped at Eason's on O'Connell Street to let two people off and two on, when a distraught lady soaking wet at the bus stop said to the driver,

'This is a disgrace, you're really late, I've been waiting here for ages in the rain, there's supposed to be a bus here every 20 minutes,' to which the driver replied,

'Every eight minutes, luv!' closed the door — and drove on.

Overheard by DuffMan, no. 123 bus

Posted on Friday, 5 January 2007

Plastic bag required at back of bus

Recently while taking the no. 16 bus home I had one of the funniest encounters with a Dublin Drunk.

I was sitting upstairs on the back seat with a friend. At one of the stops the drunk got on, and managed to get up the stairs and stumble down to the back seat. The bus was jammers as usual and the only seats left available were the two between me and the drunk.

A couple of minutes later he suddenly turned to me and asked for a plastic bag. Which I didn't have. He turned back around to face the corner of the bus and started urinating.

Well, I've never seen the top of a bus empty so fast, and to this day I've been wondering would a plastic bag really have helped.

Overheard by Paul, on the no. 16 bus

Posted on Friday, 5 January 2007

Doggie bag optional

A friend of mine lives in an exclusive gated compound in Foxrock — from the outside it looks like one huge enormous mansion.

One night she took a taxi home. Upon approaching the security gate and surveying the 'estate', the taxi driver appraised the swanky property as follows:

'Shur this is the dog's b*llix!'

Overheard by VooDoo, Foxrock dinner party

Posted on Friday, 5 January 2007

Discover Ireland

While on a bus trip from Galway to Dublin, a group of friends were sitting behind me.

Girl: 'Sorry, driver, where are we now?'

Driver: 'Moate.'(Westmeath)

Girl (to her friends): 'We're in Howth, lads, deadly, sure we're nearly home.'

Overheard by Anonymous, bus from Galway to Dublin

Posted on Thursday, 4 January 2007

In times of crisis listen to your stomach

I was on a rugby tour to Milan a couple years ago and as the plane took off from Dublin, an Italian man up the front got into difficulty. There was a big commotion and the stewards laid him on the floor. After a minute the pilot came on and announced the man was having heart trouble and that we were returning to Dublin to get him to a hospital. Then, as the guy lies there, one of the old boys travelling with the team (who had been in the airport bar prior to departure) shouts out,

'If he DIES, can I have his BREAKFAST?!'

Practically the whole plane broke into highly inappropriate laughter. I don't think any Italians got it though.

Overheard by Garrett, Aer Lingus flight EI737 to Milan
Posted on Thursday, 4 January 2007

The ice-cream house

Standing outside Áras an Uachtarain and a woman is standing beside us with her child. The little girl asks, 'Mammy, what's the name of that house?'

The mother informs her child that the name of the house is 'Áras an uactar reoite' (the ice-cream house)!

Overheard by Niamh, in the Phoenix Park
outside Áras an Uachtarain
Posted on Tuesday, 2 January 2007

Boxing Day

Many moons ago one St Stephen's night I was walking down Swords Main Street and overheard two teenage girls discussing the Christmas TV.

'Did ye see "Michael Collins" last night?' enquired one.

The other, with completely the wrong end of the stick, replies, 'No, me Ma HATES boxing!'

Overheard by Hugh, Main Street, Swords
Posted on Tuesday, 2 January 2007

You couldn't make it up

Old couple queuing for the last bus on Abbey Street, 11.30, 1 January:

Woman: 'Very cold, isn't it?'

Man: 'Yes, I'd say it's the coldest night this year.'

Overheard by Bren, queuing for last bus on 1 January
Posted on Saturday, 2 January 2007

Buy drinks but you can't smoke

Was at Centra of Stoneybatter during the Christmas holidays, where two kids not more than seventeen years old were buying two bottles of Jack Daniels and two six-packs of beer. Once they paid for all the drinks, one of the kids returns to the cash point and asks for 20 Silk Cut Purple. The reply of the cashier was, 'You are too young to buy cigarettes.'

Old enough to drink, but not old enough to smoke?

Overheard by C&P, Centra in Stoneybatter
Posted on Tuesday, 2 January 2007

It's a clean machine

A few years ago, a woman, recently returned from Germany where they like things neat and pristine, boarded a no. 7 bus. Looking around the bus, she saw the discarded tickets and other litter on the floor. She turned to the bus driver and said, 'This bus is filthy.'

To which he replied without a moment's

hesitation, 'Well, get off and wait for a clean one then.'

Overheard by Anonymous, on the no. 7 bus

Posted on Monday, 1 January 2007

Dubliners' sympathy for the Yanks

Sitting in a bar in town listening to an Irish trad band with a group of American tourists. They were all really into the music and everything was nice and relaxed. After a while a young Dublin couple sat down very close to a few of the Yanks and struck up a conversation.

Dublin couple: 'So how do ye like it here?'

Yanks: 'Yes, very enjoyable.'

Dublin couple (man): 'September 11th must have been pretty shite?'

Yanks: 'Oh yes ...' interrupted by Dublin couple (woman):

'Forget that, what about the Smoking Ban ...'

Overheard by Lucy, pub in Dublin city

Posted on Friday, 29 December 2006

Ah bless

I was on the no. 17A bus last week when an old man and his grandson got on. We were stuck in traffic outside a school. The little boy looked out the window and saw three girls that looked very similar, so he shouts out,

'Grandda, are they three little twins?'

Overheard by Pauline, on the no. 17A bus

Posted on Friday, 29 December 2006

Losing weight in Finglas

Two women were chatting on leaving the local community centre after attending a weight-loss meeting.

'I don't like that instructor,' said the first woman.

'Why?' replied her friend.

'I prefer the one we had last week — she weighs you lighter!'

Overheard by Emer, outside a weight-loss meeting in Finglas
Posted on Friday, 29 December 2006

The photographer

I was on the no. 39 bus the other night, and overheard three girls, one of whom had a camera. There was a bit of a discussion as to who would take a photo.

One said to the others, 'Look, I'll take the bleedin' photo, after all I AM the photographicis!'

Overheard by Paddy, on the no. 39
bus coming from Blanchardstown
Posted on Friday, 29 December 2006

BLT without the LT please

I was in a sandwich shop in town recently. There's a guy ahead of me in the queue — didn't look like the sharpest knife in the drawer — anyway, he proceeds to order a BLT baguette.

However, he wanted it 'without lettuce or tomato' ...

Overheard by Tav, sandwich shop
Posted on Friday, 29 December 2006

Holy God!

Sitting in a church on the northside of Dublin last Christmas Eve. It was the children's Christmas mass, so full of excited kiddies. We were early so were waiting for the mass to begin and one little girl in front kept asking her Dad, 'Daddy, where's Holy God?' to which he replied, 'He'll be out in a few minutes.'

She repeated the question numerous times, while the father was getting less and less patient with her. Eventually she said, one last time,

'Daddy, where's Holy God?' to which he replied loudly,

'HE'S AWAY IN A MANGER!'

The first three rows of the church were in fits!

Overheard by Fiona, Lisa & Jamie, St Canice's Church
Posted on Tuesday, 12 December 2006

Greetings

Was strolling down O'Connell Street when three teenage skanger birds were walking by me. One of their mobiles goes off. It was obviously one of her friends and she answered affectionately, 'Howareya slu'?'

Overheard by Anonymous, O'Connell Street
Posted on Friday, 29 December 2006

The great escape

My aunt and uncle are quite strict on their children. One of the rules was that the front garden gate must not, under any circumstances, be open in case their four-year-old son got out.

I was babysitting him one day and he rushed into the room where I was watching TV, a look of sheer horror on his face:

'Patrick, come quick! The gate is open and I might get out!'

Overheard by Froosh, uncle's house
Posted on Tuesday, 26 December 2006

An ecumenical matter

While waiting in A&E in St Vincent's Hospital, people naturally have to give some personal details. I overheard a girl replying to the question 'What religion are you?' with 'Normal'!

Overheard by Anonymous, A&E department, St Vincent's Hospital
Posted on Friday, 29 December 2006

What a return!

During the summer, while Bushy Park skate park was still under construction (right beside the tennis courts), some skateboarders were kicked off the site and decided to play tennis. One of the boys was using his board as a racket.

An old posh woman who was playing with her husband/partner a few courts away came over and said, 'I don't like the way you're playing tennis with that skateboard.'

Skateboarder quickly and wittily replied,

'Well, I don't like the way you're playing tennis with tha racket!'

Overheard by Brian, Bushy Park
Posted on Tuesday, 26 December 2006

Austin Powers for kids

A couple of years ago, when *Austin Powers* first came out on DVD, I was working in Chartbusters (Phibsboro). One evening I was out on the floor tidying up the DVD display. A concerned woman came up to me with a copy of *Austin Powers*. Pointing to the age certificate, which happened to be 15s, she asked,

'Excuse me, do you have this in 12s?'

Overheard by Ciarán, Chartbusters, Phibsboro
Posted on Monday, 25 December 2006

Last chance

Best ever flight I was on was with Go Airlines a few years back. Just before take-off the air hostess was getting ready for her safety routine, when the pilot came over the mic saying,

'Ladies and gentlemen, please pay attention to the safety instructions as this may be the last chance you ever get ...'

Overheard by Eileen, Go Airlines, Dublin Airport
Posted on Friday, 22 December 2006

Cosmic Lady

Was on the Nitelink home from town last night and a woman who looked a bit crazy turned around to me and asked, 'Excuse me, do you have today's date?'

'It's the 21st of December,' I said, 'shortest day of the year.'

'Oh yes,' she replied, 'The world splits into two today doesn't it.'

What could I say to that?!

Overheard by Podge, Nitelink
Posted on Friday, 22 December 2006

Money

In the barber's the other day the barber was trying to make conversation with a young lad of about thirteen or fourteen.

Barber: 'Are you getting anything for Christmas?'

Young Lad: 'Money.'

Cue a few laughs from the people under their breath who were waiting.

Barber: 'Is that it?'

Young Lad: 'Yeah, I wouldn't trust me Ma to buy anything for me!'

Cue more laughs.

Overheard by Paul, Shaves, Balbriggan
Posted on Friday, 22 December 2006

El radio

My auntie was over in the Canaries and brought a load of stuff back for the family. She bought my Gran a small stereo for her kitchen. My Gran said she couldn't possibly have it in the house.

'Why not?' says my auntie.

'I'll buy one here … all this thing will do is play Spanish radio stations, and I like listening to Gerry Ryan in the morning!'

Overheard by Simon, family home
Posted on Friday, 22 December 2006

Birdman of Finglas

I was in the local day care centre, collecting my mother-in-law, when I noticed a man holding a Zimmer frame, slowly walking past the room I was in. He stops at the door and shouts, 'CUCKOOOOOO', then waddles off, breaking his shite laughing all the way down the corridor!

Overheard by Philip, day care centre, Finglas West
Posted on Thursday, 21 December 2006

Little cutie

Mother wheeling pram with cute one-year-old boy in Smithfield. Along comes her friend Mary (she hasn't seen her for some time):

Mother: 'Howya, Mary, this is little Paddy.'

Mary: 'Jazsus, he's a lovely little b*ll*x.'

Overheard by Brian, Smithfield
Posted on Thursday, 21 December 2006

Flying without brains

Two D4 girls at Dublin Airport, going through security. One girl walks through detectors. It beeps and she gets all afraid.

Security: 'Remove your boots, please.'

D4 girl #1: 'Oh, sorry.'

She walks through again with the BOOTS IN HER HAND! She seems surprised when it beeps again! DOPE!

D4 girl #2 goes through fine.

Security: 'Have you any fluids in your bag?'

D4 girl #2: 'No … just water.'

Overheard by Eadz nd Natz, Dublin Airport
Posted on Wednesday, 20 December 2006

Carol singers slacking off!

I was walking up Grafton Street, past some carol singers taking a rest from singing on a cold night. Two lads walked past me, and one goes to the other in a really disgruntled Dublin accent,

'Jaaaysus, I thought dey were supposed to sing for me money!'

He'd work 'em to the bone!

Overheard by John, Grafton Street

Posted on Wednesday, 20 December 2006

Interior decorating?

Having lunch with the lads while working in Dublin Airport, the conversation turns to the mots.

First Bloke: 'So how's the new mot, what's she like?'

Second Bloke: 'Ah jaysus yeah, she's lovely, has red hair!'

First Bloke: 'Really, and does the carpet match the curtains?'

Second Bloke: 'I don't bleedin' know, I was never in her gaff!'

Overheard by G, lunchtime at Dublin Airport

Posted on Tuesday, 19 December 2006

I wonder if he passed?!

I was walking past the Driving Test Centre in Finglas. There was a Dublin Bus trainee and his tester walking side by side, towards the red learner bus, obviously to do his test. I overheard the trainee saying to the tester,

'Did ya ever drive a bus yerself, Boss?'

Overheard by Bob, Finglas Test Centre

Posted on Monday, 18 December 2006

Dub uses poetic licence

Had to go to hospital the other night. I was sitting in A&E when this guy who looked like Lorcan from *Fair City* came in, shouting and roaring. The nurse asked what was wrong, and he pointed at his blood-soaked leg and said,

'Hurry up, will yiz, I'm bleeeeeeedin' bleedin!'

Overheard by Paulie, St Vincent's
Posted on Monday, 18 December 2006

Have you ever ordered a sandwich before?

Standing in the queue for a sandwich in O'Brien's in the Omni Centre:

Customer: 'Can I have a sandwich, please?'

O'Brien's Girl: 'Brown or white?'

Customer: 'What?'

O'Brien's Girl: 'Brown or white bread?'

Customer: 'White.'

O'Brien's Girl: 'Butter or mayo?'

Customer: 'What?'

O'Brien's Girl: 'Butter or mayo?'

Customer: 'Eh, butter.'

O'Brien's Girl: 'What would you like?'

Customer: 'Chicken.'

O'Brien's Girl: 'That all?'

Customer: 'Eh … cheese.'

O'Brien's Girl: 'That it?'

Customer: (silence)

O'Brien's Girl: 'Anything else?'

Customer: 'Lettuce. Oh, and coleslaw.'

O'Brien's Girl: 'Anything to drink?'

Customer: 'Tea.'

O'Brien's Girl: 'Medium or large?'

Customer: 'What?'

And so on. Needless to say, when he got to the counter to pay for it, he couldn't remember what he'd ordered!

Overheard by The Dude, Santry
Posted on Monday, 18 December 2006

A long way from home

League final 2005, Armagh versus Wexford. Was sitting in front of about six fellas from Wexford, having the craic before throw in. There was an announcement over the tannoy:

'Could the parents of a little girl who is lost please make their way to the First Aid room. Her name is Kimberley and she's from New York.'

Quick as lightning, one of the Wexford fellas says,

'New York!? Feck me, she *is* lost!'

Overheard by Lorraine, Croke Park
Posted on Monday, 18 December 2006

The complexity of shopping these days

In Dunnes Stores on Saturday, the girl in front of me at the checkout asks the checkout operator, 'How much are yizzer 30c bags?'

Overheard by Jess, Dunnes Stores, The Square
Posted on Monday, 18 December 2006

What they teach them in school nowadays

While dropping my son to school the other day, we passed by the school's large crib with the nativity scene.

My son pipes up: 'I know about baby Jesus!'

Dad: 'Really? Who was he?'

Son: 'Baby Jesus is a sheep.'

Dad: 'No, he's not!'

Son: 'Yes, he is! He's the Lamb of God!'

There's really no response to that, is there?

Overheard by Shay, at my son's school
Posted on Friday, 15 December 2006

In the bookies

Recently while putting on a bet for a mate, I heard two guys talking and the conversation went like this.

First Guy: 'Well Mick, any luck on the 2:45?'

Second Guy: 'Do you know the expression —

beat on the post by a head?'

First Guy: 'Yeah.'

Second Guy: 'Well my horse was ... beat on the head by a post.'

Needless to say, his horse came nowhere.

Overheard by Keith, betting shop
Posted on Thursday, 14 December 2006

The backwards man

A drunken, old (but jolly) man gets on the bus and sits in the wheelchair-user carer's seat, i.e. facing us all. After a few blasts of banter with a woman and her baby, he loudly asks us all, 'Why are you all sitting backwards anyway?' then continues laughing away to himself ...

Overheard by Podge, on the no. 19 bus on the way to town
Posted on Thursday, 14 December 2006

Mass circumcision

Two oul' fellas discussing the inadequacies of the Luas.

Oul' fella #1: 'They should've linked up the Luas lines.'

Oul' fella #2: 'And the DART.'

Oul' fella #1: 'And have a circle line.'

Oul' fella #2: 'They should have it circumcise the entire city ...'

Overheard by Owen, Connolly Luas stop
Posted on Thursday, 14 December 2006

What a cabbage!

Two lads get on the no. 79 bus on Aston Quay, with McDonald's food. One says to the other as he takes the lettuce out of his burger,

'Jaysus, I hate all this cabbage in me booorgar!'

Overheard by Paul, on the no. 79 bus on the way to Ballyfermot
Posted on Tuesday, 12 December 2006

Laughing in the moonlight

It was late Saturday evening and I was queuing for the AIB pass machine off Grafton Street. I noticed two tourists — a couple — asking a slightly drunk man to take their photo with the Phil Lynott statue. As they posed for the photo they asked him, 'Who is this by the way?' to which he replied,

'Oh, that's Phil Lynott — he was the first black man in Ireland!'

Overheard by Anonymous, Grafton Street
Posted on Monday, 11 December 2006

First time on public transport?

D4 girl getting on the Westport to Dublin bus. She didn't have any change so she said to the driver, 'Can I pay by Laser?'

Overheard by John, on the Westport to Dublin bus
Posted on Sunday, 10 December 2006

Get with it, Santa!

In a hairdresser in Swords last week. There was a woman with her little girl, about four, talking about writing her letter to Santa.

Little girl: 'Can we not just send Santa a text?'

Mam: 'I don't think Santa has a mobile phone.'

Little girl: 'Ah, Mam, sure everyone has a mobile phone these days.'

Overheard by JT, hairdresser in Swords
Posted on Friday, 8 December 2006

Anyone for da mouse?

Christmas time about three or four years ago, myself and a few mates were walking down Henry Street, checking out all the stalls and listening to them shouting out all their Christmas offers: 'Geta ur rapin papor three for a eura,' and so on.

Out of the blue, some auld one with a bread-board that's full of wind-up toy mice for cats on top of an old pram starts to shout, 'Anyone der for da Mouses?'

Didn't know what was funnier — the Mouses, or the fact she was selling them at Christmas. Only in Dublin!

Overheard by Hick, Henry Street
Posted on Friday, 8 December 2006

Mixed doubles

In the local on Sunday afternoon for dinner, the pub was packed with families. There were four lads playing doubles on a pool table. A little girl, about four, runs over to the pool table and starts to mess up their game. There's an almighty screech from the mother:

'Reebbeccaaaa, stop playing with those boys' balls!'

Overheard by Philip, the local
Posted on Thursday, 7 December 2006

Battle of the supermarkets

I was in the South Terrace at a soccer match in Lansdowne Road a few years ago. Niall Quinn had made top goal scorer, and a chant of 'Superquinn, Superquinn, Superquinn!' started. Just as the chant was ending, a man at the back of the crowd shouts,

'Up Tesco!'

The whole crowd burst into laughter.

Overheard by Mick, Lansdowne Road
Posted on Wednesday, 6 December 2006

Ciúnas!

Saw a sign in Image beauty salon in Ballymun:

'Noisy children will be sold as slaves!'

Overheard by Anonymous, Ballymun
Posted on Tuesday, 5 December 2006

McBreakfast

While in McDonald's early one morning, a customer asked the cashier, 'What do you have for breakfast?'

To which she replied, 'Ah, usually just a cup of coffee and a slice of toast.'

Customer was not impressed!

Overheard by Anonymous, McDonald's, Donaghmede
Posted on Sunday, 3 December 2006

He knows when you've been bad or good ...

Walking into the Blanchardstown Shopping Centre last week, saw this little kid, about three years old, running in front of me, with his mum and granny pushing a pram behind him.

Little kid twirls around and falls flat on his back. Picks himself up, no bother, but then his Granny breaks into raucous laughter.

'AHAHAHAHAAAA! That's what you get for not holding your Nana's hand. Santy did that to ya!'

Who knew Father Christmas was so vindictive?!

Overheard by TD, Blanchardstown Shopping Centre
Posted on Friday, 1 December 2006

Ah, Dublin logic ...

Two women standing at a bus stop, apparently discussing what to wear on a night out. One says to the other,

'Well, if it's cold, you can always wear those fishnet tights … you know, the ones with the holes in them.'

Don't ya just love Dublin logic?

Overheard by Ali, at a bus stop on Westmoreland Street
Posted on Tuesday, 28 November 2006

D'yerknowharimean, Bud?

Skanger telling his friend (in a nasal whiney voice) how he fools his ma:

'Sure I smoke away in the front room when me Mudder's ou a bingo. When she comes back I do have me runners off and I'm after rubbin me feet t'geder, so I am, so the smell of me fee covers up the smell of the hash. D'yerknowharimean?'

Overheard by Beatrice, queuing in the chip shop
Posted on Monday, 27 November 2006

Toilet talk

Sitting in the bog in a city-centre pub after a few scoops, the bloke in the next cubicle says, 'Howya, how's it goin'?' to which I reply, 'Ah, not too bad!' Then he says, 'Sorry!' and I say again, 'Not too bad!' Then he says,

'Listen I'll ring you back, there's some lunatic in the jacks next to me!'

I cringed — and waited 'til he left!

Overheard by Peter, Knightsbridge, Bachelors Walk
Posted on Monday, 27 November 2006

New advances in English dictation

Closing time outside a city centre pub. Argy-bargy between a group of my friends and a bunch of skangers; scuffles followed by skangers taking flight. One skanger temporarily detained and pinned to ground by friend. The skanger refutes all and any involvement in said ruckus by screaming … wait for it …

'I didn't do nuthin to no-one never!'

A double double negative!

Overheard by Anonymous, outside city centre pub
Posted on Friday, 24 November 2006

This DART will terminate in …

On the DART between Bray and Greystones, three Loreto Dalkey schoolgirls walk through the carriage. An announcement is made:

'This train will terminate at the next station.'

One of the girls lets out a little yelp, starts flapping her arms, then says loudly,

'Oh my God! Does that mean the train is broken?'

Private school education, eh?

Overheard by Alan, DART from Bray to Greystones
Posted on Thursday, 23 November 2006

Brainbox of the year

In the local boozer after work, and in the corner the *Weakest Link* was on the box.

'What's the capital of Spain?' asks Anne Robinson.

One of the locals shouts out, 'BARCELONA, ye gobshite!'

Overheard by Tony, Bottom of the Hill, Finglas
Posted on Saturday, 18 November 2006

Barbed-wire top

I was recently working at a high-class fundraiser that a good-looking woman with a big pair of breasts and a top with a low cleavage was organising. She was introduced to a new contributor (an old man):

Old Man: 'Can I compliment you on your Barbed-Wire top.'

The woman looked blank …

Old Man continues: 'It protects the property — but doesn't obstruct the view.'

Overheard by Richie, at a fundraiser
Posted on Wednesday, 15 November 2006

The Dublin chipper

Drunk guy goes in to a chipper (real Dublin accent) and approaches the counter where a guy of possibly Indian or middle-eastern descent is working:

Drunk Dub: 'Giz a ray and chips dere.'

Counter guy (in thick foreign accent): 'Flat ray?'

Drunk Dub: 'Ah jaysus no, pump er up a bih for me, will ya!'

Overheard by Abey-baby, chipper near Parkgate Street
Posted on Wednesday, 15 November 2006

Catholic guilt

On Halloween night, I was standing at my bus stop beside three guys who were off to a fancy dress party and were all dressed as priests. When the bus finally came, the three get on and ask how much. The driver tells them 95c each, only to be met with one of the lads replying,

'I remember when Dublin Bus were a friend to the clergy!'

Overheard by Jamie, on the no. 50 bus, Drimnagh
Posted on Tuesday, 14 November 2006

I'm a celebrity, get me outta here!

A few years back, I was having a conversation with a work mate. He began telling me about a party he was at that weekend. He said he arrived and knew everyone there except this one girl. He asked a friend who she was and was told that she was a bit of a smug, snobby bitch who had some claim to fame and was full of herself because of this fact.

He at some opportunity spoke to her during the night, initiating the conversation with, 'Hey, I know you somehow, I recognise your face.'

Apparently the girl began to glow with self obsession until he said,

'Did you …? Did you …? Did you serve me in Boots the other day?'

Needless to say she was disgusted …

Overheard by Stephen, Glasnevin
Posted on Tuesday, 14 November 2006

Fire safety

At work, in our previous offices, we had a sign outside the lifts advising the safety precautions to be taken in using them — fairly normal, except that, under 'In case of fire', some smart-arse had written,

'Bring marshmallows.'

Overheard by Seamus, Booterstown
Posted on Tuesday, 14 November 2006

No speekee Ingrish

Walking along Grafton Street, couple of D4 girls talking about somebody they knew who had adopted a Chinese baby. One of them perplexedly asked,

'Loike, when he grows up, will he think in English?'

Hmmmm …

Overheard by John, Grafton Street
Posted on Tuesday, 14 November 2006

Dreamland …

Sitting at home at the weekend, my girlfriend and my Mam are having a conversation about what's happening at the moment in *Eastenders*.

My Girlfriend: 'She's putting the baby up for adoption.'

My Mam: 'Yeah, it's terrible, the poor child.'

My Dad: 'It's not real life, it's only a television programme.'

My Mam (I love this bit!): 'Ah, get a life!'

Overheard by SB, at home at the weekend
Posted on Monday, 13 November 2006

The northside diet

During the summer I was driving to the airport and stopped at the traffic lights at the back of the Custom House. An Eastern European couple cross the road in front of me, holding hands. The girl was very slim and was dressed in figure-hugging white pants.

I had my window rolled down, and a taxi driver parked in the next lane shouts across in a thick northside accent,

'Jaysus, would ya look at da, all our birds do is stuff their bleedin' faces with burgers and chips!'

Overheard by Paddy, outside the Custom House
Posted on Monday, 13 November 2006

Axe-wielding bus driver

I was on the no. 65 bus to Blessington, and the top deck of the bus had been cordoned off with a bus ticket roll (much like a crime scene). Kids had smashed the upstairs windows.

Upon passing the Jobstown Inn pub, a drunk

proceeded on and stood beside the driver, talking to him through the security screen. Within the first three stops, he had asked the bus driver 101 stupid questions, which the driver was clearly getting angered by.

The drunk then asked the driver, 'What happened upstairs?'

The driver said, 'There was a murder up there earlier.'

The man clearly shocked said, 'What happened?'

The driver then said, 'On the last run there was some drunk asking me stupid questions. So I took me axe out and chopped him up! Now, have ya any more questions?'

The drunk — petrified at this stage — stutters, 'No, next stop's mine thanks.'

Overheard by Gary, on the no. 65 bus
Posted on Sunday, 12 November 2006

Apple tart

A friend of mine ordered a slice of apple tart in the Kylemore café.

'Do ya wanna eat it?' asked the girl behind the counter.

'Pardon?' said my friend.

'I said do ya wanna eat it?' repeated the girl.

'Well, yes,' he said, rather confused.

With that she threw the apple pie in the
microwave:

'Ten cent extra.'

Overheard by Exdub, Kylemore café
Posted on Friday, 10 November 2006

Cinders

I was standing outside Burger King on Grafton
Street at about four o'clock on a Sunday
morning, one shoe in my hand because my feet
were killing me.

This lad wearing a white tracksuit comes up to
me and asks me can he have my shoe.

'What do ya want my shoe for?' I asked.

'So I can find ya in de mornin!'

Overheard by Ali, Grafton Street
Posted on Friday, 10 November 2006

Guinness is good for you ...

Saw a Guinness truck go down Parnell Street
yesterday, with 'EMERGENCY RESPONSE UNIT'
written in large letters in the dirt on the back.

Overheard by Anonymous, Parnell Street
Posted on Friday, 10 November 2006

Plan B

At Croke Park. All-Ireland Hurling Final 2006, Kilkenny versus Cork. Before the end of game, an announcement comes over the tannoy about spectators staying off the pitch, and for stewards to take up their positions.

The game ends. As expected, hundreds of fans start to run on the pitch to congratulate their heroes. Over the tannoy, 'Plan B, Plan B, Plan B'.

To add to the hilarity of the moment, 'PLAN B' was displayed in huge letters on the big screen!

Overheard by the Cat, Croke Park
Posted on Friday, 10 November 2006

Know it all

Worked with a severely irritable and thick French barman in Temple Bar some time back. Because of his demeanour he was a constant target for teasing from the other staff. One afternoon he could take no more and snapped at us,

'You tink dat I know f**k nothing! I tell you dat I know f**k all!'

We died …

Overheard by Barman, Temple Bar
Posted on Friday, 10 November 2006

Brothers are great

My daughter was going to her debs. They were meeting at the Assumption Secondary School in Walkinstown to get on the coach to the hotel, so the whole family went down to the school to see her off and have a look at the dresses.

When you walk up the drive, there is a sign saying, 'Slow Pupils Crossing'. Her brother looks at the sign and says,

'I can see why you sent her here!'

Overheard by JDub12, Assumption Secondary School, Walkinstown
Posted on Thursday, 9 November 2006

Supermacs — a family restaurant

Late at night, sitting in Supermacs, I see a large biker guy walk in who is absolutely locked. He proceeds up to the counter and says,

'Gimme a family box — without the father!'

Overheard by Bob, Supermacs
Posted on Thursday, 9 November 2006

Think bigger

A little boy was in the toy shop where I work, begging for a toy. The conversation went like this:

Boy: 'Mom, can I get something small?'

Mom: 'No you can't.'

Boy (thinks for a second): 'Can I get something BIG!?'

Overheard by Brian, toy shop
Posted on Tuesday, 7 November 2006

Throwing her weight around

On the Westport to Dublin train on Sunday after the Ireland versus Australia International Rules disaster. Middle-aged woman with giant (I mean the size of a small country) rear end has just gotten on the train and is bashing into everyone as she attempts to find a seat, then throwing herself around as she tries to get her luggage onto the overhead storage shelf.

With much huffing and puffing, she eventually sits down. A young fella smartly quips,

'Coulda done with you against the Ozzies today, Mrs!'

Overheard by Gerry, Westport to Dublin train
Posted on Monday, 6 November 2006

Aussie does indeed rule

While we were getting hockeyed by Australia in the International Rules match on Sunday, there was an Ozzie woman up on the Hill who kept waving her huge flag whenever her team scored, and the people behind her were getting annoyed since it was in the way.

Then in the 4th quarter when Ireland managed to score one mighty singular point, and she kept her flag down, a voice roared after the clapping,

'Where's your flag now?'

Overheard by Bozboz, Hill 16
Posted on Monday, 6 November 2006

Tight jeans

Me and my sister were walking down Thomas Street when a woman walked by wearing extremely tight jeans. My sister is stunned for a second then just says,

'Jaysus, she must've had to jump off the top of de wardrobe to get into dose ...'

Overheard by Anonymous, Thomas Street
Posted on Sunday, 5 November 2006

Righteous indignation

My mother was doing her weekly shopping in Dunnes. A married couple with their son of about four years of age were selecting a trolley. The small boy told his mother, 'Don't pick that one, Mammy — it's f**ked.'

The mother told the child off for using bad language, only to be told in reply,

'But Daddy SAID it was f**ked.'

Overheard by Seamus, Dunnes Stores, Kilnamanagh
Posted on Saturday, 4 November 2006

Cops and robbers

I had a week off work and was washing my car in my driveway. Two boys, not more than ten years old, were playing cops and robbers on bikes. Everything seemed normal until the 'cop' stopped talking on his imaginary walkie-talkie and informed the robber,

'I don't give a f**k about my job, I'm gonna kick your bleedin' head in.'

Overheard by Seamus, Tallaght
Posted on Saturday, 4 November 2006

Long way to go

On the steps of a church after the funeral of an elderly lady.

One mourner: 'That was very sad.'

Second mourner: 'It was. I'm so depressed I just want to find a nice quiet pub and drink meself into Bolivia.'

Overheard by Anonymous, in Clondalkin
Posted on Saturday, 4 November 2006

Why townies shouldn't do agriculture

Just before the Leaving Cert, I was giving grinds to two D4 girls in Agricultural Science. One of the short questions on the paper was, 'Why would the weather forecast be important to potato farmers in Ireland?'

I would have presumed that everybody who did history in primary school would have learned of the potato famine and blight caused by the unusual muggy weather, but apparently not, as one of the girls replied to me,

'So that farmers will know when to put on sun screen?'

God be with the next generation …

Overheard by K, giving grinds
Posted on Friday, 3 November 2006

World Vision

While walking through Temple Bar with my mother, this guy approached and asked would she like to hear more about 'World Vision'. She replied,

'No tanks, luff, I don't need any glasses.'

She didn't cop on until long after the man had walked by that he wasn't talking about Vision Express ...

Overheard by Rosso, Temple Bar
Posted on Thursday, 2 November 2006

Wise words from a Finglas head

I saw this overweight middle-aged guy out power-walking on Ballygall Road in Finglas. A youngfella from the other side of the road shouts over,

'Hey mister, you'd want to do less of the power eatin!'

Fair play to the big guy, he just laughed and kept booting along.

Overheard by S, Finglas
Posted on Friday, 27 October 2006

That'll learn him

Overheard on Hill 16:

Dublin were all over Roscommon but were failing to hit the target and were running up a high amount of wides. After the tenth or so such wide, some well-mannered educated chap (clearly out of place on Hill 16) pipes up and says,

'Come on, Dublin, let's convert our superiority into scores!'

A reply came from a cider-drinking yobbo,

'Do yiz hear f**king Shakespeare down dere!'

Overheard by Diego, from Hill 16 A5 section
Posted on Wednesday, 25 October 2006

Happy birthday

I was in a pub in town at the weekend, a pretty rowdy pub, when two female guards walked in to verify a reported disturbance. A girl sitting near the door shouts out,

'Whose birthday is it? Get yezer kits off, girls!'

Overheard by Jayo, the International Bar
Posted on Wednesday, 25 October 2006

Edible underwear

The Southern Cross Business Park in Bray. A
company called 'The Butlers Pantry' (a food
manufacturer) had recently moved in to the
estate. The driver of a delivery truck comes over
and asks us smokers outside,

'Sorry lads, can you tell me where I can find the
Butlers Panties?'

Overheard by Barney, Bray
Posted on Wednesday, 25 October 2006

The cheek!

Walking to work this morning on Dawson Street,
spotted a Garda standing beside an illegally-
parked van, writing a ticket. Van owner runs out
of a local shop and says, 'Is there a problem,
Garda?'

Garda: 'Yeah, would you look at that, some eejit
is after putting a footpath and double yellow
lines under your van — the cheek of them!'

Overheard by Aine, Dawson Street
Posted on Wednesday, 25 October 2006

Feckin' immigrants

I'm Aussie, but lived in Dublin for a few years.
Anyway, two weeks or so after I arrived, I got a
job, and having walked out of said successful
interview at about 2 p.m., thought that I should
celebrate with a few jars.

Went into a pub near Aungier Street and ordered
a pint. It was almost empty so I started chatting

with the barman. A few pints later, he's having one or two himself and we've become new-found best mates. He's going on about how great Australia is, and congratulations on gettin' de job, young lad, and you keep your nose clean now. He even buys me a pint to 'celebrate ye gettin yer start in Dooblin'. Grand.

Then this Polish girl comes in and asks, in fairly broken English, 'Do you hev job I can take, yes?'

He rudely tells her no, and as soon as she leaves, he throws her CV in the bin and says to me, in all seriousness ...

'Feckin' immigrants, comin' here and takin' all our jobs.'

Utter genius!

Overheard by Rory, an unnamed pub
Posted on Saturday, 21 October 2006

BIMBO

Sitting chatting with the gurlies. We were talking about Heather Mills, and one of my friends said, 'Oh yeah, that's the one married to Paul McCartney with the PROSTATE leg!'

Overheard by Wen, straight from a mad mate's mouth!
Posted on Friday, 20 October 2006

Decimalisation

Walking through Phibsboro on the North Circular, a small old woman shouts to a rather large black man, 'I have tha' two shillin's for ya!'

He looks at her confused and shrugs.

'The two shillins — the euro I owe ya!'

Overheard by Gar, Phibsboro
Posted on Friday, 20 October 2006

What's wrong with a knife?

Earlier this year I was working in Habitat. This very southside Dublin girl in her late teens, dressed in designer clothes, walked up to me and asked,

'Do you sell bagel slicers?'

I said I didn't even know such a thing existed and, no, the store never stocked them. She said in all seriousness, as if I had been living in the Dark Ages and the store was some throwback to 50s Ireland,

'Well, like, they have them in *The OC* ...' and then turned and walked away.

Television really is warping this generation's minds!

Overheard by Anonymous, at work in Habitat
Posted on Friday, 20 October 2006

Bright spark!

Whilst in Woodie's wandering about, as is a handyman's wont, I came across a salt-of-the-earth Dublin family. They had just passed a stand with solar power lamps on display when the mother got rather excited:

Mother: 'Ah Tom, wouldn't dem lamps be lovel-illy out by de roses in de drive?'

Tom: 'Not bad alright, how much are dey?'

Mother: 'Only €9.99 each.'

Son: 'Ah here, dem solar-powered lamps, I heard 'bout dem, they're a scam.'

Mother: 'Why, what's wrong wit 'em?'

Son: 'Sure dey don't work … der's no bleedin' sun at night …'

Overheard by Hick, Woodie's DIY
Posted on Thursday, 19 October 2006

Talking to yourself!

My boyfriend was upstairs on a bus to work one morning. A little girl and her father got on and sat right up the front. The little girl started to talk at the top of her voice, 'Dis is grea, Da, ya can see everythin up here, Ma never lets me si up here!'

The father, looking a bit embarrassed by the daughter's loudness, says, 'Der's no need to shout, I'm sittin righ beside you.'

The little girl replies as loudly as before, 'Righ so, I'll just talk to meself in me own head den.'

Overheard by CS, on a bus to Rathfarnham
Posted on Thursday, 19 October 2006

At the dogs

Many years ago I was at the Dogs in Harold's Cross with my parents — it was my mother's first visit.

Before the fifth race starts, my Ma has a pained expression and says, 'Ah, the poor dog, he must be tired.'

'Which one, Ma?'

'The one with the stripey jacket on, this is his fifth race!'

Overheard by Jinho, at the Dogs, Harold's Cross
Posted on Thursday, 19 October 2006

Just folly me directions

Outside a nightclub on Harcourt Street, I overheard a young fella beside me giving directions to someone how to get there. He says,

'Jaysus, will you just tell the taxi driver it's on "HARD CORE STREET"!'

Bless! These people are the future?

Overheard by Alanjo, Harcourt Street
Posted on Thursday, 19 October 2006

Hot weather, wouldn't you say!

One of those nice hot summer nights, I picked up three girls around the Ringsend area. Nice girls, chatting away on the way to Stephen's Green. In the middle of the conversation one turns to the others and says,

'Jaysus, I'm roasting tonight, this weather is killing me.'

One of the others agrees with her, and to express her feelings on the point replies,

'Yeah, I'm boiling, me knickers are wringing!'

Ahhh, Dub girls — where would you get it!

Overheard by Anonymous, in my taxi in Ringsend
Posted on Thursday, 19 October 2006

Ribena man

Drunk man on the no. 150 bus holding a carton of Ribena turns around to me and says, 'That can't be true, 95% of Irish blackcurrants grow up to be Ribena berries?'

How can you respond to that?

Overheard by Timmy, on the no. 150 bus
Posted on Wednesday, 18 October 2006

Bleedin' embolisms

Coming home from Clonshaugh Industrial Estate the other day, my pal Damo overheard two auld ones talking about multicultural Dublin:

'… Jaysus, there's bleedin' Chinese embolisms everywhere …'

Trying hard not to picture haemorrhaging on a city-wide scale, he hid his laughter and presumed she meant symbols.

Overheard by Babs, from a pal returning
from Clonshaugh Industrial Estate
Posted on Wednesday, 18 October 2006

Ferocious language

I went to Argos to buy a pocket-sized electronic thesaurus. Upon arriving I located one in the catalogue, filled in the little paper slip with the Argos code and then joined the queue. I handed the paper slip to the cashier who was a middle-aged Dublin lady, and the name of the item popped up on her screen, along with the price.

'So it's an Oxford … The … Thes …
Tyrannosaurus rex at €29.99. Now would you
like to insure him for an extra €3 for three
years?'

I shook my head and said no thanks.

"No, OK, so you don't want to insure him, no
problem love, that's grand, here's your order
number.'

Overheard by Karen, Argos
Posted on Wednesday, 18 October 2006

Friends for less

Working for Vodafone years ago, had a
promotion called Friends For Less, basically
nominate three 087 numbers you ring the most
to save money. Anyway, we'd always ask
customers at the end of the call do they want to
register three numbers. Had some muck savage
on who replied, 'Ya, sure, I'll go for 2, 6 and 8!'

!?!?!?

Overheard by Will, while working at Vodafone
Posted on Monday, 16 October 2006

Preparing for an evening of culture

In Molloys off-licence in Clondalkin last Saturday
night about eight o'clock.

This girl and her Ma came in. The Ma, of course,
was wearing her pyjamas and slippers. They
picked up a couple of bottles of Black Tower
and were looking at the crisps. The daughter
picks up a packet of fancy Thai spicy crisps with
pictures of red peppers on the bag.

'Wharrabouh dem, Ma?'

'Ah, no way. Dey look like dey'd burn yeh.'

Overheard by Austo, Molloys, Clondalkin
Posted on Monday, 16 October 2006

Monkey magic on the no. 10 bus

After waiting over 45 minutes on the NCR for a no. 10 from the Phoenix Park, the bus finally pulls up to the stop. When the door opens the old woman, a real Dub, at the front of the queue says to the driver,

'What were ye doin up there? Feedin' the bleedin' monkeys!'

The driver replies, 'Yeah, and takin' on some bleedin' monkeys as well!'

Only in Dublin!

Overheard by Joxer, North Circular Road
Posted on Friday, 13 October 2006

A T-ahem

Waiting in an ATM queue on Georges Street one weekend and one person seems to be taking quite a long time to use the machine. Man behind me shouts up to the girl at the machine,

'What are you gettin up there, a bleedin' mortgage!'

Overheard by Seán, Georges Street
Posted on Friday, 13 October 2006

Only something a Dub would say!

The day of the Liffey Swim a few weeks back, my friends and I were heading in to town on the no. 25A bus. Of course everyone was curious to see what was happening, so whilst stuck in traffic on the quays this Dublin girl got up and went over to the other side of the bus to see what everyone was staring at.

She turned around and said to her boyfriend (and everyone else on the bus),

'Jeysus, one a dem is gonna get stuck in a bleeding shopping trolley!'

Overheard by Penelope, on the no. 25A bus
Posted on Wednesday, 11 October 2006

That rhino's bleedin' sweatin'!

Overheard by a friend of mine, who was recently at a circus on the northside of Dublin. Show was in full swing, animals and everything, including a rhino which was mounted by one of the performers.

Beside him was a young couple. Conversation is as follows:

Young one: 'That's f**king horrible!'

Young fella: 'What is?'

Young one: 'Him riding that rhino, it's bleedin' sweating!'

Overheard by Moz, at the circus
Posted on Wednesday, 11 October 2006

Making it up?

Overheard the announcer on an open-top Dublin Tour bus going by Burdock's chipper.

'To your right we have Burdock's, Dublin's most famous fish and chip shop. An array of celebrities have eaten in this famous chip shop, from Molly Malone right up to U2.'

Molly Malone?

Overheard by Willy, Werburgh Street
Posted on Tuesday, 10 October 2006

Off da ...

Crowd of young lads sitting in McDonald's, possibly just back from a trip to the US, or maybe just talking about a DVD they'd seen. Phrases such as 'off da hook' and 'off da ...' one thing and the other etc. are being bandied about.

The analyst of the group pronounces, 'Off da hook is the most famous of all the offdas.'

Overheard by Mozzer, McDonald's, Ranelagh
Posted on Monday, 9 October 2006

The joy of childbirth

A while back the sister-in-law of a mate of mine had her first child. It was a big baby and had to be delivered by Caesarean section. I'm translating here, because the text I got from my mate read:

'She had a baby boy this morning. Big fella. Came out the sun roof.'

Overheard by Diego, by text
Posted on Monday, 9 October 2006

Top prize?

Watching the Ireland versus Cyprus game on Saturday in the Bankers pub in town.

Coming near the end of the game, Ireland losing 5-2, the commentator says that after the game they will be doing their 'Man of the Match' competition. He said, 'The top prize is two tickets to Ireland's next match.'

Cue somebody shouts out,

'Yeah more a f**kin' booby prize!'

Overheard by Mac, Bankers in town
Posted on Monday, 9 October 2006

A G.S.O.H. essential

Two scobie types sitting on the no. 78A bus behind me, talking about a pet dog they used to have.

Scobie 1: 'Ye'd miss him around though, wouldn't ye?'

Scobie 2: 'Ah yea, he was a mad little b*stard, wasn't he?'

Scobie 1: 'Yeah. D'ya remember the time he left a shite on the bed and then when you were cleaning it he took another shite on the floor?'

Scobie 2: 'Yeah, he was gas . . .'

Overheard by Sue, on the no. 78A bus
Posted on Thursday, 5 October 2006

Rural resettlement

Picked up two women in my taxi in Ballymun. One asked to go to the City Council buildings at Wood Quay. They got talking on the way in, and one says to the other,

'Jaysus, I'm going in here to see about rural resettlement. I'm goin to tell them I want a dormant bungalow in Carlow, no upstairs ...'

Overheard by Terry, in my taxi
Posted on Tuesday, 3 October 2006

True love

On the no. 150 bus going into town, a drunk couple get on and sit down the back. A few minutes pass, then the guy stands up and shouts, 'Excuse me, ladies and gentleman, I'd just like to say I love this woman!'

The woman turns her head away from him and says, 'Ah jaysus, will ye stop, you're makin' me scarlet!'

And he says, 'Shut up, ye stupid bitch!'

Overheard by JohnG, on the no. 150 bus
Posted on Monday, 2 October 2006

Where's de justice in dat?

One day while working in Dun Laoghaire Shopping Centre, one annoyed 'head-the-ball' comes running up to one of the security guards and screams at him,

'Yer man is down there accusing me of robbin ...'

The security guard looks back and the 'head-the-ball' says,

'... I wouldn't mind but I haven't robbed in here in weeks!'

Overheard by Cobs, Dun Laoghaire Shopping Centre
Posted on Friday, 29 September 2006

Never get a rickshaw in Dublin

I was getting on a rickshaw (drunk) going back to a girl's house one Saturday evening. We were in a passionate embrace and full of lust. As we passed a couple of lads on a corner, one of them shouted, 'De ye's want a knife and fork!'

Overheard by Karl, Rathmines
Posted on Thursday, 28 September 2006

Lost and found?

Overseen actually. Was walking past the Bleeding Horse on Camden Street when my boyfriend brought my attention to a small sticker on a lamp-post:

'Lost nail clippers, this is urgent, you have no idea how long my toe-nails are, information, please contact …'

You can see it for yourselves, it's on a lamp-post near the smoking area on the street!

Overheard by Leona, outside the Bleeding Horse
Posted on Wednesday, 27 September 2006

Can I take your order?

A drunk goes into the local chipper after a few scoops and orders a shark burger and chips. The disgruntled worker ignores him but the man keeps shouting up his order. Eventually the chippy shouts back, 'We don' do dem!'

Your man responds, 'Ye don' do dem? Just a shark burger so!'

Overheard by Larry, northside chipper
Posted on Wednesday, 27 September 2006

Final destination

As the Luas was approaching the Red Cow, there was the following announcement over the loudspeaker:

'All passengers will be terminated at Abbey Street.'

Overheard by Helen, Luas (Red Cow)
Posted on Wednesday, 27 September 2006

Show must go on

Queuing for a p*ss in the pub, drunk guy at urinal beside me announces, 'I have stage fright. I can't go, and I am bursting!'

Overheard by Paul, The Old Mill pub, Tallaght
Posted on Monday, 25 September 2006

What's the craic

In passport control coming back from Thailand, my boy's passport had been stolen by a prostitute. He only had an emergency passport from the embassy (which was a green piece of paper, might I add).

The passport officer kindly told us, 'Believe me, it will turn up in a few days with a foreigner coming through in an Ireland jersey, asking me what the craic is!'

Overheard by Anonymous, Dublin Airport
Posted on Friday, 22 September 2006

Balanced diet

A young boy and his mother in the Centra in Bray. The young lad picks up a carton of milk and when seen by his mother is told to, 'Put it back, don't you know you are having a can of coke with your chips!'

Overheard by Barney, Centra, Bray
Posted on Thursday, 21 September 2006

800-year struggle

Spray-painted on a wall at the entrance of my mate's estate in Donabate:

'BIRTS OUT!'

It's been there for years, uncorrected!

Overheard by Rory, Donabate
Posted on Wednesday, 20 September 2006

Euclid would be proud

I was on the ferry from Holyhead to Dun Laoghaire and I got talking with an ould pair from Limerick. It was the first time they had travelled abroad. The ould one said to me,

'We usually go on holidays to Lahinch. It's grand. It's only 50 miles from home and only 50 miles back again.'

Overheard by John, Stena Line ferry
Posted on Wednesday, 20 September 2006

Talking fruit

Girl: 'So where are you from, you sound Australian?'

Guy: 'Wales, but I do have a bit of a kiwi accent.'

Girl (laughing hysterically): 'What?! Kiwis can't talk!'

Overheard by Anonymous, St Stephen's Green
Posted on Monday, 18 September 2006

EU or not EU

Arriving recently at passport control in Dublin Airport, I overheard two English girls debating whether they should be in the queue 'EU' or 'Non-EU'.

'I was never very good at geography in school,' one of them said, 'so I don't know if England is in the EU or not.'

'Well, we don't have the euro,' the other one replied, 'so we mustn't be.'

They then joined the non-EU queue.

Overheard by Sean, Dublin Airport
Posted on Monday, 18 September 2006

Small change

Got on the bus a couple of weeks ago, having decided to get rid of all the small coins in my change jar at home. I poured my €1.35 fare, all in coppers, into the machine.

'Robbin' the piggy bank again?' asked the bus driver.

'Something like that,' I laughed.

'Or else,' he said, grinning, 'you must be a terrible singer.'

Overheard by Aoibhlinn, on the no. 18 bus
Posted on Monday, 18 September 2006

Unhappy customer

On the crowded no. 39 bus from the city to Blanch at rush hour.

A little girl of maybe four years kept screaming and crying. Her mother was wondering what was bothering her.

'Why are you so upset?'

The little bugger replied, 'Mommy, I hate f**kin' Dublin Bus.'

Overheard by Mr Winterbottom, on the no. 39 bus
Posted on Saturday, 16 September 2006

Irish Superbowl

On a recent flight from New York to Dublin, three elderly Yanks had the following discussion:

Yank 1: 'I believe it's Superbowl weekend in Ireland next weekend.' (clearly talking about the upcoming All-Ireland football final)

Yank 2: 'Wow, they play (American) football in Ireland?'

Yank 1: 'No, Irish football.'

Yank 3: 'You mean soccer?'

Yank 1: 'No, Irish football, they play with a rugby-shaped ball and wear loads of padding.'

Had to bite my lip!

Overheard by Staffy, on a flight from New York to Dublin
Posted on Friday, 15 September 2006

Language barriers

A Dub in work is queuing for a sandwich. As it's being made up, he's answering all the questions — in pure Dub — from a Polish girl, who is using what English she has to try and understand what he wants. She's wearing a completely baffled expression because she has no idea what this fella is saying, but carries on as best she can:

'You want lettuce?'

'That's deadly!' (adds lettuce).

'Tomato?'

'Nice one … tomato' (adds tomato).

'Ok, you want mayonnaise or salad cream?'

'Aw sure, it's legend as it is.'

The Polish girl tries to put mayo on, to cries from Auld Dub, 'Nah, nah, it's legend, legend!'

Overheard by Anonymous, working in Dublin
Posted on Thursday, 14 September 2006

A Dub in London Zoo

At London Zoo, my friend's sister passes by an enclosure under construction. A Portakabin behind a fence had Mifflin & Co. printed on a yellow sticker near the roof of the cabin. She calls over her two kids,

'Tom and Liam, come and see the mifflins!'

Overheard by David, London Zoo
Posted on Thursday, 14 September 2006

I'll be back

A non-national was hit by a vehicle at the pedestrian crossing on O'Connell Street. It was a minor accident, but looked all the more dramatic as he rolled off the bonnet of the car

and continued walking briskly away. Cue a stunned Howya at the lights:

'Jaysus, it's the bleeding Terminator!'

Overheard by Vincent, O'Connell Street
Posted on Thursday, 14 September 2006

Time to go home

When I was leaving Electric Picnic on the Monday morning, a guy ahead of me said, 'You know you've been here too long when you start dancing to the sound of the generators!'

Overheard by Síle, Electric Picnic
Posted on Wednesday, 13 September 2006

Mental

My friend and I were sitting in a park having a cigarette, when an old drunken man approaches us, asking for a 'spare smoke'.

Myself, whilst taking out a cigarette: 'I must warn you, they're menthol.'

Drunk: 'Ah, sure oim mental meself!'

Overheard by Creem, Ranelagh Gardens
Posted on Monday, 11 September 2006

Staying level headed

Going over the DART tracks on the upper floor of the no. 32 bus, it rocks and bounces over them, swaying dangerously. Old man who was trying to stand up gets pushed back into his seat by the movement, and mutters, 'Level crossing me HOLE!'

Overheard by Denis, on the no. 32 bus
Posted on Friday, 8 September 2006

Terms of endearment

Walking down Henry Street, two young Dublin women chatting to each other while trying to keep their various kids from running too far ahead.

One woman hands her couple-of-months-old baby to the other in order to chase a toddler who is trying a great escape, with the immortal words:

'Hold this bundle o' f**ks, while I clatter yer man.'

Overheard by Zara, Henry Street
Posted on Wednesday, 6 September 2006

Irish terror alert level

The day after the latest 'terror plot' panic in Britain, my Dad overheard a passenger who was waiting to board the ferry at Dun Laoghaire ask a harbour policeman,

'What state of alert are yis on?'

Quick as a flash the harbour policeman says, 'Barely awake.'

Overheard by Dub, Stena terminal, Dun Laoghaire
Posted on Tuesday, 5 September 2006

Anaesthesia! Bless you!

A few years ago, I had occasion to be in the casualty department of Blanchardstown Hospital, getting a cut stitched, as was the 'jaysis-howaya' chap in the next cubicle. He was being treated by a doctor of Asian origin, who had a very strong accent.

The youngfella says to the doctor as treatment started, 'Eh, d'ye moind if I don' look, pal?' to which the doctor says, 'Certainly.'

A blood-curdling scream followed, as well as every type of expletive you can think up. After this died down, the nurse that was treating me calmly called through the curtain,

'He said do you mind if I don't LOOK, not do you mind if I don't have a LOCAL!'

Overheard by Stillsick, James Connolly Hospital, A&E
Posted on Monday, 4 September 2006

Welcome to Ireland

An African gets on the no. 83 bus on Westmoreland Street, flashes his travel pass at the driver and sits down.

An auld one beside me says, '… and they've got the free travel as well …'

Overheard by Niall, on the no. 83 bus
Posted on Monday, 4 September 2006

The thin white line

My sister was driving to Dublin in the car and my father was the front-seat passenger; in the back was my three-year-old nephew. He suddenly asks, 'Mam, what are the white lines in the middle of the road for?'

My father and sister both explain the reason for white lines in the middle of the road.

There is silence in the back.

A couple of minutes later the nephew pipes up, 'But what happens when it snows?'

Overheard by Tappers, off me skin and blister
Posted on Sunday, 3 September 2006

Jesus was a joker

Two years ago when I was working in the city centre I used to meet a friend for lunch on the steps of St Mary's Pro-cathedral just off Marlborough Street (classy, I know!). So we'd sit there chatting and laughing our heads off, a little bit down from the main door where people would come out of Mass. So one day this old disgruntled pensioner woman comes over to scold us:

'You young wans have no respect, stop your laughing, this is a house of God!'

To which another woman says, 'Ah don't mind her, sure didn't Jesus enjoy a bit of messin in his day!'

Overheard by Liz, Marlborough Street
Posted on Wednesday, 30 August 2006

Get this man an atlas!

Some scumbag had been caught red-handed trying to lift cans out of the Centra/Spar at O'Connell Bridge by a 6' 10" security guard, clearly of African origin. Amidst the barrage of abuse he uttered whilst being ejected from the shop, he shouted,

'Get away from me, you big f**kin' Albanian asylum seeker b**tard, ye!'

Overheard by Hugh, Westmoreland Street
Posted on Wednesday, 30 August 2006

Love has its 'benefits'

Written on the sign at the front of the Social Welfare office on Tara Street:

'Noelle Call Me'

Only Dublin ...

Overheard by Andy, Tara Street
Posted on Wednesday, 30 August 2006

Not such an easy pass

Driving down towards the M50 toll bridge with my Dad (in my sister's car, using her Eazy Pass). As my Dad pulls up to the barrier, he holds up the Eazy Pass in front of him. Nothing happens! He's going mad pointing the Eazy Pass in all directions, all over the windscreen. Still the barrier never moves.

He rolls down the window, says to the young lad in the booth, 'This poxy thing's not workin,' to which the young lad replies, 'Hold it up behind the rear view mirror, barcode facing out!'

My dad follows his instructions and — hey presto — the barrier lifts. Then the young lad says,

'Now you see dat, mister, they're Eazy Passes, not feckin' remotes!'

Overheard by Martin, M50 toll bridge
Posted on Monday, 28 August 2006

Cat tranquillisers

On the no. 7 bus coming through Sallynoggin, two lads sitting at the back of the bus with a cat:

'Where did ya get da cat?'

'I stroked it off me aunty.'

'For what?'

'Gonna take it to da mobile vet in Tesco car park and tell the vet the fecker's depressed, ye can get animal tranquillisers off them, piece of piss.'

'Ah yeah, nice one!'

This conversation went on for another five minutes — with the top of the bus in hysterics (under their breath of course)!

Overheard by Anonymous, on the no. 7 bus
Posted on Friday, 25 August 2006

More like Thick Lizzy

At a Thin Az Lizzy gig. Girl behind me mutters to her boyfriend (obviously didn't want to be there),

'Yeah, they are good, but why are they only playing Thin Lizzy stuff?'

… errr?

Overheard by Jimmy, Whelan's on Wexford Street
Posted on Thursday, 24 August 2006

Disability of Laziness

I was on the no. 77A bus one day, coming home from town. There was a foreigner selling newspapers at the traffic lights.

Two lads down the back, one of them comments, 'Jayz, you'd think he'd get a decent job like, ya know.'

The other one replies, 'What are you saying, you haven't even got a f**kin' job!'

'Yea well … I … I have a disability!'

Overheard by David, on the no. 77A bus
Posted on Wednesday, 23 August 2006

A taxi driver who cares

A friend of mine had just arrived home after a year studying abroad, and was in a taxi heading to town from Rathmines one summer evening. He had rolled down the window to get some air.

Coming down Wexford Street, traffic was slow as a lot of people were gathered outside Whelan's/ The Village and some had spilled onto the road.

As the taxi passed the crowd, someone reached into the car and slapped my mate across the face. As if this wasn't injury enough, after a few seconds the clearly unconcerned but amused driver enquired,

'Got a bit of a slap there, did ya?'

I'm not usually a fan of taxi drivers, but this one deserves a round of applause for his compassion …

Overheard by Dan, Wexford Street
Posted on Tuesday, 22 August 2006

Crystal balls

A friend of mine was getting on a no. 11 bus on O'Connell Street when a lady boarded, obviously irate at having waited so long. She asked the driver when the next no. 10 would be along. Quick as a shot, the driver turned to her and said,

'Missus, I've got two balls, unfortunately neither of them are crystal.'

Apparently this satisfied the lady and off she got,

laughing her head off!

Overheard by Kevin, on the no. 11 bus
Posted on Monday, 21 August 2006

Top quality food

I was in McDonald's with a few friends last week. One of my friends says, 'I'll have a milkshake and six nuggets please', to which the cashier replies, 'What flavour would you like?'

Quick as a flash, my other friend says, 'Chicken!'

The group of us cracked up laughing … cashier didn't seem amused though.

Overheard by Anonymous, McDonald's, Stillorgan
Posted on Monday, 21 August 2006

Best birthday ever!

On the day of the infamous Dublin riots, I was crossing O'Connell Bridge when I passed two lads fresh from battle with the Gardaí (and presumably on their way to Leinster House). I overheard one say to the other,

'Jayse, Anto, this is the best birthday ya ever had!'

Overheard by Dan, O'Connell Bridge
Posted on Saturday, 19 August 2006

Advanced linguistics

Junior Cert French class, the fellow sitting in front of me turned around and started telling me about some match he'd been to at weekend, swearing every second word.

'Yeah, it was mad sh*t, the f**kin' defence was all over the f**kin' shop, they ...'

'Jason, stand up!' the teacher says, 'How dare you use that language in my classroom!'

Jason turns around, genuinely outraged:

'What language? English?! Just 'cos it's a French class, we can't speak English?'

Overheard by Jay, Junior Cert French class
Posted on Friday, 18 August 2006

Super disturbing taxi driver

In a taxi the other day with a few friends. The Dubliner driver must have been 20 stone at least. Somehow the conversation turns to beds. Driver starts telling us that he's got a water bed at home. Cue a lot of, 'Oh right, what's that like then?' trying hard not to picture him.

After that he says, 'Ah, you have to try different things ... y'know ... experiment, like, did you ever try jumping off the wardrobe?'

Cue laughter as this sinks in, yet another disturbing sight.

'Yeah, jumping off the wardrobe, wearing a superman outfit, ya hafta try it.'

Man, we were in fits coming out of that cab. I hope he was joking, that poor woman …

Overheard by K, in a Dublin taxi
Posted on Tuesday, 15 August 2006

Would only happen in Dublin

About two months ago while getting the no. 27 bus home, I saw a 'head-the-ball' sitting upstairs at the back of the bus. He had an X-ray in his hands and was holding it up to the window, looking at it very curiously.

I hear some fluttering, and he was examining a totally different X-ray.

Hmmm, I began to grow curious and moved a seat or two back.

He had a pile of them, I could only guess 60+.

That's what I love about Dublin. A guy wanders into some hospital, decides he would like something to play with on the ride home, and tada — he has it!

Overheard by Graham, on the no. 27 bus
Posted on Thursday, 10 August 2006

The state of Kilbarrack

Was getting the no. 29A bus at Eden Quay the other day when two of our American friends

boarded. The gentleman asked the driver,
'Excuse me, sir, where this does bus go?'

To which the driver replied, 'Kilbarrack, Bud.'

The American gentleman then enquired, 'What
state is that in?'

To which our Dublin Bus hero replied, 'It's in an
awful bleedin' state, mister.'

Overheard by Keith, on the no. 29A bus at Eden Quay
Posted on Tuesday, 8 August 2006

Six stabs = alrigh?

Young wan: 'How's Decco?'

Young fella: 'He's alrigh, got out of James's
Monday.'

Young wan: 'What happened him?'

Young fella: 'Six stabs in the chest — he's alrigh
— lucky b**tard.'

Overheard by Nicantuile, Tallaght
Posted on Sunday, 6 August 2006

Someone needs to spend more time in the office!

In Brown Thomas the other day looking at
Chloé bags, and called over an official-looking
woman to verify a price. Woman comes over and
tells us a particular bag is €478.50, and €1,032
in the same colour but with a metallic sheen.

We ask why is it nearly double for a metallic
colour and she launches into a big long
discussion about it being this, that and the other

and 'special metallic effect' and 'nearly impossible to get from any other designer'.

Then the husband came up behind her and asked if she was ready to go!

Couldn't believe she didn't even work there!

Overheard by Raychelle, Brown Thomas, Grafton Street
Posted on Friday, 4 August 2006

Hairy legs

Was in River Island on Grafton Street last week with my six-year-old niece, paying for a pair of jeans. The little brat roars out in front of a very long queue:

'Why are you buying jeans with holes in the legs of them? Sure isn't everyone going to see your hairy legs?!'

Overheard by Anonymous, River Island on Grafton Street
Posted on Wednesday, 2 August 2006

Animal noises

In Dublin Zoo last year I was walking by the farm animals. A little girl (about six) ran by us. Her Ma noticed a sheep and called after her daughter,

'Look, Kelly, a sheep ... moo ... or baah, whatever ...'

Overheard by Joey, Dublin Zoo
Posted on Tuesday, 1 August 2006

Destiny's Child

Walking past a chipper on Faussagh Avenue, Cabra, I overheard two young girls, aged about eleven, discussing one of their sisters:

'Ah sure me sister's been in a right mood since the wedding was called off, her Beyonce was doin the dirt on her!'

Overheard by Karen, Faussagh Avenue, Cabra
Posted on Sunday, 30 July 2006

Nuns Looking for heaven

I was walking down Nassau Street. Outside the Kilkenny Showrooms, there were two elderly nuns in habit, and an elderly lady looking at what appeared to be a street map. Just at that moment a middle-aged man, scruffy looking, came out of the shop, looked at the group, and spontaneously shouted across to them,

'What are you's looking for? The way to heaven?'

I laughed all the way back to work!

Overheard by Domer, outside the Kilkenny Showrooms
Posted on Thursday, 27 July 2006

Jaysis Jesus

Looking for a flat block in Dolphin's Barn complex and stopped a local man, asking, 'Can you tell me where flat 32G is, please?'

He responds, 'Is that G as in Jesus or J as in jaysis?'

Overheard by Erica, Dolphin's Barn
Posted on Thursday, 20 July 2006

Bitten on the Supermacs

I was getting the bus in from the airport and sitting in front of me were two D4 girls, one telling the other about her friend who was attacked by a dog (or loike a massive wolf, as she put it). She said,

'And then the wolf cornered him and, loike, jumped on him and knocked him over, then it started biting him.'

Her mate goes, 'Oh my God! Where did it bite him?'

D4 girl: 'Outside Supermacs.'

Overheard by Ian, airport bus
Posted on Wednesday, 19 July 2006

Eagle-eye cops!

I was at the Dublin versus Offaly match, and just after a steward got hit with a bottle, I overheard two Gardaí talking. One pointed to the stands and said,

'Yer man there in the Dublin top threw the bottle!'

Overheard by Steve, Croke Park
Posted on Monday, 17 July 2006

It's a long way to the top!

On Hill 16 for the Dublin versus Offaly match, group of lads come along looking for a good spot to stand. Guy leading the group keeps going up higher towards the back, when one of the lads shouts out,

'For f**k's sake, we're not on a sponsored walk!'

Overheard by Anonymous, Hill 16
Posted on Sunday, 16 July 2006

Who needs the bank manager?

Guy looking for cash on the lane beside The George, lots of punters passing by in the evening. The usual, 'Any spare change?' to which I'm ashamed to say, you normally walk on.

Then, just as you reach this particular guy, he asks, 'Any chance of a loan of €50?'

I cracked up laughing. Gave him whatever change I had (well over a fiver) and he thanked me very much — before pointing out that it was 'grand' if I couldn't rise to a 50!

Overheard by M, Georges Street
Posted on Thursday, 13 July 2006

Results!

In school, our maths teacher was asking what results we got in our Christmas exams. He gets around to asking my mate who is clearly daydreaming:

Teacher: 'What did you get at Christmas?'

Mate: 'Liverpool jersey and a watch, Sir!'

Overheard by Daz, Ardscoil Rís, Griffith Avenue
Posted on Thursday, 13 July 2006

Weights and measures

Scruffy 'arty' type punter: 'Two pints of Carlsberg, one with four inches of white lemonade and the other with one inch of white lemonade.'

Old style grumpy/sardonic Dublin barman: 'No problem, I have me measuring tape out the back.'

Overheard by DB, the Leeson Lounge
Posted on Wednesday, 12 July 2006

Small folk

My cousin's four-year-old daughter is very smart and quick to pass comment loudly in public. She was sitting on the bus with her mother when a male midget wearing sports gear got on and sat across the aisle from them. My cousin warned her daughter not to say anything, even though this was the first time she had seen a midget.

The little girl would not be frustrated, though, and after thinking about it for a few moments, said for all on the bus to hear,

'Mammy, that's the smallest tracksuit I've ever seen!'

Overheard by Erica, on the no. 10 bus
Posted on Wednesday, 12 July 2006

Free tour

Upstairs on the no. 38 bus coming into town. Old Dublin dear with headscarf, brown mac and sensible shoes, sitting behind a very tanned young girl with long black hair.

As we go by any landmark, the old dear leans slightly forward and whispers its name fairly loudly, 'The Phoenix Park', 'St Peter's Church', 'The Garden of Remembrance'. Girl is getting narked and finally turns round to old dear and says,

'I'm not a bleedin' foreigner! I just have a tan from me holidays!'

Overheard by Erica, on the no. 38 bus
Posted on Monday, 10 July 2006

KFnoChicken

About a year ago I went into KFC at lunchtime and asked for some sort of chicken meal. The assistant told me, 'We have no chicken today!'

KFC with no chicken … could only happen in Ireland!

Overheard by Nicola, KFC
Posted on Monday, 10 July 2006

A dishy name

My grandmother, a real Dub!

On the birth of my daughter Sorcha
(pronounced Sorsha):

'You're calling her what?'

'Saucer! What sort of name is that for a little girl,
she will never forgive you!'

Overheard by Paul, my Nan's house, Portmarnock
Posted on Monday, 10 July 2006

Little brown girl

A few years ago there was a street party on my
road. A woman was dancing with a load of
children in a ring! In the middle of the ring was
a little black girl. The woman enthusiastically
began to sing,

'Brown girl in the ring, tra-la-la-la-la …'

She suddenly realised what she was singing,
quickly stopped and went bright red!

Overheard by Will, Donnycarney
Posted on Sunday, 9 July 2006

I pity the fool …

In Down Under at Stephen's Green, wearing a
'Mr T' t-shirt with a picture of the man himself
saying, 'Ain't got no time fo jibba-jabba', or some
such catchphrase.

A girl approaches me by the bar, looks at the
t-shirt and says,

'So you're a big Mike Tyson fan?'

Overheard by Ciaran, Down Under bar, St Stephen's Green
Posted on Friday, 7 July 2006

Free-range

Middle-aged woman asks vegetable stall-holder on Moore Street,

'Are those onions free-range?'

Stall-holder looks at her and says,

'Yes, love, and I'm tellin' ye, they're very hard to catch!'

Overheard by Erica, Moore Street
Posted on Thursday, 6 July 2006

B.L.A.N.C.H.A.R.D.S.T.O.W.N.

Sitting in my car in southside retail park, two guys getting into car beside me. One has thick Dublin accent and the other guy was foreign:

Dublin Guy: 'No, we'll try Liffey Valley first.'

Foreign Guy: 'Not Blanchardstown?'

Dublin Guy: 'No, no, not Blanchardstown.'

Foreign Guy: 'Why not?'

Dublin Guy: 'Well … (trying to look for the words) … Blanchardstown is … eh … it's for (pronounced very carefully and slowly) s.c.u.m.b.a.g.s.'

The Dublin guy spots me smiling and, obviously worried, a minute later he goes,

'Excuse me, you're not from Blanchardstown are you?'

For the record, I don't think Blanchardstown is for scumbags (I reckon he just didn't fancy going through the toll!).

Overheard by Jo, Liffey Valley
Posted on Thursday, 6 July 2006

VH-not impressed

I was in ExtraVision a while back and two girls came in asking the chap behind the counter whether he sold video cassettes for a camera. The bloke gave them a withering look and said, 'No'.

'Well, do you know where we can get some?' say the girls.

'Try the 80s,' says the bloke as he turns his back.

Nice!

Overheard by Mugwumpjism, ExtraVision, Coolock
Posted on Tuesday, 4 July 2006

Muppetry

I was waiting to get on the bus on Dame Street, feeling slightly under the influence. The bus pulls up and the guy in front of me waves a €5 note and tries to stick it into the coin machine. The bus driver looks past him, directly at me and says, 'Once a muppet always a muppet, that's what I always say!'

Overheard by Cole, Dame Street
Posted on Saturday, 1 July 2006

Foul-mouthed toddler

Walking into the Square in Tallaght yesterday, I was met by a woman walking backwards shouting, 'I'm leav-EN, come on Way-EN,' as she went out the door. I had a look to see who she was shouting at, and spotted a young lad of about two or three, starting to run all the way back at the escalators.

As he started to run, he began that frightened crying that only a lost child can do, and began roaring.

As he came closer I finally made out what he was saying:

'Fer f**k sake, MA! Fer f**k sake, MA!' … over and over.

Everyone within earshot was in knots!

Overheard by Ross, The Squa-AH
Posted on Friday, 30 June 2006

Not a fan of ice-cream

Picture this. Stuck in traffic on Amiens Street on a roasting hot day in June — going nowhere. Some poxy truck hit a car. I had the car windows down, getting some air. About four or five young ones were standing at a doorway across the road.

One had just thrown water at the others and there was the usual talk of, 'Tracey, ya b*ll*x!' etc.

I spotted this guy walking towards them and he was eating the biggest ice-cream I've ever seen. It looked like the ice-cream seller had thrown about eight scoops onto his cone.

As he walked passed, one of the girls shouts out,

'Here, youngfella, give us a lick of your balls!'

Overheard by Damo, on Amiens Street
Posted on Thursday, 29 June 2006

Health care crisis

Standing on Hill 16 during the Meath versus
Dublin Leinster Championship game in 2005
when Meath pariah Graham Geraghty fell to the
ground, badly injured. The motorised stretcher
thing came to pick him up, and as he was being
carted away in obvious pain to a chorus of BEE-
BAH BEE-BAH, a little gurrier of no more than
seven leapt up from behind me and roared,

'I hope you're waiting on a f**kin' bed!'

Overheard by Hally, Croke Park
Posted on Thursday, 29 June 2006

Extra time at the Ireland v. Chile game

Chile were winning 1-0, and it was coming
towards the end of the game. The
announcement came over the loudspeaker that
there would be something ridiculous like six
minutes of extra time (an unusual amount for a
friendly game).

Anyhow, as it was announced, two typical Dubs
were passing:

'Jaysus, Thommo, six minutes? He must be adding that much time for when we went for burgers!'

Overheard by John, Lansdowne Road
Posted on Wednesday, 28 June 2006

Cut down to size

Having a pint in Kehoes off Grafton Street. Quiet time, when three loud Americans come in from golf. Loudest guy is 6 foot 5 inches and is flanked by two nearly-7-footers. He says to the barmaid, 'These guys are nearly 7 foot tall, and I am 6 foot 5. Guess what they call me?'

Without drawing breath she replies,

'Billie Bob.'

Cue sniggering … and a return to the quiet of the pub.

Pure class. Wish I was that quick!

Overheard by Mark, Kehoes off Grafton Street
Posted on Tuesday, 27 June 2006

Moving statue

My mate and I were killing time by watching one of the human statue street performers on Grafton Street. Just as we were about to push off, a gruff voice came from the back,

'He'd move if you ran off with his box!'

Lovely stuff!

Overheard by Shane M, Grafton Street
Posted on Wednesday, 28 June 2006

Knowing where your priorities lie

(Irate) girl on mobile: '... So you're telling me I can't see you until after the World Cup?'

Overheard by Anonymous, St Stephen's Green
Posted on Friday, 23 June 2006

While Heimlich turns in his grave

While in the Cherry Tree pub recently, a man started to cough while eating peanuts. His female companion panicked and shouted,

'Quickly — somebody use the Heineken Manoeuvre!'

Overheard by Dick, Cherry Tree pub, Walkinstown
Posted on Wednesday, 21 June 2006

Miss Education

Walking around Dublin Zoo, the year the safari park part opened, on a very hot Sunday with loads of families about. It just happened to be feeding time when we were walking by the seal

area, and people had begun to gather around to watch the feeding.

A large crane landed on one of the boulders in the middle of the pool and a small boy pointed to the crane and asked his mother, 'What's tha'?'

The mother says with a big smile on her face, 'Oh tha', tha's a boird!'

God love the yout!

Overheard by Kate, Dublin Zoo
Posted on Wednesday, 21 June 2006

Space Knickers

I started working in Dublin Airport recently. While talking to my supervisor, a group of Ryanair air hostesses passed by. I enquired if the airport staff mingled with the airline's hostesses. His reply was,

'Ah yeah, the Ryanair girls are sound, but the Aer Lingus girls must have space knickers on 'cos they think their fanny is out of this world.'

Overheard by Dav, Dublin Airport
Posted on Friday, 16 June 2006

The Fashion

Two old dears talking on the no. 19A bus last night:

Old dear #1: 'Do you see the kids in the runners these days?'

Old dear #2: 'I do, yeah.'

Old dear #1: 'The thing they do now is they put the laces into the runners.'

Old dear #2: 'They don't?'

Old dear #1: 'They do!'

Old dear #2: 'Do they?'

Old dear #1: 'They do. It's the fashion.'

Old dear #2: 'They don't tie them?'

Old dear #1: 'They don't. Just put the laces into the runners.'

Old dear #2: 'That's the fashion, I suppose.'

Overheard by Shango, on the no. 19A bus
Posted on Friday, 16 June 2006

That's not HELP!

When I was waiting for the train in Connolly Station, my insanely bushy-haired friend had his bag stolen. He anxiously runs to the help desk:

'I'm sorry but my bag has been stolen.'

The person behind the desk smirks and replies,

'Did it contain a hairbrush?'

My friend stares at her, not amused.

Overheard by Donal, Connolly Station
Posted on Friday, 16 June 2006

Attention to detail

Was watching the start of the Italy versus Ghana match, when my Mum walks into the room. One or two of the Ghana players had tops with 'Germany '06' written on the front. Mum spots this and pipes up:

'Isn't that great, look at the German team, they're all black.'

Overheard by Richie, at home while watching the World Cup

Posted on Thursday, 15 June 2006

Religious bankers

While walking behind three office types toward the Green, I overheard them talking about the office:

Banker #1: 'How's work these days?'

Banker #2: 'You know the story in the Bible about the man who was being constantly annoyed at home? He went to a wise man for advice and was told to get a goat and to keep it in the house. The goat made a load of noise and a major mess so things got worse. The man went back to the wise man to complain, and was told to get rid of the goat. Once the goat was gone things didn't seem so bad. Well, the goat's on holidays.'

I think we've all been there …

Overheard by Mike, Baggot Street

Posted on Thursday, 15 June 2006

She's lovely

I was in a petrol station one day when a bunch of students came in. There was a bit of a queue forming as we were all waiting for the cashier to reappear from the back.

Anyway, I overheard one of the students boasting to his mates: 'You should see the one who works in here, she is f**kin' lovely.'

Just then the cashier comes into the front of the shop. He is fat, bald and in his 50s. The other students turn around and say,

'Oh yeah, she's a f**king stunner.'

Overheard by John, Bray
Posted on Thursday, 15 June 2006

Romance lives

One night, watching a movie with Brad Pitt in it.

My mother says, 'Ooh, I wouldn't throw him out of bed for eating nuts,' to which my dad replies,

'If he was in bed with you, he *would* be nuts!'

Romance lives!

Overheard by Lorraine, at home
Posted on Wednesday, 14 June 2006

Patience of a prisoner

My friend worked as an electrician in Mountjoy Prison and heard this one morning. There is a shop in there which is open to the prisoners. One morning the shop was late opening, and as the shopkeeper came along to open it, a prisoner shouts from his jail cell,

'About f**kin' time, I've been waiting ages!'

Overheard by Derek, Mountjoy
Posted on Wednesday, 14 June 2006

No sugar coating required

In Swords, two women bump into each other.
One says,

'Jaysus, you're like our John — you're gone
HUGE!'

Overheard by Bridie, Swords
Posted on Tuesday, 13 June 2006

A solution to Africa's problems

While watching an ad for Concern, the voiceover
says, 'These people have to walk for three miles
every day just to get water,' to which my five-
year-old nephew replied,

'Why don't they just move closer to the water?'

Overheard by Derek, while watching TV at home
Posted on Monday, 12 June 2006

Miniature euros

I was getting fags in our local Spar for myself
and my pal Eve, when I decided to get a box of
chocolates for the pair of us. The chocs are
behind the counter so I asked the young cashier
for 'the big box of Miniature Heroes'.

She asked me what I wanted and I repeated,
pointing out where they were to the mystified
girl.

She walked over to the shelf, stared at it for a
few moments and mumbled something to the
other cashier, who kindly pointed them out to
her.

She returned red-faced, announcing:

'Ah, jaysus, I thought you asked for Miniature Euros, and I was sayin' to meself "What the f**k does she want them for?!"'

Overheard by Lainey, Spar, SCR
Posted on Thursday, 8 June 2006

Women's Mini Marathon

'Ow! I'm never doing that to anyone again!'

Man on having his bra strap pinged during the Women's Mini Marathon.

Overheard by Ann, 2006 Women's Mini Marathon
Posted on Tuesday, 6 June 2006

B and Queue

Standing in the queue for the till in B&Q last Saturday, buying a step-ladder. There's only three people in front of me, but it's taking the hapless cashier about ten minutes to deal with each customer, what with a dodgy scanner and barcodes not in the system.

As she left the till for the third or fourth time to ask a colleague what to do next, the bloke behind me looks at the one item I'm getting and says to me,

'Bet you wish you'd just stood on a f**kin' chair now!'

Overheard by Gary, B&Q, Liffey Valley
Posted on Tuesday, 6 June 2006

Ah yes, the charms of the Dublin taxi driver

I was standing outside Bewley's Hotel in Ballsbridge. There were three women nearby. A taxi pulled up and the driver got out. One of the women said to him, 'Are you a taxi?' to which he replied, pointing to his car,

'That's a taxi, luv, I'm a human being!'

Overheard by Áine, Bewley's Hotel, Ballsbridge
Posted on Monday, 5 June 2006

Excuse me, love ...

I was downstairs on the no. 78 bus a couple of months ago and spotted a young one talking happily away to herself. I thought, 'Ah, God love her,' until I realised she was using a hands-free phone.

Just then an oul' one leaned over to her and said,

'Excuse me, love, but yeh look like a feckin' eejit!'

The young one appeared mystified and slightly startled as the rest of us sniggered. She began to talk again to whoever was still on the phone, when the oul' one leaned over again and said,

'Excuse me, love, yeh didn't hear me. Yeh look like a feckin' eejit!'

Howls of laughter!

Overheard by Dave, on the no. 78 bus
Posted on Sunday, 4 June 2006

Shortage of smarts in ICU

A woman was talking vehemently to her friend about nurses in intensive care units:

'They just don't have the brain cells to know who's wellest.'

THEY are short on brain cells?!

Overheard by Anonymous, in a café in Glasnevin
Posted on Saturday, 3 June 2006

The lights are on but nobody's at home

My boss was assisting one of the shop-floor girls with the Christmas lights for the window, and they were having problems with the electrics. My boss went in the back to the fuse box, and called out to the girl,

'Well, are they workin' now?'

To which she replied,

'Oh, yeah! They're on now! … Oh … wait, off again … Oh, back on again!'

My boss could barely get out the words to explain to her the purpose of 'twinkling fairylights' …

Overheard by Alison, at work in Swords
Posted on Saturday, 3 June 2006

No sign of the directions

Came back to Dublin in January this year after many years away. Anyway, I couldn't find the DART station on Amiens Street (access is now different). I asked this guy working there for directions. I mention to him there are not many signs, to which he replies,

'Sure, we don't bother with signs as most people know where it is.'

Overheard by Anonymous, Amiens Street
Posted on Friday, 2 June 2006

The bouncer scale

One of a group of young-looking lads to the bouncers outside a lap-dancing club:

'So, on a scale of one to ten, how much am I not allowed in?'

Overheard by David O'C, outside Club Lapello on Dame Street
Posted on Friday, 2 June 2006

Dog's abuse

Dublin man to his dog, after it did a huge poo at the entrance of Trinity College:

'What are ya? … That's right, a fecking eejit!'

Overheard by Robin, outside Trinity College
Posted on Thursday, 1 June 2006

The singer

An ould drunk on the DART on Saturday evening, trying to convince some Dutch tourists to sing with him:

'I'm a singer,

Sure my whole family were singers,

My mother was a singer,

My father was a singer,

Even the sewing machine was a Singer …'

Overheard by Ruairi, on the DART
Posted on Tuesday, 30 May 2006

Wha's up?!?

In HMV Henry Street yesterday and there were
two very white lads, about sixteen or seventeen
years old, in the middle of doing an
unnecessarily complicated handshake. As I
walked by them, they finished and one said to
the other,

'Right! Now we're black.'

Overheard by NM, HMV on Henry Street
Posted on Tuesday, 30 May 2006

You don't rip off an old lady

I was standing outside Clery's, waiting for a bus. Beside me was an oul' one (in her 70s) with one of them shopping bags on wheels. She was staring into Clery's window and shaking her head. She looked up at me and pointed at a hat in the window.

'Who the feck would pay tha' much for a jaysus haah?'

Overheard by Anonymous, under Clery's clock
Posted on Tuesday, 30 May 2006

High-pressure job?

In a busy furniture shop in Liffey Valley the other day. One of the sales guys was rushing past me when I said to him, 'Under pressure, yeah?'

To which he replied, with a smile on his face,

'Son, pressure is only for tyres!'

Overheard by Adrian, Liffey Valley
Posted on Tuesday, 30 May 2006

Decent boss

We have quite a 'hands on' boss — Pat. He has no problem taking over from a worker if they need a break etc.

One day the phone rang, and it was a customer looking for the boss. I put them on hold and asked a few of the factory boys who were in my office, 'Any sign of Pat?'

They told me he was out in the factory giving

one of the lads a break. So I pick up the phone and said (still can't believe I said this!),

'I'm afraid he's out on the floor, relieving one of the Polish boys!'

Overheard by Anonymous, at work
Posted on Thursday, 25 May 2006

Child protection services, anyone?

A guy at work asking one of the office cleaners about her Spanish holiday:

'So was it any good?'

'Oh yeah, it was brilliant, out on the piss every night until five, and English breakfasts every morning.'

'And did you get a babysitter?'

'Ah no — the child was out with us too — she wouldn't go home!'

Overheard by Anonymous, at work
Posted on Thursday, 25 May 2006

There's always some Anto in the crowd

I was at a Celtic supporters' club meeting a couple of years ago and the Chairman warned us not to leave our belongings on the buses outside Parkhead, because recently the buses were getting robbed during the game.

A couple of issues later the Chairman announced, 'The little nuns of Glasgow are no longer making charitable fund-raisers at Parkhead.'

Some headcase in the crowd called Anto shouts out,

'They don't have to — they're robbing the f**kin' buses!'

Overheard by B, Fraziers, O'Connell Street
Posted on Thursday, 25 May 2006

Give up the day job!

Getting a taxi from Dublin Airport one night and I was half-listening to something on the radio about fighting between India and Pakistan over Kashmir.

The cabbie looks back at me and goes, 'The Indians are on the warpath again, wha?'

Comedy genius!

Overheard by Johnno, cab from the airport
Posted on Sunday, 21 May 2006

What sport is that?

On the DART through Sandymount one day and there is a group of girls playing hockey in the grounds there. An American boy behind me asks,

Boy: 'Mommy, what sport is that?'

Mom: 'I dunno, Sweety, it looks kinda like ice-hockey outside.'

Dad: 'It's called Gaelic soccer …'

Overheard by Liam, on the DART
Posted on Saturday, 20 May 2006

How does milk come out of those?

Little boy, approx. seven years old, in the women's changing rooms in the gym, says to his mother, 'How does milk come out of those?'

To which the mother replies, 'Oh, it's when you have a baby,' and leaves it at that.

The child then laughs and says out very loud, 'I used to suck on them, haha!'

Overheard by Aoife, Westpoint Gym
Posted on Thursday, 11 May 2006

The cry of the common man

Charity mugger (with the usual dreadlocks): 'Excuse me, sir, do you have a second to talk about Oxfam?'

Guy: 'Leave me alone and get a haircut, you hippy!'

Overheard by Jason, Aungier Street
Posted on Thursday, 11 May 2006

Top priority

Speaking of charity muggers …

Chugger: 'Excuse me, could I just ask you for a minute of your time please to talk to you about …'

Guy: 'I'm sorry but I really need to do a poo.'

Chugger just stands there, speechless …

Overheard by Andy, outside Stephen's Green Shopping Centre
Posted on Thursday, 11 May 2006

Vegetarian friendly?

I was in a chipper with my friend, both of us being vegetarians, and she asks the Chinese guy behind the counter,

'Are spice burgers suitable for vegetarians?' and the guy goes,

'Well, there's not MUCH meat in them, it's mainly fat and other shite, so they're kind of vegetarian!'

Overheard by voodoogirl, chipper in Bray
Posted on Thursday, 11 May 2006

Chelsea who?

On the no. 46A bus recently surrounded by noisy D4 boys and girls. I overhear a guy slagging his friend (who was obviously a Man United fan).

Guy: 'Ha ha! Chelsea won!'

On hearing this one of the girls says, 'What, the X Factor?'

Overheard by Anonymous, on the no. 46A bus
Posted on Thursday, 11 May 2006

Excuse me

I was on the Luas the other day, getting off at Heuston Station, very busy, rush hour. Anyway I was making my way through the packed-out Luas, saying 'Excuse me please' etc., when this 'howya' girl shouts all over the place,

'Will yis move outta da f**kin' way, da young

one is tryin to get da hell outta here, now
F**KING MOVE!'

Well, I was 'scarlet'.

Overheard by Kayla, on the Luas
Posted on Wednesday, 10 May 2006

The eccentrics

Upstairs on the no. 150 bus home from town
one evening about seven o'clock, and these two
lads in overalls, half-pissed on the back seat,
were quite loudly fighting over a can of Bud.
Finally they settled down and still quite audibly
began leafing through the *Star* newspaper
together, when one of them pipes up,

'What's this bleedin' word here? Egg-sentrick?'

His mate replies, 'Eccentric, ye bleedin' dope ye,
it's eccentric ... (dramatic, pensive pause) well it
kinda means you're a bit strange and ye do all
sortsa mad stuff. Like yerman Richard Branson
going around the world in a bleedin' balloon
and all that shite. He'd be an eccentric. Ye have
to be rich to be an eccentric, though. If I went
around like that they'd just say I was a mad eejit
and I was crazy … (further philosophical pause
for effect). Yeah, that's it. If you're rich you're
eccentric, if you're poor — you're just crazy ...'

Overheard by Shane, on the no. 150 bus
Posted on Monday, 8 May 2006

A Dub in a London college

A professor to student, explaining the double
negative:

'… and nowhere in the English language does a double positive mean a negative …'

To which a Dub voice at the back of the lecture room pipes up,

'Yea … right …'

Overheard by BC, a Dub in a London college
Posted on Monday, 8 May 2006

Free Fanta

Me and a few friends were walking around Dun Laoghaire recently. We heard rumours that there were free bottles of Fanta being given out as part of a promotion, but we didn't know where.

While searching for the free Fanta around the streets of Dun Laoghaire, a typical auld fella runs across the road towards us, grabs me by the arm and says,

'Do yez want free drink?' (opens a Superquinn bag with about 30 bottles of Fanta) 'They're given dem out down there.'

Overheard by Hoop, Dun Laoghaire
Posted on Saturday, 6 May 2006

Gambling problem?

I was walking home from the pub one night when a mother ran to catch up with her teenage daughter.

Mother: 'Mary, I've got your jacket here, why the f**k are there betting slips in the pocket, you stupid cow, you must be spending a grand a week in that f**king bookies!'

Mary (not missing a beat and screaming): 'That's not me f**king jacket, ya eijit, you f**king lost me bleeding coat!'

Overheard by Antoinette, in town
Posted on Thursday, 4 May 2006

Mackerel-economics

Before I started college, I got a letter from the college with a list of the subjects I would be studying, one of which was Macroeconomics. I was in the kitchen talking to my Mom and said, 'What's Macroeconomics?'

At which point my Dad came in, a wee bit drunk from the pub and shouts,

'Sure mackerel's a bleedin' fish.'

Right so, Dad.

Overheard by Voodoogirl, in my kitchen
Posted on Tuesday, 2 May 2006

Tongue-tied

Standing at a bus stop on the South Circular, I happened to notice a young couple kissing with

a degree of passion, but not what you'd call X-rated by any means, when a guy cycles past with a friendly,

'Get your f**king tongue out of her mouth!'

And they say romance is dead?

Overheard by Deebs, South Circular Road
Posted on Sunday, 30 April 2006

Gender bending in Inchicore

I used to get my hair cut in this very old-fashioned barber shop in Inchicore. I'm in there one afternoon — there's only me, the barber, a couple of auld fellas and a young mother with two sons. The black and white movie that was on telly finishes up, and Shirley Temple Bar comes on screen with the bingo numbers.

This causes a certain amount of discomfort with the auld fellas. They mutter a bit but the TV stays on. Then one of the young kids asks his Mammy, 'Mammy, is that a man or a woman on TV?'

His mother replies, 'It's a f**kin' eejit is what it is.'

Overheard by Baz, Inchicore
Posted on Saturday, 29 April 2006

Dancing sparks?

Seen this written in a toilet on a building site. Being a sparky myself, found it funny:

'Here come all the sparkys, dressed as ballroom dancers,

One in ten is qualified, the rest are f**in'
chancers!'

Overheard by Ric, building site, Dublin
Posted on Tuesday, 25 April 2006

More than he bargained for!

In Busaras the other day, in one of the shops. A
young guy queuing in front of me had ordered a
cup of tea with milk and no sugar. The foreign
girl behind the counter asked him,

'Would you like your bag squeezed?'

The guy replies,

'No, I'll just have the tea.'

He managed to keep a straight face — unlike
myself who had to leave the shop!

Overheard by Stephen, shop in Busaras
Posted on Monday, 24 April 2006

Oh, suits you!

I overheard two gay guys on Georges Street
(where else?). One was admiring the other's
jacket.

Gay guy #1: 'I love your jacket, what make is it?'

Gay guy #2: 'Gucci.'

Gay guy #1: 'Oh! Gucci, Gucci, Goo!'

Overheard by Anonymous, Georges Street
Posted on Monday, 24 April 2006

Health health health!

In a Spar in the Liberties, mum with screaming brat:

Child: 'Ma, Ma, I want crisps … crisps, Ma … I want some crisps … crisps … crisps, Ma!'

Mother: 'No! You're not getting crisps, they're bad for you.'

Shopkeeper: 'Can I help you?'

Mother: 'Ten Marlboro Lights, please.'

Overheard by Paul, Spar
Posted on Friday, 21 April 2006

Leinster fans …

I was queuing last Friday at Donnybrook for tickets for the Leinster versus Munster match. My friend came over to keep me company, and the guy behind me asked my friend if he was going to the match.

He said no, he wasn't all that interested in rugby, and if he went he'd probably spend the time reading the newspaper, listening to his i-Pod and texting his mates. The guy behind said,

'Ah, you'd fit right in, so.'

Overheard by Anonymous, Donnybrook
Posted on Thursday, 20 April 2006

Inappropriate!

At a 5-a-side soccer tournament in UCD a few weeks ago, great craic. Afterwards, the referee declares, 'That was great, lads, I haven't had as much fun since I buried the mother-in-law …'

Overheard by Louise, UCD
Posted on Thursday, 20 April 2006

Senior Cup

I was on the no. 46A bus on the way out of town. A bunch of lads from Blackrock get on at RTÉ. They started talking about their school rugby team and how they were playing in the middle of the mocks.

Jock #1: 'It's so unfair that they're expected to play in the middle of their mocks.'

Jock #2: 'I know, you'd think they'd move the mocks. You can always repeat the Leaving — you only get one shot at the Senior Cup.'

Overheard by Mick, on the no. 46A bus
Posted on Thursday, 20 April 2006

Interracial bonding

About 2 a.m. at the late-night window of a Texaco garage in Blackrock. Scumbag gets out of a van and waddles up to the window. There is an Asian man working there. The scumbag then roars aggressively at him in his best Asian accent,

'CHING BA PHAN DOO WAH' … followed by … 'DOES DAT MEAN ANYTIN' TO YOU, DUZ IH?'

Overheard by Rob, Texaco garage, Blackrock
Posted on Thursday, 20 April 2006

In the chipper

Standing in a chipper waiting for my order and a bloke walks in and orders the following:

'Will ye give us a bag of chips and two sausages and will you batter the f**k out of them for me, cheers?'

Overheard by Rob, chipper in Palmerstown
Posted on Thursday, 20 April 2006

All tracksuits are the same

Woman holds up two Reebok tracksuit tops and goes to her husband, 'Which one do you prefer?'

He says back to her, 'Don't take offence, love, but they all look the f**king same when they're on ya.'

So true. So true.

Overheard by Alan, Lifestyle Sports, Ilac Centre
Posted on Thursday, 20 April 2006

Brave eejit

Sitting on the no. 13A bus to Ballymun on Thursday surrounded by snivelling junkies and wreathed in clouds of hash smoke. Well-dressed gent beside me answers mobile phone and wife asks where he is:

'I'm on the skanger ride from hell,' he says, without batting an eyelid.

Overheard by a 13A victim, on the no. 13A bus
Posted on Wednesday, 19 April 2006

Confused?!

I was working at the information desk when a little boy about age three came up to my work colleague, looking lost, and asked her,

'Have you seen a woman going around without a boy that looks like me?'

Overheard by Beth, Shankill Shopping Centre
Posted on Wednesday, 19 April 2006

Music to watch the girls go by

Picture this. It's Tallaght, da boyz are in their car, blaring the tunes, rippin' around the estate like a dog on fire, shades on (even though it's nearing dark), equipped with those reflective blue light thingys that racer boys have under their set of wheels, beeping at anything in a skirt, about six fellas roaring, 'Wahey, luv, show us yer tits,' to every passing girl under the age of 30.

But there's something not right. Whilst I was waiting for my bus, they circled the estate several times, blaring one tune on repeat. It's not Scooter, it's not DJ Quicksilver … it's …

Shania Twain, 'Man, I feel like a woman' …

Overheard by M, Tallaght
Posted on Tuesday, 18 April 2006

You'd either love it or hate it

Was at the UCI Cinema in Coolock with a few mates last weekend and we asked the cashier guy about the films that had just started. We asked about one film in particular, to see if it was worth watching, and his reply was …

'I actually just saw it last night, it's a film you either love or hate. I thought it was alright.'

Overheard by ILLB, UCI Cinema Coolock
Posted on Tuesday, 18 April 2006

Hot stuff

Was in the Northside Shopping Centre looking for a present for my brother when I heard two oul' ones talking about a lava lamp:

Lady #1: 'Look at da, wharisit?'

Lady #2: 'It's a lava lamp.'

Lady #1 (touching it): 'It's very warm!'

Lady #2: 'Course it is, there's lava in it!'

Overheard by Kevin K, Northside Shopping Centre
Posted on Tuesday, 18 April 2006

Like mother, like son

My friend accompanies his father on a shopping trip for his Mum's birthday. While in a lingerie shop, the assistant asks the father if she can help. After some general questions, the assistant asks the father what size he is buying for. The father turns to his son (my pal) and loudly asks,

'Colin, what size are you?'

Overheard by Pocket Rocket, from my friend
Posted on Monday, 17 April 2006

Yes, no, Coke ...

Standing behind a woman in line for KFC. She orders (along with other stuff) a 'Coke'. The young Asian clerk behind the counter replies, 'I am sorry, we have no Coke.'

Woman: 'You have no Coke?'

Asian clerk: 'Yes.'

Woman: 'So you've got Coke?'

Asian clerk: 'No, we have no Coke.'

Woman: 'You have no Coke?'

Asian clerk: 'Yes.'

Woman: 'So you've got Coke?'

Overheard by Lamont, KFC at Clare Hall
Posted on Monday, 17 April 2006

The beautiful accent

Behind a group of French kids in McDonald's on Grafton Street. They pool their money together, and the best English-speaker is chosen to go to the counter and put the order in.

'Three Big Mac meals and two McChicken sandwiches, please,' says the chosen kid.

'Is dah ih?' replies the girl on the counter.

The French kid looks confused.

'Three Big Mac meals and two Mc ...'

'Yeah, I've got dat. Is dah it? Anyting else?'

After some chattering amongst themselves, they

just hand her a bunch of money and stare at her, bemused.

Overheard by Rory, McDonald's, Grafton Street
Posted on Monday, 17 April 2006

Colours, sizes, locations ... all too much!

Staff guy at Tan.ie serving some girl.

Guy: 'OK, nine minutes. You're in room no. 2, just press the blue button on the wall when you're ready to start the sunbed.'

Gal: 'Wha?'

Guy: 'When you're ready to start the sunbed, just press the blue button on the wall.'

Gal: 'Awwwwwww, right.'

Few minutes later she emerges from the tanning rooms:

Gal (shouting): 'It didn't come on!'

Guy goes in and checks while Gal stands in shop, bitching about why it's all a scam.

Guy emerges from rooms:

'It didn't start 'cos instead of pressing the Small Blue Button on the wall labelled "Start", you pressed the Large Red Button on the inside of the bed labelled "Emergency Stop".'

Overheard by Justin, Tan.ie (Chartbusters) in Clare Hall
Posted on Sunday, 16 April 2006

Rear 'em right

An auld granny pushing the young wan's baby in the pram. Granny leans over and goo-es at the baby and says, 'Giv us a luv!'

Baby gurgles. Encouraged, Granny leans in again and with a little more enthusiasm says, 'Ah gwan, giv us a luv!'

Baby beams responsively, Granny gets into the moment, leans over again, tickles baby and says, 'Ah, gwan, giv' us a f**kin' luv!'

Overheard by Wu, Irish Life Mall off Talbot Street
Posted on Sunday, 16 April 2006

Politically incorrect

Late 1990s and a few mates of mine were working as security guards on the door of shops on Grafton Street, watching out for shop-lifters. As you know, security guards have their own lingo for most things.

My mate on radio: 'Jim, there's a few knackers gone into Monsoon.'

Controller to all units: 'For the last time, lads, don't be calling them knackers, we could get into trouble for that.'

My mate: 'Right, Bud. Jim, there's a few cream crackers gone into Monsoon.'

Overheard by John, Grafton Street
Posted on Sunday, 16 April 2006

Has it all except Irish Times

A guy goes up to the newsagent counter and the girl behind it asks, 'What do you want?'

He replies, 'Thanks to a good education and wealthy parents, I want for nothing, however I do require a copy of the *Irish Times*.'

Overheard by Derrick, at a shop beside the Four Courts
Posted on Saturday, 15 April 2006

The auld ones

Old Lady #1: 'Did you hear what happened to Bernie yesterday morning after mass?'

Old Lady #2: 'Someone told me she took sick …'

Old Lady #1: 'Mmmm. Got up and ran straight to the vestry after the communion.'

Old Lady #2: 'My God, what was wrong with her?'

Old Lady #1: 'Coleslaw!' (followed by a knowing sniff)

301

Old Lady #2: 'Oh no! That happened to me before.'

Old Lady #1: 'Mmmm, yes.'

Old Lady# 2: 'Mmmm, coleslaw, yes. It's lethal.'

Overheard by Liz, on the DART passing through Killester
Posted on Saturday, 15 April 2006

If ignorance is bliss, then meet the happiest girl in the world

In school, one of my nearest and dearest friends was telling us about the Ireland match she and her boyfriend had been to see the night before. We all asked her how it was and did she have a good time, to which she replied,

'I enjoyed it an' all but I was lost in the second half.'

I asked her why? Her answer was,

'Well, the gobshites changed sides.'

Overheard by Toni, Dublin school
Posted on Friday, 14 April 2006

Paying for a good education

While observing a case in the Four Courts last year. The girl in question was a past pupil of a well-known large south-Dublin fee-paying school.

Defence barrister: 'Is this where you were residing at the time?'

Girl: 'Sorry, what do you mean by residing?'

Her parents must be so proud — that was money well spent!

Overheard by observer, Court 24, the Four Courts
Posted on Friday, 14 April 2006

Buttered up by an Asian girl

I asked the Asian-looking girl behind the deli counter for a roll with sausages, rashers and tomato ketchup. As the girl replied too quickly and loudly for my ears to discern what she was saying, I asked her to repeat herself again and again and again.

Still unable to make out what she was asking me after her third attempt to communicate with me, I thought she was going to flip when she took a few deep breaths, composed herself and said:

'BUH ER? D'ya want Buh er on yar roll?' in the thickest Dublin accent imaginable. I said yes and thanked her very much. I left smiling to myself — completely forgetting to pay for the roll!

Overheard by Aidan, Spar
Posted on Thursday, 13 April 2006

Maxin' relaxin'

I was in a hospital the other day when I heard this guy from the next room shouting for ages. He then screamed, 'Oh God, somebody help me!'

I told a nurse that was walking by and she just said, 'He's crazy.'

Two minutes later a doctor went in to calm the man down.

Doctor: 'Would you relax?'

Patient: 'I'm gonna f**king relax your head against the wall in a minute.'

Overheard by Sean, St James's Hospital
Posted on Wednesday, 12 April 2006

Multi-talented George Foreman

I was watching the film *Ali* with my girlfriend and it came to the 'Rumble in the Jungle' between Muhammad Ali and George Foreman. Bear in mind this was a documentary of Ali's life.

Ring announcer: 'In the left corner we have George Foreman!'

Girlfriend: 'Oh my God, I can't believe he is an actor *and* a chef!'

Overheard by Niall, Star Century
Posted on Wednesday, 12 April 2006

Kids in the pub

We were just after leaving a pub on Paddy's Day that was full of kids watching their parents getting rubbered. So we got talking about how much of a waste of a day it was to have the kids locked up in a pub.

Heading home we jumped in a taxi. The taxi driver was full of chat and was asking about what we'd done for the day.

One of the lads — for the craic — says, 'Ah, nothing better then bringing the kids to the pub and having a few pints on Paddy's Day,' and the taxi driver goes,

'Ah God yeah, you're right, sure I was there this morning with them.'

Overheard by Deco, in a Dublin taxi
Posted on Tuesday, 11 April 2006

Half price!

Walking down the road, man on push bike with Tesco bags. The man just cycling, minding his own business, when a car slows down by him, window rolls down, and girl with a doll in her hands holds the doll out, screams out, 'HALF PRICE AT TESCO ...'

Only in Dublin!

Overheard by Anonymous, city centre
Posted on Tuesday, 11 April 2006

Wear them and die?

Old dear (dealer) on Henry Street: 'Get the last of the Terminal underwear!'

Overheard by Wally, Henry Street
Posted on Tuesday, 11 April 2006

Not the sharpest tool in the box

In Superquinn in Walkinstown last night. I was at the checkout and the checkout girl says, 'If any of you have less than five items you can go to the checkout at the off-licence.'

A woman behind me with one item in her hand (big piece of meat) says to me,

'I have less than five items, don't I?'

Overheard by Mossy, Superquinn, Walkinstown
Posted on Monday, 10 April 2006

Politically unaware

On the no. 42 bus to Malahide, couple of young ones. Passing by a house:

Young one #1: 'That's Charlie Haughey's house.'

Young one #2: 'Who's he?'

Young one #1: 'You're a bleedin' thick, sure wasn't he the President of Ireland.'

Overheard by Barry, on the no. 42 bus
Posted on Monday, 10 April 2006

Skangers versus D4s

Was coming out of Dundrum Shopping Centre on Saturday, three D4 head girls walking towards me (with the quiffed hairs and the UGG boots).

There was a gang of skangers sitting on the wall at the fountain, and one of them wolf-whistled over at the girls. They giggled and turned around to soak up the praise, but to their obvious dismay, the whistling skanger shouted,

'Wasn't wistlin' at yous, yiz uglee bitches!'

All the skangers fell about the place laughing … class.

Overheard by David, Dundrum Shopping Centre
Posted on Monday, 10 April 2006

Coming off bread

Two sales assistants discussing what to get for their lunch. The first girl says to her mate, 'I'm trying to give up bread, it's bad for me.'

The second girl replies, 'Yer dead right, I was reading the ingredients on a packet of bread the other day, it's full of bleeding addictives!'

Overheard by Sinéad, clothes shop
Posted on Sunday, 9 April 2006

I had to ask!

I was waiting for the bus from Busáras to go to the airport, but the CityLink bus which is supposed to be very regular hadn't appeared in over 30 minutes. When I eventually got on the bus I raised my voice over the traffic to ask the bus driver,

'How regular are you?' — no sooner had I said it I knew it came out wrong — to which he replied,

'At least once a day!'

Overheard by KL, Busáras
Posted on Sunday, 9 April 2006

Hail to the bus driver

Getting on the no. 46A bus heading towards town. Pulling change out of my pocket for fare. I had €1.10 and a €2 coin. The fare was €1.05. I popped the €2 coin into the machine. The driver looks at me and says,

'This isn't a savin' scheme I'm running here!'

Overheard by Stebag, on the no. 46A bus
Posted on Sunday, 9 April 2006

Begging techniques

Was walking towards Grafton Street when this old homeless lad shouts out, 'Here! Give us some money or I'll give ya a box!'

I turned round to see him standing there with a cardboard box in his hand — and a big smile on his face. Had to give him some cash after that …

Overheard by Kev, St Stephen's Green
Posted on Saturday, 8 April 2006

Classy

Couple in their 40s get on the bus and she goes upstairs. He asks the driver for change of €20, and then holds up the whole bus, arguing with the driver that he hasn't any more money.

From upstairs you hear her shouting, 'Darren, will ye hurry up!'

Next she shouts, 'If I hafta come downstayers there is gonna be some amount of trouble.'

Then you hear her stomping downstairs, screaming at the bus driver, 'I'm f**kin' disabled. I'm f**kin' disabled. What's your problem, it's not coming out of your bleedin' pockeh!'

She then grabs the man and storms back upstairs, still shouting at the driver.

At Cork Street she screams again, 'Get your bleedin' hands off me,' stomps downstairs again,

smoking a smoke, gets off — and lies down by
the railings!

Overheard by Sarah, on the no. 77A bus
Posted on Saturday, 8 April 2006

Erectile dysfunction

A good-looking girl was walking ahead of me
through town. We were passing a building
covered with scaffolding. One of the workers
was leaning against the scaffold near the path.
He winks at the girl as she passes, sweeps out a
dramatic hand gesture towards the scaffold and
says,

'Wha de ye tink o' me massive erection, love?'

Nice!

Overheard by Anonymous, Mercer Street
Posted on Saturday, 8 April 2006

Spare change

I was queuing for the ATM on Grafton Street one
night, and as per usual there was a beggar,
sitting in between both machines, sure to get
some attention.

Beggar: 'Hey mista, any spare change,
pleeaaasss?'

Me: 'Sorry man, all I have is a fifty.'

Beggar: 'No worries, I'll give ya change!'

Overheard by Peter, Grafton Street
Posted on Friday, 7 April 2006

Prazky: crazy-old-drunk-approved

At Ranelagh Luas stop there was this old drunk sort of talking to himself. I was carrying a six-pack of Prazky. Suddenly the old drunk shouts at me, with much enthusiasm,

'Prazky! By God, that's the way to do it, boy!'

Overheard by Dan, Ranelagh Luas stop
Posted on Friday, 7 April 2006

ALLIGATOR

Walking through Temple Bar last Saturday, I noticed a bit of a commotion and headed towards it. Two lads appeared to be in a bit of a scrap and the Garda asks one of the lads, 'What are the allegations you are making?'

To which the man replies, 'No, he's the alligator (pointing toward other lad) …'

FACT!

Overheard by Andy, Temple Bar
Posted on Friday, 7 April 2006

Telling it as it is

On the Luas last night just before the stop for Heuston Station, all of a sudden the driver slams the brakes and we screech to a halt, cue shrieks and general confusion as everyone thought we had crashed. The driver then switches on the intercom and announces ever so politely,

'Sorry about that, ladies and gents, some GOBSHITE just ran a red light right in front of us!'

Overheard by Ciara, Luas Red Line
Posted on Friday, 7 April 2006

Who's driving who?

On the no. 4 bus to Ballymun.

Bus stops at the top of Parnell Square, driver sticks his head out and shouts down the bus at the passengers,

'Any a youz use dis route regular? How do I get to Phibsboro from here?'

Everyone just laughs and wonders if they'll make it home at all!

Overheard by Anonymous, no. 4 bus to Ballymun
Posted on Friday, 7 April 2006

Discourage them while they're young

I was in the Ilac Centre Library and there was a mother in there with her young child. The child picks up a book and starts looking at it. The mum yells,

'PUT THAT BOOK DOWN, YOU KNOW YOU CAN'T READ!

What encouragement …

Overheard by Anna, Ilac Centre Central Library
Posted on Thursday, 6 April 2006

Blondie & Blondie

Two quite pretty blonde girls (around 19) sitting in the ground floor café in the Jervis Centre, talking (I thought) about the Iraq war. One (the one wearing a pink hoody amazingly) says, 'It's so terrible about Iraq,' to which the other replies,

'Oh my God, I know, the dust storms are awful there, women have to cover their heads so their hair doesn't get ruined …'

Overheard by Rick, in the ground floor café of the Jervis Centre
Posted on Thursday, 6 April 2006

Disgusting!

I was in Barcode on Paddy's Night and my friend and I went to use the ladies. As we made our way to the toilets we passed a group of lads playing pool. On our way back from the ladies one of the lads yells,

'I would have loved to be the toilet seat you two sat on!'

Overheard by K, Barcode
Posted on Thursday, 6 April 2006

Sound advice

While standing in a queue in a shop on South Circular Road I overheard a D4 girl ask for a cylinder of gas. She then asked,

'Like, how long will this bottle of gas last?' to which the shopkeeper quickly answered,

'Well, darling, if you never turn the cooker on it will last forever!'

Overheard by Gerry, shop, South Circular Road
Posted on Thursday, 6 April 2006

Shamrock shake

I was near Christ Church with my friends from America who were sampling a Shamrock Shake, which of course comes out around Paddy's Day every year.

A courier is cycling by quite fast and somehow spots the milkshake in my hand. As he cycles off into the distance he shouts back in a thick Dublin accent,

'Here, Bud, is that a Shamrock Shake?', to which I shout back, 'Yeah.' Courier shouts back enthusiastically from the distance, 'NICE ONE!'

Overheard by Dara, Christ Church
Posted on Wednesday, 5 April 2006

Paddy's Night mayhem

'I've lost the will to live.'

A clearly fed-up Garda expressing his feelings to another Garda.

Overheard by Fiona, in Temple Bar on Paddy's Night
Posted on Wednesday, 5 April 2006

Thick as thieves

Two blokes outside Paddy Powers having a smoke; one was asking the other if he knew 'John', to which the other replied,

'Of course I do, I've done loads of robberies with him.'

Overheard by Anonymous, outside Paddy Powers in Rathmines
Posted on Wednesday, 5 April 2006

Zero tolerance

Stressed out Posh Mother to misbehaving child (about five years old): 'Right, okay, right, that's it, that's final, that's absolutely final. You're getting no new toys and no McDonald's for a WHOLE WEEK.'

Overheard by DB, Tesco, Nutgrove Shopping Centre
Posted on Wednesday, 5 April 2006

Taxi humour

In a taxi with my boyfriend going out to DCU. We're chatting away to the taxi driver and he asks me what I'm studying. So I tell him about my course and he says, 'Ah, dat's great.'

Next thing he turns around, looks at my boyfriend and says, 'Jaysus, what are you studying to be — a heart-throb?'

We were both in hysterics. Yet another example of razor-sharp Dublin taxi driver wit!

Overheard by Dom, taxi
Posted on Wednesday, 5 April 2006

English lessons needed

Walking down Camden Street past two vegetable stalls. At the same time a man in his 20s was walking a bike with a flat tyre past the stalls.

Woman behind stall shouts out: 'Mister, yur chain is flaa!'

Man replies in French accent: 'Excuse me?'

Woman replies: 'I said, yur chain is flaa!'

French man replies: 'I do not understand.'

Woman behind stall replies: 'Ahh, come back to me when you learn English.'

Overheard by Anonymous, Camden Street
Posted on Tuesday, 4 April 2006

Banguard

I was out for lunch with a girl from work. She is not the brightest spark. She was telling me about a mutual friend who had gotten engaged.

I said, 'Oh yeah, she's marrying a guard, isn't she?'

The dope said, 'No, she's actually marrying a *banguard*.'

Confused, I said, 'Sorry?'

She replied, 'Yeah, he is in the Garda Band —
banguard, see …?'

Overheard by Nicola, Blanchardstown
Posted on Tuesday, 4 April 2006

A culchie thing to do

I was on the Luas Green Line going from St
Stephen's Green, and suddenly this old man
reeking of gin pushes in beside me on the seat.
As soon as he did this, he turned to me, scanned
me with his eyes and goes, 'You a culchie?'

I just said no, and started listening to some
music.

When the Luas stopped in Beechwood, a black
man tried to bring a bicycle onto the Luas, and
immediately the driver announces that he wasn't
allowed to bring a bike on the Luas. The old
man looks back, tuts at the black man, then
turns to me and goes,

'A bike on the Luas … that's a real culchie thing
to do.'

Overheard by Cian, on the Luas, Beechwood Station.
Posted on Tuesday, 4 April 2006

Fashion statement

Nice-looking girl wearing a t-shirt with a pair of
eyes printed across the chest, walks by a group
of road workers in yellow jackets.

On cue, one of them says, 'Nice eyes!'

Overheard by Robbo, Pearse Street
Posted on Monday, 3 April 2006

Dangerous woman

My brother had a bit of heartburn and was asking some people at work if they had anything for it. A nice older woman kindly assists, looking through her handbag of drugs saying, 'I have some of that semtex in here.'

Think she meant Zantac …

Overheard by Anonymous, workplace
Posted on Monday, 3 April 2006

In touch with his inner self

Some years ago, I was walking along near Stephen's Green on a gorgeous, sunny summer morning. It seemed that everyone was out enjoying the day. The street was fairly crowded with women pushing prams, school-kids, a bit of everything.

To one side of the path, there was a huge pile of Bord Gáis, bright, canary-yellow PVC pipes, piled in a pyramid about 6 foot high, about to be installed somewhere nearby. There must have been over a hundred of them, and they really were striking in their 'yellowness'.

Of course, a crowded Dublin street would not be complete without the friendly neighbourhood nutter, and sure enough, one came bouncing along, talking to himself.

When he came within view of the pipes, he froze and suddenly started shouting at the top of his lungs,

'YELLOW! YELLOW! YELLOW!'

Overheard by Heather, near St Stephen's Green
Posted on Sunday, 2 April 2006

He's right!

An old drunk, sitting singing on the bus, glared out at a billboard for 7 Up Free and shouted, 'F**king sham — 7 Up's not free!'

We were all in stitches ...

Overheard by Paul, the no. 130 bus coming home from town
Posted on Sunday, 2 April 2006

Getting out

Was out in the Red Cow Hotel playing a poker tournament recently, and during a break I had the following conversation with a true Dub:

Me: 'I've seen you at every poker tournament I've been at lately, do you ever not play, you know take a break?'

Guy: 'Do you ever wonder why I play so much?'

Me: 'You're making money!?'

Guy: 'No it's not that, but if you saw the mutt I had waiting for me at home you'd get out of the house as often as you could too.'

Overheard by Patrick, Red Cow Hotel
Posted on Saturday, 1 April 2006

Immaculate contraception

At the no. 77 bus stop, two youngish girls, maybe sixteen years old, discussing the contraceptive implant:

'It's like a match stick, goes under your skin, don't protect you from dem STDs though.'

'Wha abou' STIs?'

'What's dem then?'

'You know, a sexually transmitted injury?'

Overheard by Anonymous, at the no. 77 bus stop
Posted on Saturday, 1 April 2006

Where'll I meet ya so?

Walking out from Irish Life on Abbey Street for my lunch break and pass by a young yobbo with a phone glued to his ear, yammering away, trying to meet up with his friend. It went something like this:

Yob: 'Yeah, I'm outside Irish … eh? … Roight I'm on Abbey … F**k! Roight! You know the Spire? Grand, cause I'm nowhere near tha!'

Overheard by John, Abbey Street
Posted on Saturday, 1 April 2006

The invisible car

After leaving the Dew Drop in Kill slightly worse for wear, we walked down the road towards my sister's boyfriend's house. After a few minutes a Garda car pulls up beside them. The window rolls down.

Garda: 'Are you driving?'

Well …

Overheard by Ian, Kill (near Dublin)
Posted on Saturday, 1 April 2006

Good observation

While walking through the Square in Tallaght, I noticed two Tallaghites standing at the top of an escalator which wasn't moving. They were staring in bemusement at the motionless stairway, when after a good few minutes one looked up and said,

'I think we're going to have to walk.'

Overheard by Pete, Tallaght Square
Posted on Wednesday, 29 March 2006

From the mouths of babes …

We all know how small children can REALLY embarrass adults, but this to me took the biscuit.

Little girl in the checkout queue was throwing a mega tantrum because Mammy wouldn't buy her sweets. When screaming, shouting, crying, lying on the floor and kicking didn't achieve the desired result, she stood, drew herself up to her full height, and yelled at the top of her voice,

'I saw you kissing Daddy's willie!'

I needn't tell you that one VERY embarrassed mother dropped her shopping and fled! I'm still laughing about it a year later!

Overheard by Anonymous, Tesco, The Square, Tallaght
Posted on Wednesday, 29 March 2006

Hmmm bop! or bus?!?

On the no. 16 to Rathfarnham when the bus pulls up at a stop. Three D4 young rugger heads that look like Hanson (remember them?) wannabes are standing half on/half off the bus debating something, when the bus driver vents his rage at them:

'Come on, girls, will ye?!'

The Hanson boys started blushing and the bus started laughing …

Overheard by Chops, on the no. 16 bus
Posted on Wednesday, 29 March 2006

Fag area?

Was at a gay night out a few years ago with a male friend. We decided to go out for a smoke, and my friend (who is wearing a dress, stilettos, wig and makeup) asks the bouncer,

'D'ya know where the fag area is?'

Poor bouncer was still laughing when we passed him ten minutes later …

Overheard by Annette, the Ambassador
Posted on Wednesday, 29 March 2006

Canal rescue

Along the canal at Baggot Street, a guy running past had managed to fall in. A large crowd gathered to watch the rescue operation which involved about 30 policemen, an ambulance, a rescue unit and two fire brigades.

The attempt to get him out using a rope had failed because he had pulled it in on top of himself, so they lowered a ladder. For some reason the (stoned or drunk) guy in the water swam around the back of the ladder and was screaming, 'Ouch me legs, me legs are freezing!'

At this stage the fireman lost his temper and shouted down, 'Shut up moanin' and climb up the ladder, ya f**kin' eejit!'

We were all thinking it!

Overheard by Stacy, Grand Canal at Baggot Street
Posted on Tuesday, 28 March 2006

A1 maths student?

On the bus home from work and a trio of secondary students pile on to an already packed bus. Their conversation is about their impending Leaving Cert exams this summer and one of the girls exclaims, 'I sooo need to get an A1 in maths to get my course.'

The conversation continues and then leads to talk of their mocks in April which prompts one of the girls to wonder how long they had 'til then. The A1 student pipes up,

'Don't worry that's, like, 20 weeks away.'

Overheard by AMB, on the no. 41 bus
Posted on Tuesday, 28 March 2006

Jim Apple

In Dubray Books in Dun Laoghaire I overheard a secondary school student enquiring about a school book at the desk. 'Do you have Jim Apple?'

'Jim Apple?' the confused clerk replied.

'Yeah, Jim Apple, it's a French book,' answered the teen.

'Oh, *Je m'appelle*,' the clerk replied, holding back a smirk. 'I'll just get it for you now.'

Let's hope there's a chapter in that book on pronunciation.

Overheard by Jack, Dubray Bookshop, Dun Laoghaire
Posted on Tuesday, 28 March 2006

Who needs the FBI

A while ago I was watching *Crimeline* on RTÉ and one of our finest was going through the details of a robbery that took place. He picks up a small green petrol tank and the rest goes like this.

Presenter: 'What's that you've got there?'

Garda: 'It's a green petrol container found at the crime scene and we believe it was used to carry petrol.'

I know you're thinking: 'Made up.'

I wish it was …

Overheard by Jimmy, *Crimeline*, RTÉ TV (Donnybrook)
Posted on Monday, 27 March 2006

Bulimic ... classic Dublin!

While out walking my dog a couple of months ago I passed a group of early teens talking about and getting ready for the upcoming night's merriments. One lad in particular was at one of the girls to come out and get trolleyed with them.

He pestered her until she got annoyed and gave the definitive answer:

'I told ye no! If me Ma catches me drinking again she'll go bulimic!'

Overheard by Will, Dundrum
Posted on Monday, 27 March 2006

Fashion police

I was in a sports shop last week in my civies when some aul' one taps me on the shoulder. As I turn around she barks, 'Size five, love, I'm in a rush,' to which I reply, 'Sorry I don't work here.'

Instead of her walking away rather sheepishly, she shouts, 'What, you mean they're your normal clothes? You're mad!'

Overheard by Roger Le Mont, The Square
Posted on Monday, 27 March 2006

Irish v. Germans

Guy on the bus asks for the fare *as Gaeilge*.

Bus driver (in a thick Dub accent): 'Nie sprecken de Irish.'

Overheard by Tom, on the no. 46A bus
Posted on Monday, 27 March 2006

Urinal traffic management

In the cinema a few months back. Movie ended and the scramble to the gents began. The toilets were crowded, as a number of films ended together, and there was a queue of two or three lads behind each urinal.

Then from the back of the queue, a random man in his best Dublin authoritarian voice shouts:

'Right, lads, have 'em out and ready when approaching the urinal!'

The guys didn't know whether to laugh, or pretend they couldn't hear!

Overheard by P, Savoy Cinema
Posted on Sunday, 26 March 2006

When the customer is a 13-year-old boy

I was at the local Spar, and this 13-year-old was at the counter buying a bottle of Pepsi.

He was counting one, two and five cents out, really slowly, just to annoy the girl behind the counter. When he finally got to the right amount, he threw the rest of the change down, grabbed his bottle and said,

'Keep the change, get yourself a decent haircut.'

He walked out — leaving me and the poor girl speechless!

Overheard by Katelynn, local Spar
Posted on Sunday, 26 March 2006

Good enough excuse as any

Walking along the street I noticed a young man being searched by a guard. Garda said to him,

'I'm arresting you for being a dickhead!'

Only in Ireland …

Overheard by Shauna, beside St Stephen's Green Shopping Centre
Posted on Sunday, 26 March 2006

Beer goggles

My brother and his mate sitting at the bar in their local, where the people within earshot heard the following conversation.

Brother: 'Mick, you're drunk.'

Mick: 'Feck off. What do you mean?'

Brother: 'You're pissed, I can tell when you've had too much.'

Mick: 'Ah stop messing and keep your voice down, you're very loud.'

Brother: 'I'm just telling you the facts, just ask anyone.'

Mick: 'How are you so sure that I'm drunk?'

Brother: 'You're gone all blurred …'

Overheard by Higgs, The Royal Oak
Posted on Saturday, 25 March 2006

Tasty

I was in the queue for breakfast in Jurys Ballsbridge last summer, when these two Yanks came back up for seconds.

'Scuse me, waiter,' she says, 'What are those black things? They were really delicious. We got nothing like that back home. What is it?'

Waiter: 'It's black pudding, very nice.'

'What's it made from?' she asks.

'Pig's blood,' comes the forthright reply.

American gent: 'I think we'll just have the eggs ...'

Overheard by Shamo, Jurys Ballsbridge
Posted on Saturday, 25 March 2006

Patriotic pub customer

Elderly patriotic gentleman goes into his local pub much later than usual on a Sunday night about four years ago. He has obviously been drinking.

The barman says, 'Well, Johnny, we've been missing you. Where were you at all?'

'I was at a funeral,' declares Johnny.

'Who's funeral?' asks the barman.

'Kevin Barry's!' shouts Johnny.

'Jaze, I didn't even know he was sick,' replies the barman.

Overheard by Anonymous, Leeson Lounge
Posted on Saturday, 25 March 2006

Medical help

Young girl at bus stop on mobile phone:

Girl: 'I'm in town. Will you meet me?'

'Where are you?'

Girl: 'I'm opposite a shop. It's "The V ..., V ..." '

(Interrupted by man next to her) Man: 'It's the "VHI", love!'

Overheard by Anonymous, it happened to a friend of my daughter
Posted on Friday, 24 March 2006

Blondes

Two young wans sitting behind me on the no. 43 bus, discussing the merits of dyed hair, when one says to the other,

'If I had me hair dyed blonde and I was pregnant, would the baby be blonde too?'

Overheard by Anonymous, on the no. 43 bus
Posted on Friday, 24 March 2006

Surely there was a better place to make this call ...

Picture it: no. 10 bus going home from work the other evening. Young Dublin boy in front of me decides to call some girl that he had obviously only met the previous weekend. Conversation goes something like this:

Dublin Boy: 'Hi, Joanne, it's Danny!'

Girl: 'Danny who?'

Dublin Boy: 'Danny ... remember? The guy from last weekend?'

There's a couple of seconds of a pause:

Dublin Boy: 'Hello? Hello ...?'

She had hung up on him.

Everyone on the bus was in fits of laughter and the red-faced young fella got off at the next stop.

Overheard by Jonathan, on the no. 10 bus

Posted on Friday, 24 March 2006

Your tube

I was standing at the bus stop this morning, and two elderly men were having a chat. I overheard one say to the other, 'I had the tube down my throat — hope it wasn't the same tube you had up your arse!'

I had to turn away so they wouldn't see me laughing ...

Overheard by Darren, Inchicore
Posted on Friday, 14 March 2008

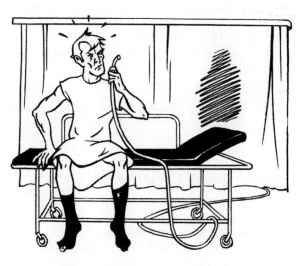

I love Parmesan cheese

Enjoying a meal in Flanagan's restaurant on O'Connell Street. At the table beside me were a young Dublin 'howya' couple out for a special night. The girl had ordered a bowl of spaghetti.

As the waiter was passing by, the young Dub girl pipes up, 'Hey, Mister, ya don't have any of dat Palmerstown cheese for me pasta, d'ya, love?'

Overheard by SJ, Flanagan's restaurant, O'Connell Street
Posted on Friday, 14 March 2008

Cluedo on the Nitelink

I was on the Nitelink coming home from town when two lads in their thirties stood up to get off at Dundrum. One of them was wearing a pair of yellow trousers. Some Head-the-Ball down the back of the bus shouts out,

'Colonel Mustard, in the billiard room, with the trousers!'

Yer man wasn't impressed!

Overheard by locko, Nitelink, Dundrum
Posted on Thursday, 13 March 2008

Caught doing a 'Martin Cahill'

On the Luas last week, three skangers bunk on at Inchicore bridge and only travel two stops. They spotted two gardaí walking along the footpath across the road. One of the youths replicates the hand-over-the-face gesture that was made famous by the late Martin Cahill, aka The General.

One of the gardaí spotted this and returns the gesture back to the youth.

If this wasn't funny enough, the youth then says, 'I'm gonna text Johnor te tell him wah happened.'

Just as they were getting off, he turns and asks his mate, 'How de ye spell "caught"?'

His mate replied, 'C–O–T, ya f**ken doughnut!'

Overheard by Danny, Luas
Posted on Thursday, 13 March 2008

Mahon Tribunal issues statement

Seen rather than heard.

Written on a T-shirt in Temple Bar:

Been there

Done that

Bought the Taoiseach

Overheard by K, seen on a T-shirt in Temple Bar
Posted on Wednesday, 12 March 2008

Motion over the ocean

I was recently on a very turbulent flight from Tenerife to Dublin and was feeling out of control and nervous. Five or ten minutes into this turbulence, two lads in their forties, who looked like they liked their booze, began to sing:

'Oh, I'd like to know where you got the motion, rock the boat, don't rock the boat, baby!'

And of course the rest off the plane joined in, which then made me laugh and sweat like crazy and even more nervous.

Could only happen with a plane full of Dubliners on the way to Dublin!

Overheard by David, mid air over the Atlantic
Posted on Wednesday, 12 March 2008

Never been to Lesbinia!

On the no. 77 bus coming home from work during the summer, there was a large group of female Spanish students. As the bus travelled along the route, the group got smaller and smaller as each got off at their respective stops.

As one girl was saying goodbye to her friend, she turned and kissed her on the cheek. In front of me, a Cork culchie (obviously only in Dublin for the day!) turns to his mate and asks, 'Are they lesbians?'

Without even batting an eyelid, or turning his head, the other culchie replies, deadpan,

'No — they're Spanish!'

I nearly folded!

Overheard by Arty, on the mighty no. 77 bus!
Posted on Tuesday, 11 March 2008

Genital chips

Standing in the local chipper waiting for my food. Guy in front of me is waiting for his bag of chips.

Guy behind the counter gets his chips and asks him, 'Would you like salt and vinegar?'

Guy waiting on chips replies, 'Yeah, salt the bollix out of them.'

Overheard by Dubliner, local chipper
Posted on Monday, 10 March 2008

Work benefits

Overheard in Tesco, mother to young son:

'I am *not* payin' €4 for Sellotape when I have some in work!'

Overheard by Elaine, Tesco, Bray
Posted on Saturday, 8 March 2008

'Show me the money!' Gerry Maguire

Text to friend last week:

'Pint? I'm meeting some of the lads in Doyle's at nine. Hope you can make it.'

Instant reply from mate:

'You had me at "pint".'

Overheard by Paulo, by text
Posted on Sunday, 9 March 2008

Overheard incorrectly in Dublin

It was my first week working in a supermarket during the school holidays and I was busy packing shelves. An old lady asked me for the jacks, so I brought her to the ladies and said I'd wait outside. She looked puzzled and asked me why I brought her there. I said, 'It's because you asked for the bathroom ...'

She said, 'I'm looking for AJAX!'

I still cringe every time I think of it!

Overheard by Breda, SuperValu, Killester
Posted on Friday, 7 March 2008

Outta his head

I was out in town one night when three heads walk by, one of them far more drunk than his two mates who were propping him up in the middle.

Suddenly he pipes up loudly: 'Here, lads, come on and we'll go to the George for a dance, wha?'

His mates clearly embarrassed: 'No, Mick, we're heading home, come on.'

Two mates whisper over the top of his head to each other: 'F**k sake, if he could hear himself!'

Mick: 'F**k sake, man, what's the harm in havin' a dance to a bit of Kylie? Good music that is!'

Friend: 'Jaysus, his Ma was right — wine and beer do make him feel queer!'

Overheard by Niamh, Temple Bar
Posted on Tuesday, 4 March 2008

Androgynous rocker

While practising for a gig, the next band had a very feminine, long-haired rocker type waiting for his turn to play. One of the girls who was hanging around pipes up: 'Do you ever get mistaken for a girl?'

His quick-witted reply: 'No, do you?'

Overheard by yamadyoke, community centre
Posted on Tuesday, 4 March 2008

You're in Dublin now

Was over from England last weekend visiting family. We were sitting on the Airlink bus when a crowd of foreigners got on, dumped their luggage and stood next to the luggage racks. Inspector gets on and says, 'Youse lot go and sit upstairs, your bags are perfectly safe, you're in Dublin now!'

Overheard by Tommy, Dublin Airport
Posted on Monday, 3 March 2008

How to fail an eyesight exam in spectacular style

My sister recently had to go for a medical for work. During the eye test she was asked to look into this machine and call out the last line on the screen, so she started calling out, 'a ... g ... h ... pass ... pass ... r'.

Then the doctor asked her to call out the next line up from that one. She called out, 'd ... t ... e ... f ... n ...', slightly happier with herself for her ability to read this line.

She had struggled on one or two on the last line so she knew the doctor wouldn't exactly praise her sight, but nothing could have prepared her for the doctor's comments:

'Madam, I'm afraid we will have to investigate your eye sight in more detail — there were no letters on that screen — they were all numbers ...'

Overheard by Anonymous, from my sister
Posted on Thursday, 28 February 2008

336

The different stages of drunkenness ...

Two blokes who passed me by on Nassau Street gave me a whole new insight into classifications of inebriation.

First Guy: 'I can't believe you said that to her!'

Second Guy: 'I know man, I know!'

First Guy: 'Were you drunk or what?'

Second Guy (thinks for a second): 'Well ... not "drunk" drunk. Just sort of "shite at pool" drunk.'

Overheard by Ella, outside the Spar on Nassau Street
Posted on Tuesday, 26 February 2008

IT genius

During my retirement, I offered to help out one day in a PLC college, teaching IT technology.

I hear a growl of annoyance from a young female, who cannot sign into her messenger.

She troubleshoots and then shouts,

'It says der's sumting wrong with me poxy service!'

(proxy server!)

Overheard by Don, PLC college
Posted on Tuesday, 26 February 2008

Not a leg to stand on

I recently brought my uncle, who is in his late 70s, to his local doctor, as he was complaining of numbness and loss of feeling in his right leg.

My uncle, who has been a heavy smoker all of his life, was becoming a regular visitor to the surgery and knew the doctor on a personal basis.

Doctor: 'Well, Tony, what's the problem?'

Tony: 'It's this bloody leg of mine, I can't walk very far without my leg becoming numb and dead.'

Doctor: 'Well Tony, it's a combination of smoking and old age, these things happen as we grow older.'

Tony: 'Old age?'

Doctor: 'Yes, Tony, do you understand?'

Tony: 'Not really. The left leg is the same age and I have no problem with that one ...'

Overheard by Higgs, local GP, Kimmage
Posted on Tuesday, 19 February 2008

Digital milk?

I used to work in a newsagents, and Avonmore were doing a promotion for digital cameras where you collected tokens from milk cartons. One customer comes over to me and asks,

'What's the difference between digital milk and low fat milk?'

Overheard by Anonymous, Finglas
Posted on Monday, 18 February 2008

Gender confusion!

Shopping in town, I passed two women talking on the street. One of them had a baby with her.

Woman #1 (with baby): 'Have ya met me little grandson?'

Woman #2 (peers down at baby): 'Ah lovely — is it a boy or a girl?'

Overheard by Aisling, in town
Posted on Monday, 18 February 2008

Happy Valliers!

I was sitting waiting for the bus to move off from my stop the other day. The entire bus was pretty quiet apart from the hum of the driver's radio. Suddenly, the local 'Anto' gets on and livens the whole place up with this phone conversation:

Anto: 'Howya, €2 please, cheers!'

Anto (on phone): 'Sorry der, love, wha were ya sayin?'

Anto (in a shocked voice): 'WHA?! A DIVORCE?! WHA ... WHY?! Hell ... hello? hello?'

Anto marches off the bus muttering to himself: 'Great, now I have to learn how to wash, cook, clean ...'

Although we felt sorry for him, the entire bus (including the driver) CRACKED up laughing.

Overheard by Thomas, bus terminus
Posted on Monday, 18 February 2008

Where there's a will there's a way

My friend, who is a diabetic, is doing a 48-hour fast for charity. I asked her how she manages, when diabetics are supposed to eat something every few hours. 'That's easy,' she said, 'I just do it in three-hour stretches!'

Overheard by Anonymous, from a friend in Walkinstown
Posted on Saturday, 16 February 2008

Communication breakdown

I guess we just take our rights for granted ...

Walking through Dunnes in town I see an Asian girl carefully stacking the shelves. A young Irish manager walks confusedly up to her and asks her why she's still working.

She mumbles an answer, to which the manager replies, 'No, no, that's just my sense of humour, I was only joking when I said you didn't work hard enough for a lunchbreak!'

Overheard by Lindy, Dunnes, Georges Street
Posted on Friday, 15 February 2008

Stinger

A couple of years ago, a friend of mine, about 20 at the time, stumbled out of the Big Tree pub one night onto Dorset Street. Totally pissed drunk with some random bird on his arm, he hailed a taxi. Both of them jump in the back and my mate says, 'Beaumont please.'

The taxi driver replies, 'I know where you f**kin' live Tomas!'

My mate: 'Oh ... sorry, Dad!'

Overheard by Stephen, taxi
Posted on Sunday, 13 January 2008

Homicidal seats

On the bus, sitting on the top deck.

Drunk woman stands up to get off and walks into a seat. She shouts at the seat, 'Ya dirty whore, what'd ya hit me for?!'

Failing to receive an answer, she turns away still shouting — and falls down the stairs! Only in Dublin!

> Overheard by flyingcabbage, on the top deck of a bus
> Posted on Monday, 11 February 2008

Terminate her!

I am an Austrian guy, tall and quite a big build. Was in the Oliver St John Gogarty's celebrating New Year's Eve with my Irish girlfriend and some friends. It was packed as usual with the normal mixture of Irish and tourists.

Went to the bar to order some drinks. An English girl standing beside me who obviously overheard my accent turned, and the conversation went something like this:

Girl: 'Oh, you must be American?'

Me: 'No, actually, I'm Austrian.'

Girl: 'Wow, really? I could've sworn you were American, you sound exactly like Arnold Schwarzenegger.'

Overheard by Alexander, Oliver St John Gogarty, Temple Bar

Posted on Friday, 8 February 2008

A slight exaggeration

Walking down Georges Street in Dublin, an elderly Dublin man with a stick stopped me and said, 'Here young fella, ya wouldn't help me across the road, me sight isn't the best.' I said no problem and walked the man across.

Half way there, he turned and said, 'Jaysis, thanks young fella, the last time I tried to cross the road I got flattened by a bus!'

Overheard by David, Georges Street, Dublin

Posted on Sunday, 3 February 2008

Irish Lessons

My friend Liam was in the company of a few native Irish speakers in a pub in Connemara recently when a discussion began about what the correct Irish terminology was for a variety of different sexual activities.

One of them then asked an old guy in the corner who was obviously eavesdropping on the conversation if he knew the correct Irish for cunnilingus.

Quick as a flash he comes back with, 'Níl mé in ann smaoineamh ar faoi láthair ach bhí sé ar barr mo theanga ar maidin.'

(I can't think of it now but it was on the tip of my tongue this morning.)

And they say Irish is a dead language!

Sales meeting

My uncle Frank was talking to his manager about a sales meeting. The manager was trying to give him some wickedly insightful judgment about all involved.

The manager goes off on a rant that Frank was facetious, that it's fair to say the other people at the meeting were also facetious, that out of the four people there he himself was the only one who wasn't facetious.

To which Frank interjected with, 'Do you know what "facetious" means?'

Manager asks, 'Frank, do you think I am using words out of contents?'

Pure LEGEND!

Dirty birds

Heard this from the mother at the weekend. She had just got on a train at Heuston, and a hen party of the roughest-looking women you've ever seen (plus one blow-up doll called Roger wearing Y-fronts) came through the carriage, screeching and laughing and skulling cans of Satzenbrau.

Anyway, in the midst of all the merriment came this little gem:

'Heeyor! Whatcha mean ya need de tylet!? Sure I have a cup here ya can use — look!'

Overheard by Morticia, Heuston Station
Posted on Wednesday, 30 January 2008

Wakey majakey

I was at the recent Terenure v Belvedere match in Donnybrook. I then see this young wan in a Belvedere jersey chatting to her mate on the phone and she says in the biggest D4 accent,

'And the Terenure guy took down his trousers and waved his wakey-majakey at me!'

Me and my mates were in stitches!

Overheard by Tom, Terenure v Belvedere match, Donnybrook
Posted on Tuesday, 29 January 2008

Enough to make you sick!

Called in to see a friend in hospital the other day. She had no complaints with the service there, except for one thing:

'Long after I'm gone to sleep at night, around half eleven or quarter to twelve, some nurse wakes me up to give me a sleeping tablet!'

Overheard by Anonymous, in a Dublin hospital
Posted on Sunday, 27 January 2008

Toilet training Granny

Yesterday as I went into Dunnes, a child, mother and Granny came in behind me. It was pouring rain, and Granny said, 'Oh, my pants are all wet, I'm soaking.'

Little kid, aged about three, turns to Mammy and said,

'Oh no, Mammy, I think Granny had a little accident!'

Overheard by Anonymous, Dunnes Stores
Posted on Friday, 25 January 2008

The times are changing

Back in Ireland on holiday last summer, having lived abroad for many years, I was at a BBQ chatting with friends about how much Ireland has changed over the years.

One of my friends who lived abroad for as long as I had says, whilst looking at the barbeque, 'Be Jaysus, when I left Ireland we used to eat inside the house and shite outside. Now they f**king eat outside and shite inside!'

Overheard by Niall, at a BBQ
Posted on Thursday, 24 January 2008

Fancy name

I was sitting in a waiting room in hospital beside this man when an orderly walked in who knew him.

Orderly: 'Jaysus, Mick, how's it going? Haven't seen you in a while!'

Mick: 'Ah, not so bad now, not so bad.'

Orderly: 'C'mere, are ya still working with your man, what's his name?'

Mick: 'Who's that now?'

Orderly: 'Ah you know him, jaysus it's a fancy name, on the tip of me tongue it is, kinda foreign is it? He's about that height (gesturing with his hands), ah you know him, a real fancy name, could be foreign, start with a T or something does it?'

Mick (very hesitantly): 'Tom is it?'

Orderly: 'Ah Tom — that's it!'

Overheard by Niamh, St James's Hospital
Posted on Tuesday, 22 January 2008

Have some respect!

One day I got on the mighty no. 123 bus, when an older man around 70 starting pushing myself and the others onto the bus, saying, 'Come on will ya move up the bleeding bus.' After a few minutes I hear him shouting again from the top of the bus saying and pointing, 'You, Missus, are you getting off? Make way everyone, will you f**king move and let the woman through.'

At the next stop a guy gets on the bus, a totally normal guy carrying a bottle of 7Up, and the old guy starts yelling, 'Jayus! You can't bring that on the bus, have some f**king respect for the bus driver will ya,' and grabs the man's 7Up!

Then when he finally gets off the bus he looks at the bus driver and says, 'See ya soon boss,' and gives him a salute.

Think he thought he worked for Dublin Bus!

Overheard by Therese, no. 123 bus

Posted on Monday, 21 January 2008

The sad state of 'reality'

Girl: 'Did ya see *You're A Star* the other night?'

Guy: 'Nah, me Gran died so we didn't get a chance.'

Girl: 'Did ya vote for it though?'

Guy: 'Yeah, Granny was there dead in the bed an' we were all textin' over her ...'

Overheard by Anonymous, on the no. 16A bus

Posted on Monday, 21 January 2008

Too good for you

My Mam was on a no. 77 bus going home to Tallaght, when she heard a group of boys trying to chat up some girls about the same age (15 or 16) down the back of the bus.

As the girls got to get off the bus, one of the fellas asked for their phone number.

Stepping down the stairs one of the girls replied (very loudly), '085 22 2 good for u.'

Everyone was in stitches!

Overheard by Anonymous, bus to Tallaght

Posted on Monday, 21 January 2008

It's really just a mart for culchies

I was walking up Harcourt Street on Friday just
after leaving work. Outside Coppers was some
kind of sewerage truck with a long pipe going
downstairs into the night club. One of the girls I
was with says,

'Oh my god, are they sucking the shite out of
Coppers?'

Overheard by Brian, Harcourt Street
Posted on Monday, 21 January 2008

Area code prejudice!

A woman was browsing in an expensive tile
shop. She asked the sales assistant, 'How much
does it cost to lay tiles?'

The assistant replied, 'Well, it depends on the
area.' The woman asked, 'Oh, so if you lived in
Ballsbridge, would it cost a lot more?'

Overheard by Anonymous, a tile shop on the south side
Posted on Tuesday, 15 January 2008

George Orwell would turn in his grave

I was in Eason's in O'Connell Street today,
looking for George Orwell's *Animal Farm* for
school. I couldn't find it in the school novels
section so I asked the assistant where I might
find it.

He looks at me blankly for about 15 seconds and

then says, 'Well, in Pet Care, over there, I suppose ...'

Right ...

Overheard by Anonymous, Eason's
Posted on Sunday, 13 January 2008

The no frills airline (really!)

On a Ryanair flight to Edinburgh a few weeks ago, the air hostess kept pausing during the safety demonstration.

'In the event of a drop in cabin pressure, oxygen masks will drop down. Pull mask down and place over your face.' Pauses. Young lad down the back shouts, '... and insert €2 for oxygen!'

The whole plane was in stitches —everyone except for the air hostess!

Overheard by Steven, on a Ryanair flight
Posted on Tuesday, 8 January 2008

Xmas cheer

I was in the Statoil garage in Cabra on Christmas Day when I overheard a young lad of about 15 talking to his mates about what his father had given him for Christmas.

Young Lad: '... me Da gave me €250 for Christmas ... I swear to God I nearly hugged him!'

Overheard by Mr.X, Statoil, New Cabra Road
Posted on Saturday, 5 January 2008

Shell suits to sea

In a packed off-licence, a young lad was standing in the queue in his finest white kappa tracksuit and a cardboard box full of cans in his arms. The bottom of the box gave way and his cans went everywhere, beer pissing out of half of them.

While he was deciding what to do with his jaw hanging down, a pissed aul' lad leans in and says, 'That's what you get for wearing a tracksuit!'

Overheard by Whelo, Malahide
Posted on Saturday, 5 January 2008

He got a right de-bollicking!

I work in a veterinary clinic and I answered a phone call one day:

Woman: 'I need to have my dog's stitches out.'

Me: 'Okay, what did your dog have done?'

Woman: 'Oh, what's this you'd call it ... I suppose he was de-bollickated. Is that what you'd say?'

Me: 'Well, I'd say neutered ...'

Overheard by Anonymous, veterinary clinic
Posted on Friday, 4 January 2008

The lunatics are running the asylum

My pal to a head of lettuce she was rinsing in the sink:

'Goin' anywhere nice on your holidays, love?'

Overheard by Anonymous, kitchen
Posted on Thursday, 3 January 2008

And they're off!

Some years back while walking down Baggot Street after an evening out, we were 10 yards behind a family of American tourists making their way back to their hotel. As they passed a bookies shop, one of the group pointed at the sign over the window and exclaimed,

'Hey! Look at that! "Baggot Racing"! What the hell's a Baggot?'

We had nearly recovered from laughing when 50 yards further on they passed a laundrette called 'Baggot Cleaners' and one says,

'Jeez, they must race them back there and then clean them in here ... We gotta come back and see this tomorrow ...'

Overheard by Pucfada, Baggot Street
Posted on Thursday, 27 December 2007

The concerned thief

I was awoken about 4.30 a.m. the other week by the sound of someone trying to break the lock on my side gate to steal my moped which was in the rear garden.

Rather than corner the bloke, I went around the front of the house and shouted at him as loud as I could, 'What the f**k do you think you're doing?'

The look on his face was priceless but he then climbed over the wall into my neighbour's garden and I continued shouting after him, at which point he stopped, turned around and said,

'Will ya shut da f**k up, yer gonna wake everyone up!'

Overheard by Fran, Firhouse
Posted on Thursday, 20 December 2007

Crazy dress code

A few years ago, I went to a fancy-dress party at a pub as a pint of Guinness. I was under a big cylinder covered in black bin liners, with my arms and legs sticking out. Had a cream collar and a harp on my chest.

I approached the door and the bouncer stopped me. He looked me — a pint of Guinness — up and down, and said deadpan,

'Sorry, pal, I can't let you in here wearing runners.'

Overheard by AG, Tara Street
Posted on Monday, 17 December 2007

No, the feathered two-legged type!

At a table quiz in work.

Quizmaster: 'Name the bird of peace.'

Random shout from a table: 'Mother Teresa!'

Overheard by Doots, work table quiz, The Vaults
Posted on Friday, 14 December 2007

Poor Mikey ain't getting time off?

Not so much heard as seen!

Was having a slash in the toilets at UCD and as I was washing my hands I noticed the check sheet which states when and who check the toilets to make sure they're clean, etc. Reading down I saw many signatures and dates when they were checked. One of the latest read:

Date: 11/12/07

Checked by: Mikey from Boyzone

Overheard by Shaggy, UCD
Posted on Tuesday, 11 December 2007

Plane logic

During the safety demonstration on board a Ryanair flight from Dublin to Leeds, there's two real Dubs sitting next to me. The cabin crew get to the bit about the life-jacket, and one fella turns to his mate and says:

'Why the f**k do they give ya a life-jacket on a plane, f**k sake, that's like given ya a bleeden parachute on a boat.'

Overheard by Steve, on a Ryanair flight from Dublin to Leeds
Posted on Saturday, 8 December 2007

Operation Freeflow my arse!

Garda at a set of lights in Drumcondra, directing traffic with one of those glow-sticks. Lights were green but the garda was directing our lane to stop. My brother drives straight on through the lights past the garda, and I pointed out that he was supposed to stop.

He replies,

'I'm not stopping for some fucking culchie with a light sabre.'

Overheard by Anonymous, Drumcondra
Posted on Thursday, 6 December 2007

A long time ago in a romper room far far away

Had brought my daughter to Play Zone in Celbridge, a kind of padded room for toddlers with ball pits, climbing frames, slides etc. Heard another father trying to coax his son into sliding down one of those enclosed, tube-like slides.

Son looks into the dark hole at the top of the slide and goes to Dad, 'But I don't want to go down the dark slide.'

Dad thinks about it then goes, 'Only by conquering your fears can you ever hope to defeat the dark slide.'

Son still wouldn't slide down it!

Overheard by Bet Down Dad, Play Zone in Celbridge
Posted on Tuesday, 4 December 2007

Who am I?

Well, what you have to know first to understand the story is the fact that I have naturally blonde hair and blue eyes. For years I've had people mistaken me for being from Sweden and over-pronouncing words thinking I can't understand their English (even though I've been born and reared in Dublin!).

Yesterday while shopping I was waiting for my sister so I sat down on a bench and a real 'aul' one' sat down beside me.

This conversation actually happened:

Old Woman: 'If you don't mind me asking, love, what country are you from?'

Me: 'Ha! No, I'm Irish, I'm from Dublin.'

Old Woman: 'Oh jaysus, sorry, love.'

Me: 'It's grand. I actually get that a lot ...'

Old Woman: 'I'd say ye do, love. Ya look Swedish or Dutch or somewhere far away like that. Are sure you're from Ireland, pet?'

Me: 'Yeah!'

Old Woman (while getting up to leave): 'I'd check your birth cert if I were you ...'

Overheard by Kimberly, The Square, Tallaght
Posted on Thursday, 29 November 2007

Forgiven and forgotten

My cousin was talking with two friends at the front door about her son's waster of a father:

'Ah, but ya gave birth to lovely kids considerin' ...'

'I have a very forgivin' fanny!'

Overheard by bobby, Clondalkin
Posted on Monday, 26 November 2007

Kitty

A few weeks ago we were sitting watching TV in the living-room. There was myself, me Da, Ma and brother. Suddenly the cat walked into the room with a €5 note in its mouth (obviously dropped by somebody because I don't think the cat's working yet). Then me Da comes out with a classic:

'Who put the fiver in the kitty?'

Brilliant!

Overheard by Fred Flintstone, Ballyfermot
Posted on Sunday, 25 November 2007

Getting what you can

A few years ago when I was in sixth year there was a panto going on. In the changing rooms during the interval I overheard two first-year lads about 12 years old talking about other first-year girls. One delivered this killer line:

Lad: 'Shut up, Gav, you're gay! You went out with yer one Aine for two months and got nothing off her!'

Gav: 'So?'

Lad: 'I went out with her younger sister, and got CDs!'

Overheard by Charlie, panto changing rooms, school
Posted on Sunday, 18 November 2007

Just blame it on the aul' wans

Was standing in UCD waiting for a no. 17 bus. One of those new 07 buses pulls in with no one on it. The front left-hand side of the bus smashes into the kerb, the driver hops out, examines the damage, lights up a smoke, glances at me and says,

'F**k it, sum aul' wan reversed inta me,' and walked on!

Overheard by Jonny, UCD
Posted on Sunday, 18 November 2007

Horny Harney

Myself and my wife were watching the news. An interview with the Minister for Health was followed by one about children sharing pornographic images on mobile phones and via websites like Bebo.

Thinking she would spare herself from the usual questions ('What's pornography' etc.), my wife asked our seven-year-old daughter to get something upstairs.

A couple of minutes later she re-entered the room behind us and declared, 'I'm horny!'

Stunned, we turned around to find her wearing a black wig and a smile, repeating, 'I'm Mary Horny!'

Overheard by Macker, our sitting-room
Posted on Sunday, 18 November 2007

Miss Guided?

Having presented some junior Girl Guides with their badges etc. at an investiture ceremony, the Guide leader was really warming to her theme. When it came to the award for the most senior of the girls, the leader gushed,

'... and not only is she great at taking care of the Girl Guides, she's well known for looking after the Boy Scouts around the village!'

Overheard by Anonymous, Guides investiture in Cabinteely
Posted on Sunday, 18 November 2007

Boneless

Arrived at the butcher's first thing one morning, to find him roaring laughing at a note some woman had shoved under his door.

It said, 'Paddy, please take the bone out of my leg!'

Overheard by Anonymous, Duffy's butchers shop, Clondalkin
Posted on Friday, 16 November 2007

Cringe TV

Watching RTÉ the other night about new apartments in Ratoath being developed so that everyone with any disability can live there, hassle free etc. They were giving disabled people a tour of the apartments and the foreman walks into one of the apartments with a blind girl and her guide dog.

First thing he says to her: 'As you can see, the lights come on automatically.'

Silence from the blind girl ...!

Only on Irish TV!

Overheard by Anonymous, Blesso
Posted on Friday, 16 November 2007

That should narrow it down

At a recent wedding a friend who was seated at our table went out to the hotel foyer where she encountered a small boy, also a wedding guest, crying while sitting on the stairs. She asked why he was crying and he said he had lost his Mammy.

'Okay, no problem,' she says, 'what's her name?'

'MAAMMMMY,' replied the boy.

Overheard by lenny, at a wedding in Dublin
Posted on Thursday, 15 November 2007

Foreign nationals need Dublin Bus to lead them to their Promised Land!

Just yesterday, whilst RTÉ *Drivetime* were interviewing people in Finglas regarding the effects of the Dublin Bus dispute, one lady was concerned about 'the foreigners'. She said, 'Sure they don't know their way around, how will they get to their destiny?'

Overheard by Anonymous, RTÉ *Drivetime*, 12 November 2007
Posted on Tuesday, 13 November 2007

F word

Being a teacher, I hear some strange stories from students but this one tops them all. The girls had a different teacher for sex education last year, and one of my 10 year olds came back mortified:

'Miss, ya'd never guess wha da teacher sed! She sed da F word!'

Worried at what this word might be, I told her to tell me later. At the end of the day I asked her what this F word was.

'Ah, Miss, ya wouldn't believe it ... da teacher said FANGINA!'

Overheard by miss c, school in Dublin 12
Posted on Monday, 12 November 2007

John Player ewwww!

Couple of years ago at a party with a bunch of mates, we ran out of smokes. So wandered up to this chubby middle-aged woman I hadn't met before, smoking, and politely asked, 'Wouldn't have a spare smoke, would ya, please?'

Her response, deadpan, deadly serious with glazed eyes: 'Give us a lick out, would yeh?'

I bought some instead ...

Overheard by Eamo, the Noggin Inn
Posted on Monday, 12 November 2007

Cats stuck together?

Walking down Grafton Street with two D4 type girls in front of me: 'So, are Siamese cats, loike, stuck together?'

Overheard by Bekah, Grafton Street
Posted on Sunday, 11 November 2007

Lessons in Irish

I live in Germany and was talking to a friend who had just returned from three years of working as a translator in Dublin. During the conversation she mentioned that she'd learned some Irish while she was over there, then rattled off the numbers one to ten, just to prove it.

I asked her how she got interested in Irish. 'Well, the Irish drop so many Irish words into English that I had to keep asking people what they meant,' she replied. 'After that it was just the same as learning any other language. You watch what people do and listen to what they say.'

I asked her for an example 'Well, when someone opens the door and sees the weather outside, listening to them taught me how to say, "It's raining" in Irish.'

After checking to make sure I could remember how to say it myself, I said, 'Go on then, how do you say it?' Without batting an eyelid she says, 'Aah for f**k sake!'

Overheard by Gapper, by my friend
Posted on Saturday, 10 November 2007

Toilet humour

I work on a building site near Heuston Station. The toilets are forever getting new literature on the walls, getting painted over, before new material appears. I saw a new one recently saying 'Polish workers — GO HOME'! The next day, below this some one had added, 'But leave your women'. The next day someone else had come in and scribbled '... and take ours with you!'

Overheard by Neil, construction site, Kilmainham
Posted on Saturday, 10 November 2007

An oldie?

A fat bloke came into work yesterday to collect an order he had previously made. My young colleague went out back to the warehouse to get the bloke's order. He was gone some time and then eventually emerged with it and said to the fat bloke, 'I'm terribly sorry about the wait.'

To which the fat bloke replied, 'Don't worry, son, it's not your fault, I eat too much!'

Overheard by Anonymous, work
Posted on Thursday, 8 November 2007

Learning from Dad

Little girl on the bus, after spotting a fly (roaring): 'Look, Dad, a bastard!'

Overheard by Anonymous, on the bus
Posted on Thursday, 8 November 2007

Russia versus Ireland

My Dad overheard this on his coffee break in work.

Russian Guy: 'In Russia, only women put milk in their tea.'

Smart Ass Dub: 'Well, in Ireland only women drink vodka!'

Overheard by Traykool, from my Dad
Posted on Monday, 5 November 2007

Nice one Grandad!

Kid: 'Grandad, how long is a minute?'

Grandad: 'Depends on which side of the toilet door you're standing.'

Overheard by Anonymous, half-time in Croke Park
Posted on Sunday, 4 November 2007

Forgetting the wife

An elderly man and lady were getting ready to get off the bus. When the bus pulled in to the stop, the man got off but the lady didn't.

When the bus began to pull away again the man ran after the bus and began banging on the window. The bus driver stopped and let him on the bus, with the man shouting: 'I forgot my wife!!'

Overheard by Greg, 46A
Posted on Monday, 5 November 2007

Dublin's future

I was walking through the Liberties with a little three year old I was minding. She had no buggy with her, and half way to where we were going

she sat down on the side of the road, with her hands on her face.

When I asked her what she was doing she looked up at me and said, 'Sitting!'

I asked why. She replied, 'Cause I'm f**kin' bollixed!'

Now, that's Dublin!

Overheard by Conor, outside Kevin Street Garda Station

Posted on Friday, 2 November 2007

Flat bus

Was waiting around for my bus yesterday evening when a lad comes up to me and asks, 'Has the braless bus gone yet?'

I was like 'What ...?' And he asks me again, 'Has the BRALESS bus gone yet?' I was like, 'Sorry, I don't know what you're talking about,' and he asks,

'For fook's sake, the bleedin' no. 32A bus, love, has it gone yet or wha?'

Took me a few minutes to work out what he meant!

Overheard by Chloe, no. 32A bus stop

Posted on Wednesday, 31 October 2007

Getting 'Felt'

Many years ago I worked in a large hardware store in Capel Street. One day a lady walked into the store and enquired of the young sssistant at one of the counters, 'Excuse me, young man, can you tell me where I can get felt?'

He replied with a smirk on his face, 'In the basement, Madam.'

The lady took offence, called him rude and insolent and asked to speak with the manager, who politely informed her that yes, she could get felt in the basement!

We laughed about this for days!

Overheard by angie, Lenehans in Capel Street
Posted on Monday, 29 October 2007

The Dublin divide

Skanger: 'Ten Silk Cut Purple, please.'

Posh Assistant: 'Em, don't ya mean John Player Blue?'

Skanger: 'Give me the box of Silk Cut or I'll box ye in the face.'

Posh Assistant: 'OK ...'

Overheard by LongMileRoad, town
Posted on Saturday, 27 October 2007

Now there's a compliment

'What's wrong with you today? You've a head like a burst couch.'

Overheard by Anonymous, at home
Posted on Saturday, 27 October 2007

Can't get no satisfaction

Was queuing outside Coppers last night and ahead of me were two girls from Dublin who were very skangery (if that's a word). They were clearly over 21 but the bouncer was looking for an excuse not to let them in.

Bouncer: 'Sorry, girls, but if you don't have ID, I can't let you in.'

Girl: 'But I'm 26 for f**k sake.'

Bouncer: 'I don't care how old you are. I need to see ID to satisfy myself that you are old enough.'

Girl: 'I'd say you have to satisfy yourself full stop — ya ugly pig!'

Overheard by Len, outside Copper Face Jacks
Posted on Friday, 26 October 2007

All-Ireland Final day

After the 2006 All-Ireland Football Final (Mayo v Kerry) which Kerry won. Two Mayo women were walking through a residential street when they were approached by two local girls (about six and eight years old). The little girls got in their faces and started chanting 'You're shit! And you know you are. You're shit! And ...'

The Mayo women found this funny and started trying to reason with the girls saying, 'Ah come on now, we beat you in the semis,' but the girls were having none of it and began chanting 'Hill 16 is Dublin only, Hill 16 is Dublin only. Who are ya? Who are ya?'

At this point the girls' father strolled out of his front door. Realising what was going on, he clapped his hands together and roared over at the top of his voice, 'Hill 16 is Dublin only, Hill 16 is Dublin only.'

Overheard by Niall, outside Croke Park

Posted on Thursday, 25 October 2007

Stick it where?

Was with my Granny (about 70 years old, very Catholic, never curses) and two nephews in the park on Sunday. We got talking about how many young girls have kids but the kids' Dads are not around.

We both agreed that the men have it a lot easier in that situation, when my Gran said to me, 'Sure, they're just a randy lot — they would stick it in a keyhole if they could.'

Overheard by Pixi-b, Marley Park

Posted on Thursday, 25 October 2007

Numeracy building site style

Walking past a building site today and two foreign lads were filling a skip. They had a large 8x4 slab of wood between them.

One turns to the other and says, 'We go on 2. 1—2—3, OK, go!'

Overheard by Phanom-Anom, Dublin town

Posted on Thursday, 25 October 2007

Bodes well for the future

Was dropping the little lad into the crèche this

morning. After making sure he was okay, I said to him, 'You be a good boy for Sarah today.'

To which he replied, 'Don't worry, Daddy I won't be a little bollix like David over there!'

My lad is three!

Overheard by Santos L Helper, local crèche
Posted on Monday, 22 October 2007

The beer-bellied revolutionary

On returning from a Che Guevara 40th anniversary do, one of the regulars walked into the pub wearing a Che T-shirt. It was about three sizes too small and was stretched tight over his massive beer belly.

The barman took one look at him and shouts over, 'Jayses, Paul, I never knew Che's head was that big!'

Overheard by Anonymous, Celt Bar, Talbot Street
Posted on Saturday, 20 October 2007

The honest taxi driver

I was coming home from town in a taxi the night of the Junior Cert results in September. While chatting to the taxi driver he was telling me about how shocked he was at how well his daughter did.

'Well, she certainly didn't get the brains from me ... The milkman must've been a clever f****r!'

Overheard by Sean, back of a taxi
Posted on Saturday, 20 October 2007

The scholar

My friend bashed his head last week and got ambulanced off to Blanch. He's 69 years old, and studying as a mature student in NUIM. The ambulance fellas who brought him in told me that when they revived him after his accident (he was unconscious for 15 minutes) they asked him his name and what he did.

When he said he was a student, they thought the bash on the head had really done some serious damage. It took him quite a while to convince them he hadn't lost it altogether!

Overheard by Rudy, James Connolly Memorial Hospital
Posted on Friday, 19 October 2007

When you still think your passengers are kids

Three of us take turns driving into work. One morning we were getting picked up by Libby (who is a mother of three young children). On the way to work she must have forgotten who was in the car with her, because she suddenly pipes up in an overly excited voice, 'Ohhhhhhhhhhh wow, look at all the diggers over there,' thinking she had her kids in the car!

Overheard by Fiona, in a car on the way to work
Posted on Friday, 19 October 2007

Blooming brilliant!

Working in a florist, my manager was thinking of a poster to put in the window to grab people's attention. She told me she had a great idea and the next day she came in with the poster.

It was a big picture of a cactus and below it,

'NOT YOUR USUAL BUNCH OF PRICKS'!

Overheard by Daisy, work
Posted on Friday, 19 October 2007

First-time caller, long-time idiot

Message left on my mobile:

'James? ... JAMES, pick up ... I know you can hear me ... pick up the phone.'

Overheard by James, on my mobile
Posted on Friday, 19 October 2007

Foot & Mouth, or foot in mouth?

My sisters in-law from Wales were travelling over to Dublin by car ferry. It was at the time of the Foot & Mouth outbreak in the UK and Irish authorities were on high alert, spraying down all cars and asking passengers if they'd been on farms etc.

Disembarking in Dublin Port their car was stopped by an official. 'Any dairy products?' he asked, to which the driver replied in complete seriousness, 'No thanks, we're staying in a hotel and breakfast is included.'

The rest of the car erupted in laughter — still to the confusion of the driver!

Overheard by Gar, Dublin Port
Posted on Thursday, 18 October 2007

Say cheese

Was in the All Sports Café and there was a couple sitting at the next table. The waitress brought down two cocktails to them and left. The fella said to his girlfriend, 'We should have got a pitcher', to which she responds, 'But we don't even have a camera?!'

Overheard by Stroker, Temple Bar
Posted on Thursday, 18 October 2007

Claustrophobic holiday

An American tourist couple sitting on a park bench. The lady says to her husband, 'Don't you just get so claustrophobic in these small countries?'

Overheard by Paul, St Stephen's Green
Posted on Wednesday, 17 October 2007

Sap

Was walking past the newsagents when I see a young father of 25 reprimand his son of about seven who was attempting to follow his mother into the shop. I overheard this brief conversation:

Father: 'Yer not goin' in there, yer waitin' ouhh here wih meee!'

Son: 'Whyyyyyy?'

Father: 'Ya know why, I told ya why a minute ago why, what did I tell ya? Why can't ya go into the shop wih yer Mammy?'

Son (hangs head): 'Cos I was acting the f**kin' sap.'

Father: 'Exactly, ye were actin' the f**kin' sap.'

Overheard by cactus, Summerhill
Posted on Wednesday, 17 October 2007

Irish Rail, having a laugh

Public Address: 'We wish to apologise for the late boarding of the 07:30 hours service to Waterford. Boarding will commence in approximately 10 minutes.'

Irish Rail staff on the platform: '10 minutes!' — and then raucous laughter!

Overheard by Anonymous, Heuston Station
Posted on Wednesday, 17 October 2007

Service with a smile?

At the Police concert, ordering a hot dog.

I asked the woman serving,

'Could I have some onions on the hot dog?'

Her reply, 'Where the f**k do you think you are, America?'

Classy!

Overheard by Little Larry, Croke Park
Posted on Wednesday, 17 October 2007

A city of contrasts

Last August I was in Dublin for a couple of nights with a friend, staying in Buswells. One night we decided to take a taxi to the Omniplex, and discovered the driver lived on the southside but was from Wicklow originally (you know the way taxi drivers have that amazing talent of telling their entire life story in less than five minutes).

Realising he has a pair of culchies with him, he started on about how Dublin isn't half as bad as the media make out, and how in all his 20 years of living here he's never been robbed or had any sort of trouble and that we were as safe here as we would be back in our little village.

All very well and good, two hours later we were getting a taxi back. Driver was a northsider this time, took a different route back to the hotel. Driving down a narrow street with feck all light and quite a bit of graffiti, he announces, 'Hauld on to yer handbags, ladies, this is where da druggies hang out.'

Overheard by Effy, taxi ride from the Omniplex to Buswells Hotel

Posted on Wednesday, 17 October 2007

Hopes and dreams

Years back in primary school the teacher asks, 'What would you like to be when you grow up?'

Student #1: 'Policeman.'

Student #2: 'Fireman.'

Student #3: 'Sex machine ...'

Overheard by m0ngch1ld, primary school
Posted on Tuesday, 16 October 2007

Southside liberalists

Was sitting in the Elephant & Castle restaurant with a few friends recently and there was a loud group of attractive southside girls (early 20s) seated beside us. Listening to them discuss the merits of new mothers breastfeeding in public, we hear one of them exclaim loudly, 'Well they're just FOCKING exhibitionists if you ask me!'

Overheard by Aoife, Temple Bar
Posted on Tuesday, 16 October 2007

Brotherly love

On the no. 10 bus, two brothers about seven years old:

Brother 1: 'Gimme one!' (sweets)

Brother 2: 'No!'

Brother 1: 'Gimme one or I'll fart on your face when you're asleep.'

Brother 2 hands pack of sweets to Brother 1!

Overheard by Dee, no. 10 bus
Posted on Monday, 15 October 2007

There's something about Mary

When Mary McAleese walked out onto the pitch to meet the players at Croke Park at the Ireland v Germany, one bloke shouted from the back of the Canal End, 'Go on, Mary, ye ride!'

Overheard by colin, Croker
Posted on Monday, 15 October 2007

FAI stuck in a time warp?

I was at the Ireland v Germany match at Croke Park. The Germans were making a substitution.

FAI announcer: 'Substitution for WEST Germany (ironic laughs from the crowd) ... eh, sorry, for Germany ...'

Overheard by G, Croke Park
Posted on Sunday, 14 October 2007

National stereotypes!

While driving four lads from Crumlin village to the Ireland v Germany game at Croke Park, the conversation got around to how sullen and devoid of humour the Germans are.

Guy in back of car: 'Bleeding Germans, no poxy fun, a grumpy shower altogether.' To which front-seat passenger pipes up these words of wisdom delivered without a trace of irony:

'You're dead right, Anto. Look at that Hitler fella, a right touchy bastard.'

I nearly wrote off the car trying to keep in the laughter.

Overheard by Damian, in my taxi on the way to Croke Park

Posted on Sunday, 14 October 2007

Post it note

I was in the queue in a post office and there was an aul' wan ahead of me. She says to the post mistress, 'Give us the stamps so I can post this parcel.'

The post mistress weighed the parcel and gave the aul' wan the parcel and the stamps. The aul' wan looked at the post mistress and asked, 'Will I stick 'em on meself?'

The post mistress says, without any hesitation, 'No love, stick them on the parcel!'

I nearly folded!

Overheard by Bello, post office in Clanbrassil Street

Posted on Sunday, 14 October 2007

At least he asked

A mate of mine was on the Nitelink a couple of years back, heading to Clonsilla. The bus was packed upstairs as it was 3 a.m.

A man up towards the top of the bus stands up and asks,

'Does anyone mind if I take a piss?'

At that, everyone lifts up their feet towards their chests, nothing said ...

Overheard by spilly, Nitelink to Clonsilla

Posted on Saturday, 13 October 2007

She'll give you a lift ...

Was visiting a friend in the IFSC. Stepped onto a lift with a few well-dressed financial types and, right at the back, there's two blokes in overalls covered in paint.

Female voice from lift: 'Please select floor.'

Bloke 1: 'Howya luv, that's a sexy voice ...'

Female voice from lift: 'Going down ...'

Bloke 2: 'Feckin' tease ... rawwrrrr ...'

Overheard by Fred, IFSC
Posted on Friday, 12 October 2007

Red-head

Eight-year-old Dub kid cycles by a guy with red hair and shouts, 'Here, Mister — do you read?'

Red-head says, 'Eh, yeah.'

Boy shouts, 'Have ye red pubes?'

Brilliant — even the red-head had to laugh!

Overheard by Anonymous, said to red-headed friend of mine
Posted on Friday, 12 October 2007

Decapitated?

Walking through Temple Bar, a group of young lads talking to a bouncer.

Lad: 'Here, mate, do you know where the Turk's Head is?'

Bouncer: 'I'd say it's probably on his shoulders!'

Overheard by Jean-Pierre, Temple Bar
Posted on Thursday, 11 October 2007

Two onions in a hanky

I was back home in Dublin on holidays recently, visiting my family. I was in Northside shopping centre with my mother. She was talking to a friend of hers whose husband had just died.

My Mother: 'That's terrible, I am very sorry to hear that.'

The woman replied: 'That old bastard, I am glad he's dead ... I needed two onions in a hanky so I could cry at the funeral!'

Overheard by Anonymous, Northside shopping centre
Posted on Thursday, 11 October 2007

No fingers all thumb

A mate of mine lost the four fingers of his right hand in an accident at work. After a couple of days we went to visit him in hospital and my brother asked if he would still be able to drive.

'Don't know, but I'd imagine so,' he answered.

My brother kept looking at him real serious and said,

'Sure, if you can't, you can hitch-hike everywhere!'

Overheard by Paul, hospital
Posted on Thursday, 11 October 2007

All on tap

My friend's sister came over to visit with her new baby. My friend's kids aged three and four were delighted with their new cousin. After a while the baby began to cry and the mother started to breastfeed.

The kids looked at each other in amazement. Not used to the spectacle, the four year old asked, 'What are ya doing?' and he was told, 'Feedin' da baby,' to which he replied,

'Do yis do Coke?'

Overheard by Bello, from my friend in Whitehall
Posted on Thursday, 11 October 2007

Finglas slang?

Some terms needed to understand: Locked = Drunk;

Boot = Ugly Girl

A girl and three lads were getting out of the car. The driver shouted to his friends, 'Is the boot locked?' and his friend answered, 'No, she's only had a couple of pints!'

Overheard by zazo5000, Finglas
Posted on Thursday, 11 October 2007

On the Nitelink

Stumbled onto the Nitelink home last Saturday night only to be caught in the crossfire between a group of skangers slagging each other off, from one side of the bus to the other.

The mouthy bird shouts to some fella, 'You were bleedin' shoii in bed anyway, so shut yer gob.'

To which he replies,

'Ah would ya ever f**k off, sure I only rode ya in me car.'

Overheard by Martha Focker, no. 42N bus
Posted on Thursday, 11 October 2007

Knickerbocker glory

I finished up work and went out shopping with my Mam. There was a girl that we kept seeing around the shop, and people kept assuming mistakenly that she worked there. While she was in the queue the security guard tapped her on the shoulder.

She, assuming someone was about to ask again, shouted at the top of her voice, 'I DON'T BLEEDIN' WORKKK HEERRRREEE WILLL YEEE EVERRRR CHANGEEE THE STUPIEH UNIFORMMMSSS.'

The security guard obviously didn't take to her shouting, and shouted back at the top of his voice,

'I KNOW YOU DON'T WORK HERE, I'M TELLING YOU YOUR SKIRT IS TUCKED INTO YOUR KNICKERS!'

The whole shop start laughing — funniest shopping trip ever!

Overheard by Carrie, Dunnes, The Square,
Tallaght, during Christmas rush
Posted on Thursday, 11 October 2007

Lovable skangers

Walking up O'Connell Street and two skanger young lads about 12 years old were chasing and beating the crap outta each other, calling each other every profanity under the sun.

Anyway, they gallop past me for the third time when one of them comes to a sudden halt beside a queue of people at a bus stop, where he spots a lady with twins in a buggy.

He shouts after Tommo, 'Tommo, Tommo, com 'ere, look at dis!'

Tommo gallops back to see what'z going on. When he sees the twins, the two skangers look at each other in amazement, all excited, and stick their heads in the buggy and start ooooh-ing and aaaing!

Tommo: 'Ah, jaysis, they're luuuvly aren't they?'

'Yeah,' says the other lad, 'they're gaargeous, Missus, luuuvly.'

But they soon snapped out of it — and proceeded to kick the shite outta each other and gallop off again!

Overheard by Dee, O'Connell Street
Posted on Wednesday, 10 October 2007

Ah, how sweat!

A friend of mine is a primary school teacher in Dublin, teaching senior infants.

One wee boy in her class is from Russia. He has fairly good English but sometimes gets a bit mixed up. One day when they were doing computers he put up his hands and shouts, 'Teacher, teacher there's no rat with this computer.'

Overheard by Anonymous, friend teaching at a
Dublin primary school
Posted on Wednesday, 10 October 2007

The passion of the Religion teacher

Sitting in Religion in an all-girls school while a very awkward male teacher tries to explain the Catholic Church's views on sex. One of our other classmates, who was supposed to be playing a GAA match, comes in and starts explaining that the other team didn't show up.

This moved into a lengthy discussion about the 'cheek' of other school, when suddenly the Religion teacher, quite peeved at being forgotten shouts,

'CAN WE PLEASE TALK ABOUT SEX NOW!'

Overheard by Darrire, Sancta Maria College

Posted on Tuesday, 9 October 2007

Hygienic!

In changing rooms in Penney's, O'Connell Street, I overheard a young wan say to another, 'Dya know whaa, I've had a shower every single day this week!'

Overheard by dee, Penney's changing rooms

Posted on Tuesday, 9 October 2007

Magic water

Was in a newsagents a few weeks ago when a customer with a bottle of water approached the man behind the till.

Cashier: 'Next, please!'

Customer (showing the bottle of water): 'Is this Still water?'

Cashier (without hesitation): 'As far as I know it hasn't changed, yeh.'

Legend!

Overheard by Howie, Tallaght newsagents
Posted on Tuesday, 9 October 2007

À la carte Catholics

My seven-year-old son is preparing for his Holy Communion. We don't go to mass, so he was a bit in awe of the goings-on. It was a folk mass so there were plenty of alleluias ringing out from the altar.

My son nudged me, pointing at the singers, and whispered (loudly),

'Mom, are they the Christians?'

One mortified mom!

Overheard by Anonymous, church in Greystones
Posted on Monday, 8 October 2007

Big shoes to fill

A friend of mine had — by the age of 15 — reached the height of a healthy 6 foot 4 inches, with a size 14 foot to boot.

Shopping in town one day he had picked out a pair of runners to buy. A young fella came up to him after a while and asked, 'Can I help you there, bud?'

My mate asks, 'Do you have these in a size 14?'

The young lad looks at him in disbelief and replies, 'Hold on till I see if we have a pair of canoes out the back!'

Overheard by Cormac, town
Posted on Monday, 8 October 2007

Kids these days

I was driving through one of the estates in Shankill.

There was a group of children playing on the road just ahead of me so I slowed down as I was passing them. When I looked out the window, one of the kids who could have been no older than five screams at me, 'Are ye startin!!'

Overheard by Susan, Shankill
Posted on Monday, 8 October 2007

Dub takes the biscuit

Amid a very stressful time for all my family in Tallaght Hospital, my very sick mother (thankfully well again) asked me to go to the hospital shop and get her some plain biscuits. Delighted that she wanted something to eat, I eagerly obliged.

In the lift going back to the ward, biscuits in hand, I met a middle-aged woman who asked, 'Are you on shop duty, love?' I replied that yes, I was. What she said next gave us all a much needed side-splitting laugh:

'Jaysus, love, the last time I done shop duty in here, I was getting biscuits for me sick aunt, but when I got back to her ward she was bleeding dead.' Then touching my arm she looked at my plain biscuits and continued, 'You'll be alright though, luv — I bought the chocolate ones!'

Overheard by Deirdre, Tallaght Hospital
Posted on Sunday, 7 October 2007

Horsing around!

One night in the Sheriff youth club, two of the boys off the football team are undecided on a night on the town. One says to the other, 'John, are you goin' out?' which was met with the reply, 'Does a rockin' horse have a wooden dick!'

Overheard by G, Sheriff youth club
Posted on Saturday, 6 October 2007

The aliens have landed

While purchasing some stock for the club in a Cash & Carry, the following announcement came over the PA:

'Will the rep from Mars please report to reception.'

Overheard by jj, Cash & Carry Store
Posted on Friday, 5 October 2007

Lethal weapon

Two security guards on Henry Street last night over the walkie talkie:

'Lad in green combat trousers coming towards ye.'

'Yeah, what about him?'

'Is that the little bollix that hit me with the cauliflower?'

Overheard by Sheriff2, Henry Street
Posted on Friday, 5 October 2007

To kill a mocking bird

While waiting for the no. 123 bus at a stop in Summerhill, I noticed a man very obviously disoriented and out of his head (drugs/booze who knows) slumped against the wall.

Two minutes later a bird perched above him and shit on his head. It looked like someone threw a McFlurry at him, yet he didn't notice for maybe a minute or so, but when he noticed he threw an absolute fit.

He started to scream obscenities at the bird, mostly incoherent, but I did catch this classic line:

'See you, come here till I tell ya, come down here and I'll shit on your face!'

The bird declined!

Overheard by cactus, Summerhill
Posted on Wednesday, 3 October 2007

Perfect strangers

An elderly Dublin lady is taking a stroll around the Irish Museum of Modern Art with a friend when she passes someone she seems to recognise on the stairs. Typically Irish, she knows it would be rude not to acknowledge this person who seems so familiar.

'Ah, howyeh!' she places a gentle hand on the stranger's arm.

'Eh, hello,' the familiar gentleman replies.

'How's it goin'? Haven't been talkin' to ya in a while.'

'Erm, no ... eh ... I'm good.'

'Ah, dat's great, yer lookin' well.'

'Eh, thanks.'

'And how's yer Ma keepin?'

'Oh ... eh ... fine, she's fine ... I have to be on my way. Bye now.'

The familiar gentleman continues on his way. Once out of earshot the old lady's friend exclaims, 'Jaysus, Mary!'

'Whah?' replies Mary

'That was Elton John!'

Overheard by Anonymous, Irish Museum of Modern Art
Posted on Wednesday, 3 October 2007

Are you there Michael??

Was in one of these 'Angel' shops the other day — you know these places that sell mystical/spiritual items such as CDs, angel cards, and also perform healing. A customer was telling a story to other customers about when she went to visit a medium to try and contact her dead husband. The shopkeeper was listening in the background. It was a very sensitive subject. She was at the part when the medium got in touch with some spirits:

Customer: 'Then the medium said that on one side she has come in contact with a person, but is not sure of his name, and on the other side she has a Mickey' (the customer's dead husband's name!).

Shop Keeper: 'Is that his only body part she had?'

Overheard by Anonymous, in an Angel shop/healers
Posted on Wednesday, 3 October 2007

Extra body parts

A little boy snuggled onto his rather well-endowed auntie's lap. While staring at her cleavage he shouts, 'Ma, Auntie Phil has a bum on her belly.'

Overheard by Greystones, Harbour Bar in Bray
Posted on Wednesday, 3 October 2007

Service with attitude

I work as cabin crew for a budget airline and one day after take-off from Dublin Airport I was serving a rather posh woman. She asked me for an OJ.

I was well aware this meant orange juice, however she obviously felt the need to explain it, quoting, 'That's an orange juice to you dear!'

Feeling quite offended by this, I decided if you can't beat them join them, and promptly replied, 'Would you like ice, Mam? That's frozen water to you!'

Overheard by trollydollyx, on a flight from
Dublin to London Gatwick
Posted on Wednesday, 3 October 2007

If you have to ask ...

Overheard in a pub off Grafton Street last week, early afternoon drink. A lady from one of the Brown Thomas make-up counters walks in, all dolled up in red uniform, full face on, looking like Mrs Bouquet. Hubbie in suit, looking beleaguered, carrying all her parcels (M&S bags, loads of them). She moves seat two or three times before finding one hygienic enough to please.

She orders a seafood something for both of them and decides to match it with a suitable wine.

Her quarter bottle arrives. 'Em, excuse me, barman,' (looking at bottle with a sigh) 'can you tell me where this "wine" has come from?'

Barman: 'The fridge ...'

She just sat down. Sniggers all round.

Overheard by Anonymous, Neary's cocktail lounge
Posted on Wednesday, 3 October 2007

The menu

Working in a restaurant in Malahide, standing talking with a colleague while waiting for a particular table to get seated. As they proceeded to check out the menu, one AJH (ah jaysus howya) turns to the other and asked,

'Ma, wha ya havin' for starters?'

The reply was, 'I was goin' to have the prawn cocktail, but I don't like the texture in me mouth, 'n anyways they don't taste the same as a package a' Skips!'

Overheard by Alan, at work
Posted on Tuesday, 2 October 2007

The Guinness gobshites

Working in a pub on the northside, two lads stand outside smoking when the Guinness delivery arrives. After taking off the large kegs, they roll a few half-size kegs past the lads.

One turns to the other and says, 'I wonder what's in them?' Without a moment's hesitation the other guy says,

'They're the glasses of Guinness, ya gobshite!'

Overheard by Nick, northside pub
Posted on Monday, 1 October 2007

Sensitive parenting

Was on the train from Dublin to Carlow. A group of women in their thirties sat near me and started discussing the bullying that was going on in their kids' school. One woman struck me as a really good mother, telling her son to tell teachers, and making him feel good.

After a few minutes, she mentioned she had run

into the kid that was bullying her son and told him,

'If you ever come near my Johnny again, I'll kill your parents with a baseball bat and bury them in the Dublin mountains and you'll never see them again.'

I nearly fell off my seat and spent the rest of the journey buried in my book!

Overheard by Eimer, on the train
Posted on Monday, 1 October 2007

Planet Ireland

In Maths class recently:

Teacher: 'Michael, what planet are you living on?'

Michael: 'Ireland …'

Overheard by Anonymous, Maths class
Posted on Monday, 1 October 2007

Latest invention

Dublin woman in Jonesboro Market at a garden ornament stall.

Woman: 'What's that?'

Salesman: 'That's a sun dial.'

Woman: 'What does it do?'

Salesman: 'When the sun shines on it you can tell the time.'

Woman: 'What will they think of next …'

Overheard by Pat, Jonesboro Market
Posted on Sunday, 30 September 2007

The art of movement

On the no. 18 bus on the Long Mile Road. The bus was packed and the driver wouldn't move until people moved back. There was a really tall man in the aisle and he was told to move or else the bus wouldn't move. Frustrated, a woman shouted at him:

'Move back! It's like movin' forwards except backwards!'

Overheard by J, no. 18 bus
Posted on Sunday, 30 September 2007

Read it

While getting my post from a busy apartment lobby the other morning a resident came in and spoke to a guy by the ESB meters:

Resident: 'You're right to check your meter — that crowd did me by €60 on my last bill.'

Guy: 'I am that crowd ... I'm the meter reader!'

Overheard by Sarah, apartment lobby
Posted on Friday, 28 September 2007

Brendan Neeson?

Last year my Mam was in my next-door neighbour's house and the *Late Late* was on. Brendan Gleeson was being interviewed and after a few minutes of watching, this conversation unfolded between the ladies:

Mam: 'Barry Gleeson is on the telly!'

Neighbour: 'God, he's the image of his brother.'

Mam: 'Who's his brother?'

Neighbour: 'Brendan Gleeson?'

Mam: 'Oh, sorry, no, that is Brendan Gleeson! I just got the name wrong!'

Neighbour: 'Oh, right. And isn't he a brother of Liam Neeson?'

Mam: (silent disbelief)

Neighbour: 'They're gettin' the picture of each other, though I'd say Liam is older.'

Overheard by Anonymous, at home
Posted on Thursday, 27 September 2007

The land of no return

On the DART home from work I overheard two elderly ladies having a chat.

Lady #1: 'It's awful, when I was coming in this morning a man collapsed on the carriage. I think he had a heart-attack. I must watch the news tonight. If he died they might give it a mention.'

Lady #2: 'Oh God, that's horrible. I hope he didn't buy a return ticket!'

Overheard by The Ballhopper, the DART
Posted on Thursday, 27 September 2007

Bertie, your people are starving

Overseen rather than Overheard

Man protesting outside the Dáil with a notice board that reads:

'On hunger strike until Bertie comes clean and tells the truth to the Mahon Tribunal.'

He was drinking a cup of coffee — with a Twix!

Overheard by Gaz, outside the Dáil
Posted on Thursday, 27 September 2007

Traffic cops

While driving on the M50 recently with my sister, brother-in-law and 12-year-old nephew, we were overtaken by a Garda Traffic Corps jeep with 'Garda Traffic Corps' in big letters down the side.

My nephew turned to me in all seriousness and asked, 'Why is there an 'R' in traffic cops?'

Overheard by Shane, M50
Posted on Thursday, 27 September 2007

Request

In the local the other day there were two lads playing guitars. After they finished a song someone shouted to them, 'Here, do yes do requests?'

They said they did.

'Well f*ck off, cause you're bleeding brutal!'

Overheard by sheriff2, Clonliffe House
Posted on Wednesday, 26 September 2007

Age is relative

Shortly after my aunt gave birth to her son, her brother Dan was speaking to their other brother Mike (who lives in the States) on the phone.

Uncle Mike: 'So, I hear Kate had a young fella.'

Uncle Dan: 'Yeah. He was fairly young alright.'

Overheard by Ether, via my Mam
Posted on Tuesday, 25 September 2007

The generation gap exposed

I was at the local supermarket when I passed a boy and his mother, he with a pack of CDs in hands and his mother angrily telling him, 'I'm not payin' a tenner for you to burn CDs, what ya wanna do that fer anyway, is it stupid ya think I am or wa?'

Overheard by Anonymous, Dunnes, ILAC Centre
Posted on Tuesday, 25 September 2007

It's in the jeans

Was sitting outside a pub in town, a couple of lads at the table beside us. A girl walks by in a

pair of Rock & Republic jeans. One of the guys at the table beside us shouts out, '€600 for a pair of jeans and your arse still looks shite!'

Overheard by keepitrim, Dublin 2

Posted on Tuesday, 25 September 2007

Like a needle in a haystack ...

I regularly have a coffee in a coffee-shop on D'Olier Street and it takes me past this nice, softly-spoken bloke from Dublin Bus. I think he must be a supervisor or something.

One day, I overheard him talking calmly into his walkie-talkie: 'And tell us, by any chance, did you ever find that bus?'

Overheard by Anonymous, D'Olier Street

Posted on Tuesday, 25 September 2007

Organ-asms!

Was in Biology class and the topic was 'organisms'.

My friend, quite ditsy but genuine, was asked a question by the teacher in front of about 50 others (lecture style):

Teacher: 'Jessica what are organisms?'

Jessica: 'Orgasms are ... '(class erupts in laughter and what was funnier was the fact that she didn't realise what everyone's laughin' at)

Teacher: 'Or-gan-isms, Jessica ...!'

Jessica: 'Oh sorry, Miss, yea, ehm, organ-asms are ...' (another eruption)

Teacher: 'ORGAN-ISMS, JESSICA, ORGAN-ISMS!'

Jessica (in a fluster): 'I KNOW, MISS, I KNOW, I
JUST CAN'T SAY IT, I JUST CAN'T SAY IT, I TRY
BUT ORGASMS KEEPS CUMIN' OUT!'

Overheard by Chloe, sixth-year Biology class
Posted on Tuesday, 25 September 2007

Misheard Lyrics

I was collecting my younger sister and her
friends from swimming lessons a couple of years
back. The song 'Brimful of Asha' was on the
radio and we were all singing happily along. All
of a sudden everyone went quiet and one of my
sister's friends was heard singing at the top of
her lungs, serious as anything,

'There was a binful of rashers on the 45!'

Overheard by K.C., my car
Posted on Monday, 24 September 2007

Utilities!

Overheard a woman saying she had no room in
her kitchen and, 'Would love to get one of those
fertility rooms built on the side of her house for
her washing machine and all the other big
appliances.'

Overheard by Catherine, Submarine Bar
Posted on Monday, 24 September 2007

Never judge a book by its cover!

Nice, polite family gathering. The topic gets
around to Superman. The kids are in full flight,

describing him to elderly Auntie. They get to the bit where they tell her, '... but as soon as he takes all his clothes off, he's Superman!'

Auntie leaves us all breathless with her instant response:

'Aren't we all!'

Overheard by Anonymous, at home,
Montpelier Gardens, Dublin 7
Posted on Monday, 24 September 2007

Left-hand Granny

Out with my grandparents a few years ago, I spotted a foreign registered car driving along. I said to my grandfather, 'Look, Granda, a car with left-hand drive.' My grandmother then says, 'God, that's great, they have everything for left-handers these days!'

Overheard by Alan, driving in Dublin
Posted on Sunday, 23 September 2007

MTV

In my local, Egans in Kilkenny, a couple of Dubs walk in, big hoop earrings, peroxide heads — you know the type. One of them spots the TV:

'Jayus, look they have MTV down here too!'

'We only have a lend of it, we have to give it back to the pub next door in an hour,' replied the barman.

'What a pity,' they say — and walk out!

Overheard by murty, Egans, John Street, Kilkenny
Posted on Sunday, 23 September 2007

A rubbish name for the Ha'penny Bridge!

Waiting to cross the road at the Ha'penny Bridge, I heard an American tourist ask another, 'What's the name of this bridge?' He spotted a word on a bin at the corner and said, 'It's the Bruscar Bridge!'

Overheard by Brenda, at the Ha'penny Bridge
Posted on Sunday, 23 September 2007

Wee Daniel

I was upstairs on the tourist bus going around Dublin. There were some English tourists from Liverpool who were quite loud.

As we drove down O'Connell Street and passed by the statue of Daniel O'Connell, the driver said, 'On our right is a statue of an important Irish figure, Daniel O'Connell.'

On hearing this, one of the English women was shocked and exclaimed in a loud voice,

'I can't believe that the Irish built a statue to that bloody singer!'

Overheard by Jacko, Dublin tourist bus
Posted on Saturday, 22 September 2007

First aid cop

Man collapses in St Stephen's Green and a large crowd gathers around him. A garda goes to his aid and is trying to help him breathe.

Suddenly a man pushes his way to the front of

the crowd and asks the cop, 'Do you need help?'

The garda asks, 'Are you a doctor?'

The man says, 'No, I'm a dentist.'

Garda replies, 'Well, when he has a toothache —
we'll call you!'

Overheard by Bob, St Stephen's Green
Posted on Saturday, 22 September 2007

Institute Geography classes urgently needed!

In the Institute last week, overheard these two
D4 girls on the corridor:

Girl 1: 'Sorry, loike, I didn't catch your name?
I'm Aimee with loike, two Es? And yours?'

Girl 2: 'It's, loike, Maria with one R.'

After a couple of 'haw haw haw haw haws', Girl
1 asks, 'I'm from Sandymount, and you?'

Girl 2: 'Oh, I'm from Cavan, big estate.'

(long awkward pause)

Girl 1: 'So is that, loike, the southside or the
northside?'

Girl 2: (just gives her daggers)

Girl 1: 'What, is it in Wicklow?'

Overheard by Anonymous, Institute of Education, Leeson Street
Posted on Saturday, 22 September 2007

In a time zone all of her own

Watching the France v Ireland rugby match in my
house with a group of friends. One of our

friends, Colm, was over in France at the time.

Richie: 'Here lads, Colm's in France and they're an hour ahead of us. Will I ring him and see what the score is?' (he was of course joking)

Charlene: 'NO! NO! NO! I don't want to know what the score is before seeing the match!'

Ha-ha — we all had a good laugh at that!

Overheard by Andrea, Dún Laoghaire
Posted on Friday, 21 September 2007

The advantage of having a wheelchair

I was standing outside a busy bar on Baggot Street with a few friends when a gent approaches in a wheelchair. He took a look towards the door, looked towards us and said, 'It looks way too busy to go in there.'

At this point my mate piped up, 'I don't know what your problem is, sure you already have a seat.'

Thankfully, the chap in the wheelchair took it well and saw the funny side!

Overheard by The Ballhopper, Toners, Baggot Street
Posted on Friday, 21 September 2007

Drunk and disorderly

Was at an ATM machine one night in Ranelagh and was hassled for change by a homeless guy. At first I was trying to ignore him but couldn't avoid overhearing his rant about how he had earlier been picked up for being drunk and disorderly.

In the thickest Dublin accent you can imagine, this is what he said:

'How the hell can ya be drunk and disorderly when you're asleep?'

Overheard by David, AIB Ranelagh
Posted on Thursday, 20 September 2007

The specialist

A true Dub, sitting at the bar, talking on his phone:

'I'm no gynaecologist, but I'll have a look!'

Overheard by James, Anseo, Camden Street
Posted on Thursday, 20 September 2007

Can I help you? Obviously not!

At Dublin Airport baggage hall a lady walked up to an airport staff member when her bags failed to appear after she arrived.

Lady: 'My bags haven't come out yet.'

Staff Member: 'Has your plane landed yet?'

Overheard by Santos L Helper, in Dublin Airport
Posted on Wednesday, 19 September 2007

Tongue tied

At work in a CD manufacturer we needed a few discs to be tested but they were in a different department. My workmate gets on the phone:

'Hi, who's that? ...

Heya, Margaret, would you be able to pull a

couple of dicks for me? Eh, COUPLE OF DISCS, sorry — a couple of discs?'

Overheard by Tucker, in work
Posted on Wednesday, 19 September 2007

Go on there, get that into your lungs!

Two auld fellas of about 60+ sitting on a park bench, enjoying a rare day of sunshine after a miserable summer.

'Jaysus, isn't life grand all the same?'

'It is too, y'know, sometimes all I need is some fresh air and a cigarette!'

Overheard by Fenster, Fairview Park
Posted on Tuesday, 18 September 2007

Classy bird

After a gig in Vicar Street, queues a mile long for the toilets. One of the lads says to his girlfriend, 'F**k this, I'm going outside.'

His girlfriend says, 'I'm not pissing on the street tonight — I'm in my nice dress!'

Overheard by berta, Vicar Street
Posted on Tuesday, 18 September 2007

Lisp and a northern accent, not a good combination

Guy comes into a builders providers on the Naas Road, with a very strong Northern Irish accent plus a bad lisp.

The man asks for 'shifter bits'.

Guy behind counter: 'Shifter bits?'

Lispy: 'Yeah, shifter bits.'

Counter Guy: 'What's a shifter bit?'

Lispy: 'Bits, bits ...'

Counter Guy: 'Like a drill bit or an adjustable spanner?'

Lispy: 'NO! NO! NO!' (getting pissed off) 'Jeshsus, shifter bits size 8.'

Counter Guy (looking confused): 'Eh, maybe it's a special tool you'd get in a motor factors?'

Lispy: 'Ah, for jeshsus shake!' (man points at a display behind counter) 'Them shifter bits there, are ya shtupid or shomething?'

Counter Guy (turns to the display): 'Aaw, safety boots size 8, no worries!' (while biting his lip!)

Overheard by Anonymous, Heiton's builders providers, Naas Road

Posted on Monday, 17 September 2007

Technugly

Overheard in Ibiza by a group of Dubs beside the pool:

Lad 1: 'Look at yer one!'

Lad 2: 'Would ya stop, big Eircom broadband head on her.'

Lad 1: 'What?'

Lad 2: 'In a bundle!'

Overheard by Stephen, Bariva Apartments, Ibiza

Posted on Saturday, 15 September 2007

A what?

I was next in line with my son to see Santa one Christmas. In front of me was a guy and a little girl and he was asking her what do you say when Santa asks you what you want from him. She says a doll, a bike and something else. It was all very cute. Anyway when she eventually got to see Santa I could overhear the following:

Santa: 'So, little girl, have you been good girl?'

Little Girl: 'Yes.'

Santa: 'So, what do you want from Santa?'

Little Girl: 'A six foot cow!'

Overheard by Anonymous, Santa's grotto
Posted on Friday, 14 September 2007

Overheard on Ballymun bus

Many years ago, I stayed in digs in Glasnevin whilst attending Bolton Street College. One morning I was upstairs on the early morning Ballymun bus into the city. The bus was jammed and a kid whose mother was at the back was running up and down the aisle with a dirty big lollipop! Everyone was pushing in as the kid passed, in case their coats got ruined by the sticky lollipop.

The mother, seeing what was happening, was screaming to the kid, 'Michael, come down here now and sit down next to me.'

After a few minutes of this, the kid turned from the front of the bus and shouted back, 'Mammy, you leave me alone or I'll tell all the people on the bus that you did your wee wee in my potty this morning.'

Overheard by John, Ballymun bus into city
Posted on Friday, 14 September 2007

Can you please abbreviate?

Friend: 'Got your mail and by the way, what does BTW mean?'

Overheard by Anonymous, from a friend
Posted on Friday, 14 September 2007

Not the brightest

Walking along the Grand Canal on a typical rainy day. My friend Jo says, 'Aw, look at the poor swans hiding under the water ... they don't want to get wet!'

Overheard by Anonymous, Harolds Cross
Posted on Tuesday, 11 September 2007

Those were the days

Really old man, hardly walking, heading down O'Connell Street, hanging off of the arm of (who seemed to be) his daughter.

'Jaynee, how things change,' says he.

She seemed to be half ignoring the poor chap.

'I remember the Nelsons Pillar, Angela. If you met a young wan there it was said that — with a little bit of luck — you'd get your nuts.'

She looked mortified!

Overheard by Anonymous, O'Connell Street
Posted on Monday, 10 September 2007

Viva Las Skerries!

Was having a few beers with friends in a mate's house and got a game of cards going. While we were getting the cards ready a friend volunteered to go to the shop to get supplies. We asked him to get a box of matches so we could use them as chips for poker.

He returned, saying that the shop had no matches — but he'd got a lighter instead!

Overheard by P, mate's house
Posted on Monday, 10 September 2007

Hard of hearing?

Walking over Portobello Bridge one morning, running late.

Pissing rain. Freezing cold. Traffic mad. Everyone miserable. You get the picture.

The path on the bridge was crowded so it was slow.

Thirty-something woman beside me says to a little auld one in passing, maybe in her seventies:

'Ah, howaya Miriam. How ye keepin, haven't seen ye in bleedin' aaages? Jayzuz, isn't eh' a'ter getting' real cold?'

To which your one goes,

'Ah, would you ever f**k off, you're not lookin' too young there yourself!'

Overheard by LongMileRoad, Portobello
Posted on Sunday, 9 September 2007

Charmer

A group of girls were sitting in the smoking room at the local pub. They were asking people who came in, 'How old do you think I am?' and so forth.

When one of the regulars came into the smoking room, he was asked, 'Here, how old do I look?'

He replied, 'I don't know, but if you sit on my face, I'll guess your weight!'

Overheard by JUNIORF, in the smoking room at the local
Posted on Thursday, 6 September 2007

Wake-up call

I was on my way to work in Dublin early one cold winter's morning a few years back, and said 'Good morning' to an elderly man as I passed him.

'Listen, love,' he replied, 'any morning I can throw me bollix out of the bed and follow them is a good morning!'

Overheard by Anonymous, Omni car park
Posted on Thursday, 6 September 2007

Kids really do say the funniest things

I'd just got home from work to find the eight year old jumping up and down with excitement at an upcoming party. She was bursting with questions: 'What will I wear? What can I bring?'

With a thousand other immediate things to do right away, I told her to wait till later — this party was the last thing on my mind.

About 10 minutes later she sidled up to me again with the question, 'Maaaaammm! Are you at the end of your mind yet?'

Overheard by Anonymous, at home, Dublin 7
Posted on Thursday, 6 September 2007

Foot in mouth!

A DIY-er in a major hardware outlet, discussing the size of an extractor fan he wanted for his kitchen.

DIY-er: '... not sure about the size ...'

Assistant: 'Well then, wouldn't you like to go home and measure your hole?'

Overheard by Anonymous, B & Q
Posted on Wednesday, 5 September 2007

Bad choice of words?

Arrived in the village to post a letter, only to find a postman crouched on his hunkers emptying the letterbox. To my absolute horror I heard myself say, 'Do you mind if I give you one?'

Couldn't get away fast enough!

Overheard by Anonymous, a village somewhere in County Dublin
Posted on Tuesday, 4 September 2007

Foreigners?

At a bus stop in Ringsend, two true-blue Dubs having a conversation about their work colleagues. The boyos appeared to be builders of some sort, and one said to the other,

'Jaysus, dis lad I'm workin' wit, I can never understand a word he is saying.' The other responded, 'Why? Is he foreign?' to which the other replied, 'No, he's English!'

Overheard by Louis, Ringsend
Posted on Saturday, 1 September 2007

Nice compliment

During the Dublin and Kerry match last week, Diarmuid Murphy the Kerry keeper was getting a bit of stick from the Dubs on the Hill when someone shouted down,

'Diarmuid, you have a head like a melted welly!'

Overheard by Eoin, Hill 16
Posted on Thursday, 30 August 2007

Political confusion

At the recent match between Dublin and Derry, I had the pleasure of standing in front of an opinionated Dub fan, with an obvious abundance of political ideology. His first rant was directed clearly at the Garda Band at half time: 'FREE STATE BASTARDS'

He's clearly of a republican persuasion, I thought, but his republican credentials were somewhat tarnished when he began his second rant, directed at the Derry fans: 'BLEEDIN' ENGLISH BASTARDS, SHUDIN' EVEN BE PLAYING FOOTBALL IT'S A BLEEDIN' 32-COUNTY ALL-IRELAND GAME, NO BLEEDIN' ENGLISH GAME'

I — along with others — was in fits of laughter at this. I had to turn around and put a face to the stupidity, and yes, he was every inch I pictured him — right down to the silly moustache.

Overheard by Dave, Hill 16
Posted on Tuesday, 28 August 2007

Well at least he had the manners to inform me

I got onto the no. 78A bus, found no seats downstairs so decided to try upstairs. I found an empty seat and was about to sit down when some bloke yells,

'HERE, MISSUS, I wouldn't sit there if I were you, I just pissed there!'

Overheard by Roisin, no. 78A bus
Posted on Tuesday, 28 August 2007

Fallen comrades

Me: 'Hi, I'm hoping to get a taxi back to Glasnevin.'

Woman: 'Okay, where are you now?'

Me: 'Terenure College.'

Woman: 'Okay, where's that?'

Me: 'Em, Terenure.'

Woman (sighs then sarky): 'Thanks ...'

Me: 'No, sorry, I'm not being smart, I'm not from here. I just know it's Terenure College. I don't know the street names outside.'

Woman: 'Well can you not look at the signs?'

Me: 'Afraid not, the main gate is a good distance away from where I'm standing now.'

Woman: 'That wasn't very clever. How are we going to find you?'

Me: 'It's a school ... you can come up the drive. I'll be the only person standing around.'

Woman (laughs now): 'But WHERE in Terenure is the school?'

Me (laughing): 'You guys dropped me here this morning from Glasnevin. You lot stranded me out here in the first place, so SOMEONE there knows where it is.'

Woman (laughing): 'Fine ... be half an hour.'

When I get in the cab, the driver gets on the radio: 'Mary, have found Lost Northsider and am returning to base ...'

Mary: 'Roger that, Sean ... we never leave a man behind.'

Overheard by Fred, Terenure College
Posted on Sunday, 26 August 2007

Tiger Kidnapping

My 18-year-old brother was playing footie on a green in Swords with his mates, this was during the whole 'tiger kidnapping' scandals with the bank managers and stuff. Anyway, on this particular day one of the kidnappings occured in one of the houses on the green where he was playing so the police call him in for questioning as a possible witness.

Garda: 'Now, tell me what you saw, anything suspicious, anyone just hanging around that you didn't recognise?'

Bro: 'No, saw nothing really, mad though, I wuda thought I'd hav noticed "that" like!!'

Garda: 'What do you mean by "that"??'

Bro: 'Well deffo wuda noticed if I saw a tiger around Swords, didn't think people could have tigers as pets ... deffo not playing round there again, I'd be sh***in' meself if it escaped!!'

Overheard by Jenny, Swords
Posted on Friday, 25 August 2007

Location Location Location

I rang a restaurant during the week to book a table. I wasn't quite sure of the location so I asked, 'Where exactly are you?' The waiter replied,

'I'm standing in front of the till next to the door!'

Overheard by kopfile, Little Caesars
Posted on Friday, 24 August 2007

Very Lost

Outside a bus stop in Trinity College an American came up to me with a map and asked,

'Which road do I take to get to Belgium?'

Overheard by Tom, bus stop outside Trinity
Posted on Friday, 24 August 2007

Pizzas and buckets

Was in an Italian restaurant on Dame Street the other night. Two girls sit down at the table next to me and my girlfriend, and one of the girls ask for a pizza.

Girl #1: 'How big are your pizzas?'

Waiter: 'Nine inch, 12 inch ...'

Girl #1: 'How big is the 9 inch?'

Waiter laughing: 'About the size of the plate in front of you.'

Girl #1: 'And what's the difference between the 9 inch and the 12 inch?'

Waiter: 'Three inches!'

Girl #1: 'I don't know, I'll just order chicken wings.'

Girl #2: 'I'll have those as well and will ya give us one of those things that comes in a bucket with the ice as well?'

Waiter: 'A bucket?'

Girl #2: 'Ye know, the bottles.'

Waiter: 'You mean wine or champagne?'

Girl #2: 'Yeah one of those, the nicest ones.'

Waiter walks off ...

Girl #1: 'Bleeding Italians don't having a bleeding clue what they're talking about.'

Overheard by John, Dame Street
Posted on Friday, 24 August 2007

Clear as ...

Walking through the corridor in St Aidan's CBS, Whitehall, when I overheard a teacher called Mr McCrystal giving out to a young lad.

Mr McCrystal: 'Now I won't have that anymore, you got that, never again. Am I clear?'

Young Lad: 'Yes, sir, Mc-crystal clear.'

Overheard by Dunid, St Aidan's CBS, Whitehall
Posted on Friday, 24 August 2007

My Nan

My Nanny is chatting to her friends in the pub:

Nanny: 'My nephew is living in Australia for the

past 12 years, he's a paedophile.'

People didn't know what to say ...

Nanny: 'Ye, he drives an ambulance!'

Oh, *paramedic*!

Overheard by Sheriff2, pub
Posted on Friday, 24 August 2007

Metric spuds

Overheard in fruit & veg market:

Old Lady: 'Can I have five pounds of potatoes, please.'

Market Trader: 'Sorry luv, it's now kilos.'

Old Lady: 'Ok, can I have five pounds of kilos please!'

Overheard by RayG, fruit & veg market
Posted on Thursday, 23 August 2007

A worse alternative?

Sitting at home with me niece one morning and she asked for some popcorn. Me Ma turns around and says, 'No, no, love, it's too early for popcorn. Do you want some cake instead?'

Overheard by Nx, at home
Posted on Thursday, 23 August 2007

Culture differences

I was out having a smoke in the local when I overheard three heads having a heated discussion about the recent turban-wearing Sikh garda, and heard this classic:

'Sure, give them a few years and they'll be patrolling O'Connell Street on elephants!'

Overheard by phil, the local
Posted on Wednesday, 22 August 2007

Kids are mad!

Was talking to my friend the other night, with his three-year-old son who's a very cheeky chappy indeed!

I took out a packet of sweets and offered the kid one. After taking it, his father asks, 'Now son, what do you say if a stranger offers you sweets?' The kid replies 'Yes!'

Disgusted at his reply my mate says in a very firm tone, 'What! No, that's not what you say! What do you say if a stranger offers you bleedin' sweets?!'

Kid shoots back, 'Yes ... PLEASE!'

Overheard by Anonymous, mate's house
Posted on Wednesday, 22 August 2007

A caring Dub

One half of a mobile phone conversation, in Abbey Street yesterday:

'Ah, how's it going, John?'

PAUSE

'C'mere to me, were ye caught in the hurricane?'

PAUSE

'Ye big sap!'

Overheard by Dean, Abbey Street
Posted on Wednesday, 22 August 2007

Ty-ezz fer by-ezz

I went into a children's clothes shop in Tallaght and asked the shop assistant if they stocked ties, as my young son wanted one.

She said, looking at me as if I had several heads, 'Ty-ez? Yer lookin' for Tyy-ezz?'

'Yes', I answered, 'do you have any?'

'We don't have any roo-em for ty-ez.' She then added, 'There's the biggest tie shop in Ireland round the bleedin' corner, for f*** sake.'

It took me a moment to realise she was referring to Smyths, the TOY shop!

Overheard by Katie, Tallaght
Posted on Tuesday, 21 August 2007

Motherly instinct

Sitting in front of me on the Luas, a small lad about three or four years old is talking to his grandmother: 'Nan, my Ma says I'm never to talk to strangers.'

'Yes, your mother is right, love,' says Gran.

After a fairly long pause of about two minutes the kid says to Gran, 'Nan, what's a stranger?'

Overheard by Phil, Luas Jervis Street
Posted on Tuesday, 21 August 2007

Burglars

When one of my brothers was in primary school, it was the first day back after the summer and the teacher was asking the kids about their holidays. One girl shot her hand in the air, gasping to tell her most exciting news.

'Miss, our house was burgled!'

'Oh, that's terrible, Fiona, do they know who did it?'

'My Daddy said it was gobshites!'

Overheard by Kev, St Mary's primary school
Posted on Monday, 20 August 2007

In the Know

On the FM104 radio phone show there was a heated discussion about the case of the Sikh man who was refused entry into the Garda reserve force unless he stopped wearing his turban on duty.

This Dublin young fellah gets on and drawls, 'The garda were right, I mean if he arrested me I'd wanna see the top of his head so I know what's goin' on like, you know what I mean?'

The mind boggles ...

Overheard by Sara, FM104
Posted on Monday, 20 August 2007

Like father like son

A very long time ago when I was on a school outing we went to the National Gallery. One of the lads, Tom,* was the son of a notorious Dublin criminal, who was in hiding at the time. We had a guided tour and at the end we had some time to ask some questions. Tom got really excited and asked the tour guide a million questions.

'Which painting is worth the most?'

'Are there sensors on the walls?'

'How many security guards are on at night?' (you get the picture)

The tour guide was really impressed by his enthusiasm ...

*Name changed for obvious reasons.

Overheard by C, The National Gallery

Posted on Monday, 20 August 2007

Star struck

11 August, two young girls on the bus.

Girl 1: 'Do you want me to read you out your stars?'

Girl 2: 'No, I don't believe in them.'

Girl 1: 'What ... they are soooo true.'

Girl 2: 'Go on so.'

Girl 1: 'OK then, what's your sign?'

Girl 2: 'Virgo.'

Girl 1 (ruffles through the page looking for Virgo then in absolute amazement): 'I don't believe it!'

Girl 2: 'Oh my God, what is it, what's it say?'

Girl 1: 'A hectic time; with your birthday only around the corner, plans need to be made ...'

Girl 2 interrupting: 'It knows about me 18th?'

Girl 1: 'I told ya, it's always right.'

Overheard by Dunid, bus in Drumcondra
Posted on Monday, 20 August 2007

Big mouth Dad

I was waiting for the bus on Dame Street and was explaining to my Dad (who is English) how southsiders and northsiders generally tend to slag each other. Being from the southside, I told him how we say all the scumbags are from the northside (not true of course, there's plenty on the south!).

We get on the bus and sit down. Dad looks around and says in a really loud voice in his posh English accent, 'This bus looks like it's full of northsiders!'

All I could say was 'Shhhhhhhhhhhhh!' and just glared at him, stared straight ahead and hoped nobody heard a thing!

Overheard by Anonymous, on the bus
Posted on Friday, 17 August 2007

Elevated

An elderly woman steps from the DART at Glenageary station and looks slightly unsure of her bearings. A young Chinese man in an Iarnród Éireann top is in the elevator, so the elderly woman approaches him.

Elderly Woman: 'Is this Glenageary?'

Young Chinese Man (clearly with little comprehension of English): 'What?'

Elderly Woman: 'Is this Glenageary station?'

Young Chinese Man (baffled): 'What?'

Elderly Woman (increasingly flustered): 'Is this the DART stop for Glenageary?'

Young Chinese Man (triumphantly): 'No, this is elevator!'

Doors shut, elevator goes up ...

Overheard by peter, Glenageary DART station
Posted on Wednesday, 15 August 2007

The dearest

While driving my taxi I had an elderly passenger who said, 'You're the dearest taxi I have ever got from this shopping centre, €6.47 and we haven't even left the shops!'

I looked at her and said, 'That's the time you're looking at — not the meter!'

Overheard by Anonymous, in my taxi
Posted on Tuesday, 14 August 2007

Mis-heard in Dublin

Was out in the pub last Friday with a few mates from work. One particular guy brought his brother in with him. His brother, who is gay, and himself recently bought an apartment together, something I'm also in the process of doing. So I saunter up to my mate's brother (who I shall call Dave) and the following exchange takes place:

Me: 'How's it going, Dave? Question for ya.'

Dave: 'Sure.'

Me: 'You're a home-owner now, right?'

Dave: 'What? I'm a homo?!'

Me: 'Home-owner! HOME-OWNER!'

Overheard by Pete, pub in the city centre
Posted on Tuesday, 14 August 2007

An audience with the commode

I spent some time in hospital at Christmas. The ward was full of elderly women. One woman was unable to walk so needed to use a commode (she called it the po). One morning she started screaming that she needed the po.

I rang the bell for the nurse, who was Filipino. She started explaining to her that it was very early — it was only 6.30 a.m. I thought that this was a bit cruel, so I called the nurse over and told her that the woman was looking for the commode.

The nurse put her head in her hands, started laughing, and told me she, 'thought the woman was saying she wanted to see the Pope!'

Overheard by Anonymous, Beaumont Hospital
Posted on Monday, 13 August 2007

When I + I doesn't ADD up

Talking to my sister about a relation of ours, I said, 'I think he has OCD.'

She says, 'No, he has ADD.'

I said, 'What's the difference?'

She said, 'OCD means you have to keep cleaning everything around you, and ADD means you're a little bollix!'

Overheard by Intel, at home having a few drinks
Posted on Monday, 13 August 2007

I guess this adds to the continuity

More overseen than overheard. On the train line between Connolly and Clontarf there's some graffiti saying 'CONTINUITUITY IRA'.

Some genius having trouble knowing when to *stop* spelling the name of the group they support is a new one on me ...

Overheard by Cian, the DART between Connolly and Clontarf
Posted on Friday, 10 August 2007

Mis-heard

Many years ago, repeating the Leaving Cert in Ringsend, I was taking in some quiet study time in the school library, in preparation for the exams. In walks the principal and utters what I thought was, 'Terrible stuffy in here.'

I replied, 'Yes, indeed,' and left it at that. Then once again the principal repeated what I thought was, 'Terrible stuffy in here.'

Again I replied, 'Yes, indeed.' I was asked by the principal to step outside and explain my cheek!

Getting to the bottom of it, she wanted to know if Terrence Duffy was here ... Confused or what?

Overheard by Emmet, Ringsend Dublin
Posted on Thursday, 9 August 2007

The 'M' word

In Biology class many years ago, studying the female reproductive system, the teacher asked what was the name for this monthly occurrence.

Johnny starts, 'Sir, sir,' really eager, which was unusual for this individual but obviously it was one of those rare times when he knew the answer and he wasn't going to miss out.

Teacher: 'Yes, Johnny?'

Johnny: 'Sir, sir, the masturbation cycle!'

We pissed ourselves ...

Overheard by seahorse, school
Posted on Thursday, 9 August 2007

Dublin schoolboy wit

Teacher at the end of Biology lesson:

'So, boys, what causes an erection?' (expecting the answer 'bloodflow to the penis, etc.')

Loooong embarrassed pause. Boy down the back of the class:

'YER MA!'

Overheard by Mrs Mogsey, local Bro's school
Posted on Wednesday, 8 August 2007

First date conversation

Was in a restaurant on Georges Street at the weekend and overheard the following conversation between a young couple sitting at the table next to me who looked as if they were on a first date.

Initially there is one of those long, awkward silences until the girl pipes up in her D4 accent, 'So, do you like jogging?'

There is another long silence until the guy, clearly confused by the question goes, 'Uh ... ya.'

To which she replies, 'Oh, I love jogging ... it's so much quicker than walking.'

Overheard by jonnyfu, restaurant on Georges Street
Posted on Tuesday, 7 August 2007

Don't argue with the gay flight attendant

My flight was being served by a camp flight attendant, who seemed to put everyone in a good mood as he served us food and drinks.

As the plane prepared to descend, he came swishing down the aisle and told us, 'Captain Marvey has asked me to announce that he'll be landing the plane shortly, so, lovely people, if you could just put your trays up, that would be super.'

On his trip back up the aisle, he noticed that an extremely well-dressed and exotic young woman hadn't moved a muscle.

'Perhaps you didn't hear me over those big brute engines, but I asked you to raise your tray, so the main man can pop us on the ground.'

She calmly turned her head and said, 'In my country, I am called a Princess and I take orders from no one.'

To which the flight attendant replied, without missing a beat, 'Well, sweet-cheeks, in my country I'm called a Queen, so I out-rank you. Tray up, Bitch.'

Overheard by beets, Delta flight to New York
Posted on Tuesday, 7 August 2007

Off to Funtasia

My brother's friend was over and was telling us he's going on holidays next week.

I asked where he'll be going and he said, 'Funtasia.'

He's actually going to Tunisia ...

Overheard by L, at home
Posted on Monday, 6 August 2007

Chips with everything

In a five-star restaurant recently, my husband wanted chips with his meal, but my daughter and I insisted that — because of our posh surroundings — he ask for 'French fries'.

Having taken our order, the waiter was then asked for a side order of French fries, to which he replied that he was sorry, they didn't have any — would chips do instead?!

Overheard by Anonymous, in a five-star restaurant, no less!
Posted on Monday, 6 August 2007

Scary

On the no. 130 bus home to Clontarf, some bird on her phone:

'Hiye, yea, listen we're goin' te Skerries ... no man, Skerries ... What d'ye mean? Can ye not hear me? SKERRIES! S. C. A. R. Y. S.'

I couldn't laugh at the time for fear of getting my head kicked in ...

Overheard by Josie, the no. 130 bus
Posted on Monday, 6 August 2007

Ryanair wit

Was on the plane home from Spain the other day.

As usual, at the end when we are waiting to get off the plane, the pilot's voice comes over the speakers, 'Thank you for flying Ryanair,' etc.

Just as we think he's finished, he comes out with this:

'... and it's very rainy in Dublin this evening. If you don't have an umbrella, you might need to contact Rihanna, and ask her for an umbrella, ella, ella.'

Certainly a break away from the usual, 'Flight time is two hours ...' etc.

Cheap flights, and a bit of humour: what more could you ask for!

Overheard by cc, Ryanair flight!
Posted on Sunday, 5 August 2007

Ballyer at Heathrow

I was going through Heathrow Airport a few years ago getting a connecting flight to the States. I got talking to a guy originally from Ballyfermot who now lived in New York.

He was a rough looking guy, and wasn't too fond of the British airport authorities.

Before going through customs he told me he could guarantee that they would stop and question him.

Apparently he was always stopped.

Anyway, we arrived at the part where they check

your passport and the airport customs guy asks in his finest English accent, 'Are we going anywhere nice today, Sir?'

The bloke from Ballyfermot replied,

'Well, I'm going somewhere nice, but I don't remember f**king inviting you anywhere!'

Overheard by Anonymous, Heathrow Airport

Posted on Saturday, 4 August 2007

At the cinema

Was at the cinema years ago when Jaws came out and at the start of the film the camera is in the water looking onto a quiet beach. It's moving back and forth, we see a young couple about to come in swimming and the Jaws music is playing. Not a sound out of anyone when we overhear a voice at the front, 'Jaysis how'd they get a fish to operate a camera?'

Overheard by Alan, cinema

Posted on Sunday, 4 August 2007

The magic word ...

My four-year-old sister was asking me to get her something (I forget what) and I said to her, 'What's the magic word?'

Sister: 'Abracadabra!'

Me: 'No, it starts with P. 'P–L ...'

Sister: 'Plabracadabra!'

I think she needs some lessons in manners ...

Overheard by CoolKitty, at home
Posted on Saturday, 4 August 2007

Orange juice and coffee — together at last

In Supermac's on O'Connell Street about three years ago, I was standing at the counter and the following conversation took place.

Customer: 'Hi, see this voucher I have, "Buy a burger and get a free 7Up"?'

Guy behind the counter: 'Yeah?'

Customer: 'Instead of a 7Up, can I get an orange juice?'

Supermac's Staff Kid: 'Yeah, okay.'

Customer: 'Great. Eh, instead of buying a burger, can I buy a coffee and still get the free 7Up?'

Supermac's staff kid: 'Hold on, I'll ask someone.'

(kid explains customer query to manager)

Supermac's manager (looking annoyed): 'Yeah, okay.'

Supermac's staff kid (to the customer): 'Do you want those in separate cups?'

Overheard by Neilo Indestructibloke,
Supermac's in O'Connell Street
Posted on Wednesday, 1 August 2007

Children of Lir ...

Two girls passed me by on O'Connell Street, obviously discussing a recent History class.

Girl 1: 'And they were changed back from swans after 900 years ...'

Girl 2: 'Nine hundred years? Jaysus, imagine waking up after nine hundred years ... sure you'd be f**ked!'

Overheard by Anonymous, O'Connell Street
Posted on Tuesday, 31 July 2007

Cinderella's fella

Standing outside Burger King on Grafton Street about four o'clock on a Sunday morning, one shoe in my hand because my feet were killing me. Lad wearing a white tracksuit, baseball cap, sovereigns comes up to me and asks me can he have my shoe.

'What do ya want my shoe for?' I said.

'So I can find ya in de mornin'!'

Overheard by Anonymous, Grafton Street
Posted on Tuesday, 31 July 2007

Wherever they may rome

Waiting for a few mates on Grafton Street on Friday night, two fairly posh girls in their mid 20s walking past:

Girl 1: 'Did you hear about that Roma family on the M50 roundabout? Terrible isn't it?'

Girl 2: 'I know!' (gasping) 'And I thought Italy was a developed country!'

Overheard by The Long Fellow, Grafton Street
Posted on Monday, 30 July 2007

The art of subtlety

At the hurling in Croker over the weekend. Walking up Clonliffe Road after the games. A garda sitting on a horse which was very well endowed. Lad about thirty yards away shouts up the road,

'Would ya look at the bollox on the horse!'

Overheard by Cyril sneer, Clonliffe Road
Posted on Sunday, 29 July 2007

The 78A to Outer Mongolia

On the no. 78A bus there was the usual group of skangers upstairs, one of them is talking (very loudly) about travelling.

Skanger 1: 'Ya know wha, you never really know anythin' about life until you've travelled.'

Skanger 2: 'Yeah, like what?'

Skanger 1: 'Ya know, like about how other people live and how different life is in other places, it opens your mind, ya know!'

Skanger 2: 'No way, and where did you go?'

Skanger 1: 'Torremolinos ... it's in Spain.'

I was half expecting her to say Outer Mongolia or something!

Overheard by Jenny, no. 78A bus
Posted on Tuesday, 24 July 2007

Smoke gets in your eyes

Overheard by a Dub in Atlanta.

Four middle-aged 'chandeliers' eating and drinking and smoking like troopers. Disgusted lady at the next table bursts out in an exasperated voice,

'Gentlemen, your cigarette smoke is really bothering me.'

'It's killing me!' said the oldest and most flamboyant.

Overheard by daddyo, Atlanta
Posted on Tuesday, 24 July 2007

The flying nuns

Not so much overheard as seen in Dublin.

My Nan got tickets at Christmas time for a hymn concert being given by the nuns. On the bottom of the ticket was,

'No moshing or crowd surfing.'

Need I say more ...

Overheard by Shedevil, my Nan's house
Posted on Monday, 23 July 2007

May cause drowsiness?

In a doctor's surgery with my three-year-old daughter.

Doctor: 'Give her one 5 ml spoonful three times a day before meals and don't let her operate a bicycle ...'

Overheard by Cal, doctor's surgery
Posted on Friday, 20 July 2007

The clap

As our plane taxied to a halt at Dublin Airport a couple of months ago, the passengers broke into a spontaneous round of applause. An old dear, seated beside a retired pilot, smiled knowingly at him and was heard to say,

'I'll bet you OFTEN got the clap!'

Overheard on a plane which had just landed at Dublin Airport
Posted on Friday, 20 July 2007

Colour-blind

Girl walking down O'Connell Street wearing a purple and black stripey jumper. Scumbag shouts over to her, 'Here, Missus, watcha tink ye ar, a bee or somtin?!'

Overheard by botsy, O'Connell Street
Posted on Wednesday, 18 July 2007

An old excuse reworked

My friend walked into work a bit late one day and said,

'Sorry I'm late, me dog ate me watch,' expecting no one to believe him. Later on that day a woman in the office came up to him and said in a serious manner,

'Sorry to hear about your dog eating your watch, was it expensive?'

Overheard by turbo, work
Posted on Wednesday, 18 July 2007

Good weekend

Heard a lad shout this out of his tent to someone at the Oxegen festival:

'You can take me virginity, but yer not gettin' any of me bleedin' cans!'

Overheard by Handbag, Oxegen
Posted on Tuesday, 17 July 2007

Pub crawl

A few years ago having a few drinks in the Stork pub on Cork Street, just two doors down from Morrissey's pub. Watching United against Blackburn. Blackburn go 2-0 up.

Not long after this a bloke walks in, looks up at the telly and says, 'Ahh, f**k this, I'm going back up to Morrissey's — its only 1-0 up there!'

Overheard by John, the Stork pub
Posted on Monday, 16 July 2007

Candid camera

Walking into Oxegen last week and in the car park there was the usual collection of vendors selling their wares. As we passed, a guy shouted out, 'Get your camerits,' much to the amusement of my English boyfriend. Just as we're about to crack up, another seller in front of us shouts out the same thing!

How do we explain where the 'its' came from?

Overheard by Anna, Oxegen festival car park
Posted on Monday, 16 July 2007

Selective sunshine

On the last proper day of glorious sunshine my girlfriend and I went to Donabate beach. We were lying in the sun when I heard this bickering beside me.

Girl 1: 'It's fucken freezen!'

Girl 2: 'Let's go to the other end of the beach, it's warmer!'

Girl 1: 'Why?'

Girl 2: 'Cuz the sun is shinen down there!'

Overheard by Alan, Donabate beach

Posted on Sunday, 15 July 2007

Cheap thrills

Overheard two lads working in a lift shaft, first lad had just got off the phone.

First Lad: 'That was me mate, d'ye wanna buy a rampant rabbit for yer moth? Only 30 quid!'

Second Lad: 'What, like to breed other rabbits?'

First Lad: 'What?'

Second Lad: 'Like a sex-mad rabbit?'

First Lad: 'Are you bleedin' serious?'

Overheard by sammy, on a site in Cookstown

Posted on Sunday, 15 July 2007

The new curate

Two ladies at the hairdressers, discussing the new foreign curate:

'Ah sure, he gives LOVELY sermons. It's just a pity you can't understand the half of them!'

Overheard by Anonymous, at the hairdressing salon

Posted on Saturday, 14 July 2007

The no. 145 bus ... you've gotta love it

Getting the no. 145 bus home from town last night around 11, there was four 'head the balls' on their way home, all drunk. There were three girls and one lad. One of the girls said to the fella, 'Wat were ya in fur?'

He replied, 'Aaarmed robbery 'n GBH.'

Her reply to that was, 'I don't mind a bit of greviouslee badily herm meself!'

Overheard by James, no. 145 bus
Posted on Friday, 13 July 2007

Explaining the complexities of life

English class and we were reading extracts from whatever novel we were studying, taking turns to read. One of the lads at the back, John, was daydreaming, but was interrupted by the teacher.

Teacher: 'John, what is love?'

John (in deep thought); 'Well, Miss, love is like when a man and a woman ...'

Teacher (interrupting): 'No, John, read the paragraph starting with "What is love?"'

Overheard by flanman, English class
Posted on Friday, 13 July 2007

Best excuse ever

Two years ago when I was in school, this guy, bit of a joker, saunters into French class half an hour late. The following conversation took place.

Teacher (in her French accent): 'Mark! Where have you been?'

Mark (strong Dublin accent): 'Eh, I was down in

Mr Darcy's (the principal) office.'

Teacher: 'Yes, Mark, I know that, I was down in Mr Darcy's office half an hour ago, he said he'd only keep you for ten minutes, that was half an hour ago, where have you been since?'

Mark: 'Eh, well I bumped into Keego on the way back ...'

Teacher: 'Yes, and ...?'

Mark: 'Ah, sure ya kno yourself when ya get chattin', Miss ...'

Classic!

Overheard by Dave, Institute of Education
Posted on Thursday, 12 July 2007

Francophilia

Three girls talking up their sexual experiences.

The 1st says she'd had a 'menage a twa'.

The 2nd asks what that is.

The 3rd says, 'It's French for a rendezvous between three people.'

Overheard by Tadaa!!!, on the no. 75 bus to Dun Laoghaire
Posted on Thursday, 12 July 2007

Politically incorrect

Two girls in work discussing refugees.

Girl 1: 'There's so many African-Americans in Dublin!'

Girl 2: 'African-Americans? That's not what you call black people!'

Girl 1: 'I thought that was the PC term.'

Girl 2: 'Only if they are American.'

Girl 1: 'Oh yeah, well there's so many African-American-Irish in Dublin.'

Overheard by Cal, work
Posted on Thursday, 12 July 2007

To court or Cork?

A couple of years ago when he was four, I asked my son if he would like to go to Cork on holidays. He looked at me with a horrified face and said, 'But I've been a good boy, why do I have to go to Cork?'

I was a little confused, so I asked him what was wrong and his answer was,

'All the bold people go to Cork and the judge bashes them with his hammer!'

Overheard by emmsy, at home
Posted on Tuesday, 10 July 2007

Spoonful of sugar

In Capitol last Friday night, heading upstairs, and this girl walks down the stairs, kind of big build, large chested, and we just hear a guy shout to his mate,

'Here, have ya got any Calpol? She's very chesty!'

Overheard by The Decadent Kids, Capitol
Posted on Monday, 9 July 2007

The dog's b*ll*x

Last week my son turned around and said,

'Dad, now I know what those things are between Peanut's legs.' I looked at our West Highland Terrier, Peanut, who was lying on his back with his legs wide open.

'What are they?' I asked anticipating the answer. 'They're his balls,' he said with a grin. I smiled and said,

'That's right, they *are* his balls.' He looked at the dog and said,

'I used to think they were his brains!'

Overheard by Jay, at home
Posted on Sunday, 8 July 2007

Crash landing

Seen rather than heard.

Written on the emergency plastic card in the back sleeve of the seat on an Aer Lingus plane (the part where the man has his head bent down whilst holding on to the seat in front). Big speech bubble:

'OH SHIT!'

Overheard by Phil, Aer Lingus plane
Posted on Friday, 6 July 2007

D4 lad a little out of touch

I was walking down Baggot Street Lower outside the Bank of Ireland head office when I overheard one D4 lad say to the other country lad in a posh accent:

'Hey, do you want to go and get a few britneys (beers) after work?'

Country Lad: 'I'm headin' back home. I'm goin' baling.'

D4 Lad: 'What's baling? Is that a new water sport or something?'

Surprised, the country boy replied: 'Cutting the grass and putting it together.'

D4 Lad: 'Oh, does that still go on?'

Overheard by peter, Baggot Street Lower
Posted on Thursday, 28 June 2007

Election muddle

Heading home from work on the bus during the general election and there's a poster up of Noel Ahern (Bertie's brother).

Girl #1: 'Jaysus, Bertie looks completely different in his posters, doesn't he?'

Girl #2: 'That's his brother.'

Girl #1: 'No it's not, it says "Ahern" not "O'Hern" on it.'

Overheard by Ash, no. 17a bus Dublin
Posted on Monday, 25 June 2007

Not making a splash ...

In Briody's pub yesterday after the match, one of the kids was talking about scuba diving and asked us (quite loudly),

'Why do scuba divers always fall backwards off

the boat?' Before any of us could answer, one of the old pint-suppers pipes up — without even turning around from the bar,

'Because if they fell forwards they would still be on the boat!'

Overheard by peter, Briody's pub, Marlborough Street
Posted on Monday, 25 June 2007

Nobody Knows

On Hill 16 for the Dublin v Offaly Leinster semi-final. There was a minute's silence for a recently deceased GAA member. About 40 seconds into the minute's silence, some wise-crack said,

'I DON'T KNOW WHAT A TRACKER MORTGAGE IS ...'

Overheard by Alan, Hill 16, Dublin match
Posted on Monday, 25 June 2007

Joining in the festivities

I decided to check out Gay Pride on Saturday. I have a new camera, and I wanted to get some practice with it. These two blokes approached me, a bit of a smell of drink off them, but in good form.

'We want to be on the front page of the *Irish Times* — take our photo!'

I played along. They invited one of their female friends to join them in the picture, and I took a picture of the three of them, one of the blokes giving the other a kiss on the cheek. I showed them the photo.

'Eh, we're just in town for the day — what's this parade about?'

Overheard by Anonymous, Parnell Square East, just
before the start of the Gay Pride parade
Posted on Monday, 25 June 2007

Here comes trouble ...

A few years back I was walking through a north Dublin housing estate where I saw two women talking at a gate. A young fella walked out of the house and passed the women. Without stopping the conversation, one of the women slapped the young fella on the back of the head as he passed.

Young Fella: 'Wha was dat for?'

Woman: 'You're either coming from trouble or goin' to it so you deserve a clip round the ear for whatever you done, or whatever you're about to do!'

Young Fella: 'Ah, Maaaaaaaaaaa!'

Overheard by Anonymous, De North Side
Posted on Thursday, 21 June 2007

Tinky Winky goes to the deed poll office

Babysitting my friend's little girl the other day (she's two) and she sat down to watch Teletubbies. She was telling me all about them, so I asked her what their names were. Apparently they're now called Po, Dipsy, Lala and Winky Wanky!

Overheard by Anonymous, my friend's house
Posted on Thursday, 21 June 2007

They'll take your job next ...

St Patrick's Day 2004, my brother and I were going to the airport to meet our Mam who'd been away. We got a taxi, and in conversation with the driver we somehow got onto the fact that our President, Mary McAleese, is from the six counties.

Some time later, conversation got round to the long fellow, Eamon De Valera, who was Spanish/American.

Sometime after that, we got round to St Patrick, who was Welsh.

The taxi driver said, 'Typical, all the good jobs are taken by foreigners!'

Overheard by FrankO, taxi to Dublin Airport
Posted on Wednesday, 20 June 2007

Flirtatious in a sober drunk way

Girl 1 (to drunk friend): 'Oh my God, you are so drunk. Stop behaving like you did out there!'

Drunk Girl: 'What? I wasn't behaving? What do you mean?'

Girl 1: 'Seriously, you were rubbing your crotch against that guy over there!'

Drunk Girl: 'I was NOT! I am almost sober.'

Girl 1: 'Aaah yea! Your crotch was ALL over him. You wouldn't do that if you were sober!'

Drunk Girl: 'I totally would!'

Overheard by Anonymous, toilets at Quays Bar
Posted on Tuesday, 19 June 2007

Eye and Ear

Driving past the Eye and Ear Hospital a few years ago, my mate goes,

'Jaysus that must be a mad job to have, being one of them eyeaneers.' Confused by this, I asked him to explain himself.

'Ya know, eyeaneers, them fellas that look after your eyes.'

He thought they were like engineers! All his life he genuinely thought that!

Overheard by stevo, passing the Eye and Ear Hospital
Posted on Tuesday, 19 June 2007

Health warning

Cheeky young professional type passes a kid of about 15 with his back to a wall smoking a cigarette and says, 'Smoking's bad for your health!'

Quick as a flash the kid says, in a thick Dublin accent, 'Yeh, so's bein' a bollix.'

Overheard by Colm, Aungier Street
Posted on Monday, 18 June 2007

Life's questions

One night, we stopped off in Blackrock for chips on the way home. While I was in the chipper, handbags erupted on the street between a few south-Dublin types. Ralph Lauren, Hugo Boss and Henry Lloyd had never seen the like. It was fairly harmless stuff.

Anyway, I joined the gallery of gawkers outside, enjoying the entertainment while eating our chips. A taxi pulled up, and from the doorway of Tonic Bar tottered two gorgeous young wans, all boob tubes, glamour and mini-skirts. The lads' attention was drawn away from the minor scuffle as they all stared in awe at the visions of beauty to our left.

The guy beside me, who was a few pints in, with a chip hovering close to his lips, nudged me gently and said,

'Jazes, how would you be gay?'

Overheard by Murray, outside the Central Café, Blackrock
Posted on Monday, 18 June 2007

Dub abroad

While boarding a plane in Lanzarote, I observed a man mid 50s, very tanned from his holiday, bright yellow polo shirt, a sovereign ring on almost every finger and a very strong Dublin accent. He's walking down towards his seat with his bags when he recognises someone from home.

'Ah Jaysus, Jim, howsagoin? Yis have a bleedin' great colour — were ya away or wha?'

Overheard by Pongo, in Lanzarote while boarding the plane back to Dublin
Posted on Monday, 18 June 2007

Great nickname

Couple of young wans on the back of the no. 75 bus. They're talking loudly about a porno movie they saw the other night. Conversation goes like this:

Girl 1: 'Da noises she was makin', all dat moanin', dat was mad, like.'

Girl 2: 'Wot was mad bout it?'

Girl 1: 'Do you ever make noises like dat when you're doin' it?'

Girl 2 (very proud): 'Jaysus, they don't call me 'Emer the Screamer' for nuthin!'

Overheard by Anonymous, no. 75 bus
Posted on Friday, 15 June 2007

Even the teacher creased herself laughing

Very boring Leaving Cert English class many years ago.

Teacher (reading from novel): 'They were proud people, they stood erect and stiff ...'

(Shouted from back of class): 'They were a shower of pricks ...'

Overheard by Ted, English class
Posted on Thursday, 14 June 2007

Culture shock

Waiting for the back door of a Ryanair plane to open (people all standing at their seats with bags in hands), a man turns round and says to an Asian man in the seat behind him (who he obviously knew),

'Hey, Mahmood, I was just thinking sometimes it's great to be a Pakistani!'

'Why's that?' says Mahmood.

'Cos ye nearly always get a whole row of seats to yer self!'

The look of shocked faces was priceless — until the two of them laughed!

Overheard by Paul, Ryanair plane
Posted on Wednesday, 13 June 2007

Nature calls ... at Clery's

I was waiting for a taxi on O'Connell Street one night when I noticed a group of three girls. Two of them were dressed well, but the third ruined the image by shouting,

'I'm goin' fer a piiiiss!'

She marches up the steps next to Clery's and hoists up her skirt and pulls down her knickers. Next thing you hear is her screeching,

'F**k off! F**k off! I've a bladder infection!' at a passer-by.

Then she strolls down the steps, fixing her skirt and pulling up her knickers on the way down, and announces loudly,

'I'm going for a box of faaaags!' marching off, looking like a man, leaving the other two looking at each other in horror and disbelief.

Overheard by RandomMan, the steps beside Clery's
Posted on Wednesday, 13 June 2007

Members only

Queuing outside a night-club in Temple Bar. Two likely lads ahead of me were swaying gently from side to side. 'Are yiz members?' asks the bouncer.

'We are,' say the lads.

'I'm sorry, then. It's non-members night only!'

Overheard by Jimbo, Temple Bar
Posted on Tuesday, 12 June 2007

Objection to licence renewal

Work canteen (yonks ago), a news report comes on the radio saying how River Phoenix has died following a 'lethal cocktail' of drink and drugs.

Up pipes one lad: 'Jayus, that's terrible, they shouldn't be allowed to serve them.'

'Serve what?'

'Them lethal cocktails — they're always killing people.'

... back to quietly munching our sangers ...

Overheard by Anonymous, canteen in Tallaght factory
Posted on Sunday, 10 June 2007

On tow

A few years ago our car engine blew up. I was on maternity leave at the time so I was too broke to pay for the breaker's yard. It just sat in our garden for about a month with a big 'On Tow' sign in the back window.

One day a Traveller called to the door and asked, 'Is tha' a "For Sale" sign on the car?'

I didn't have the heart to tell him, so I said the car was wrecked but he could have it ... bless.

Overheard by Cal, my house
Posted on Friday, 8 June 2007

I know a little Latin ...

Getting off the ferry in Dun Laoghaire after a fairly rough crossing from Holyhead:

Auld Wan 1: 'That was a bit rough.'

Auld Wan 2: 'Yeah, it's nice to be back on terra cotta.'

Overheard by John, Dun Laoghaire ferry terminal
Posted on Friday, 8 June 2007

Getting on the property ladder ...

In a friend of a friend's house, queuing for a sunbed session.

Girl 1: 'It's my 21st next month, I hope you're all coming.'

Girl 2: 'You're 21 already. And you've no kids yet?'

Girl 1: 'No, why?'

Girl 2: 'Well, how the f**k are you going to get a house?'

Overheard by Barb, The Wild West (Dublin 22)
Posted on Thursday, 7 June 2007

This was on the first pint!

Watching the news a few months ago in the pub, the reporter says, 'Now over to our correspondent in Paris.' The French reporter gave his report in English.

My mate said, 'Isn't it good the way they put on the accent no matter where they are reporting from?'

I asked him to explain — kind of hoping he was joking!

He thought it was an *English* reporter putting on a *French* accent, rather than a *French* reporter speaking *English*.

I actually didn't laugh at first! I just sat there thinking — this guy has been thinking this all his life! Every time he has watched a report from anywhere, he has thought some English guy was in that country mimicking their accents!

Overheard by Fran, Pub
Posted on Tuesday, 5 June 2007

Treated like royals

Walking along the road out of Croke Park after the Dublin v Meath match. Heard this gathering phlegm and spit noise behind me. I stopped, checked my jacket, and looked beside me to see a little Dub about seven or eight.

He says, 'Don't worry, I was aiming at that Meath fella ahead. It landed on him! Sure I wouldn't do any harm to a Dub!'

Nice!

Overheard by gormdubhgorm, walking from Croke Park near Clonliffe House
Posted on Monday, 4 June 2007

Dah's great valu, wah!

Standing having a smoke on North Earl Street, overheard the following:

Fundraiser: 'Hiya, how's it going? You couldn't spare a minute for Concern, please?'

Dub Fella (mate beside him): 'Yeh, gowan, make it bleedin' quick wil yeh.'

Fundraiser (launches into speech, then she says): 'Did you know you can feed an entire family for a month for €21 in Darfur?'

Dub Fella: 'F**kin' jazis, dah's greight value, wah! I shud bleedin' muave der!'

The poor girl actually looked really amused! I think she was glad of a unique response for a change!

Overheard by doyler, North Earl Street

Posted on Friday, 1 June 2007

Watch out for toilet trickery!

While sitting on the toilet in work one afternoon, I began reading the graffiti on the door! Here someone had written, 'Do you want to play toilet tennis?'

Pondering the question I thought, 'Yes!' and read on.

It said, 'Look left', which I happily proceeded to do; it then directed me to, 'Look right', which I also did. Reading on, I continued following the same directions! It was only after 4-love that I realised I'd been had!

Overheard by Mick, Smyths Toys, Tallaght

Posted on Thursday, 31 May 2007

Long-distance runner

Some time ago I was running alone in the Phoenix Park. I saw this lone runner, head down, running hard, coming towards me. When he was just about to pass me and without stopping, he asked in his best Dub accent out of the side of his mouth,

'Are them f***ing Kenyans far behind me?'

All I could do was smile and said to myself,
'Good one!'

Overheard by Duggie, Phoenix Park
Posted on Wednesday, 30 May 2007

Raking it on the 77

Decided to be brave last night by getting the no.
77 bus home from town. At Cork Street, a
rough-looking guy ('a skanger' to be politically
incorrect) gets on carrying a garden rake.

As he takes his seat upstairs he announces to
everybody: 'If any of yous make a rake joke
you'll get it in de head.'

That bus never ceases to amaze me.

Overheard by G, no. 77 bus
Posted on Wednesday, 30 May 2007

Dope caught in the headlights

One of my colleagues came into work late one
day with this excuse:

'My car wouldn't start this morning. The
battery wasted because my electricity went last

night so I used the headlights to light up the front room ...'

Overheard by Count Cockula, in work
Posted on Tuesday, 29 May 2007

The voice of reason!

Sitting at my desk at work, another quiet and boring day in the office ... just getting on with it as you do.

My Colleague (sitting opposite me): 'Would you ever shut the f**k up!'

Me: 'But ... I didn't say anything!'

My Colleague: 'Not you! The voices in my feckin' head!'

I have since moved desks ...

Overheard by SA-Tam, in the office
Posted on Monday, 28 May 2007

Ello, ello, ello

My friend (who is a bit of a smart ass) was stopped for speeding on the Navan Road.

Cop: 'I've been waiting for you all day!'

Friend: 'I know, I got here as quick as I could!'

Overheard by Marty, Navan Road
Posted on Monday, 28 May 2007

The future is healthy

Son: 'I want tea.'

Mother (who had just ordered coffee): 'Yer not

gettin' tea, it's bad for ye ... yer getting a Coke.'

Overheard by Anonymous, Café Sofia, Wexford Street
Posted on Monday, 28 May 2007

Cheap burial

My Dad ordered a skip a couple of weeks ago and rounded up a couple of my brothers to help him move the stuff into it (trees, a shed, rubbish). Two days before the skip arrives one of my brothers rings my Dad and the conversation goes like this:

Brother: 'Da, I have a bit of a problem.'

Da: 'Wha, son?'

Brother: 'Well, ya know the way you're after getting a skip? Mrs X just died so I'm in a bit of a pickle.' (meaning he couldn't help cause he had to go to his close friend's funeral)

Da: 'Well, like, I'd love to help ya, son, but I'm sorry, the skip is gonna be full up as it is, so there will be no room for her in it.'

Very insensitive — but also very funny at the time!

Overheard by Anonymous, at home
Posted on Monday, 28 May 2007

Hurt in the fracas

Grafton Street, one of our friends was caught in the crossfires of a bit of a mêlée. The Garda came and were looking for witnesses and statements. They asked my friend, 'Were you also hurt in the fracas?' He answered:

'I don't know where my fracas is — but my lip is all bleedin'.'

Overheard by Derek, Dublin late at night
Posted on Sunday, 27 May 2007

Find X

Well, not so much overheard ...

On our really important end-of-year exams, one of the Maths questions was a triangle with lots of angles marked on. The instruction for the question was 'Find X' (you were obviously meant to calculate angle X).

However, one of the guys in my class simply drew a circle around X and wrote, 'Here it is!'

Classic!

Overheard by CoolKitty, school
Posted on Saturday, 26 May 2007

Broken clouds

Pilot giving his spiel before take-off, Aer Arann, Dublin to Kerry:

'The weather in Kerry is similar to here, 15 degrees, light winds with broken clouds, though we hope to have the clouds fixed by the time we arrive.'

Overheard by Kevin, Aer Arann flight, Dublin Airport
Posted on Friday, 25 May 2007

Kissing rules

Walking around an estate, I overheard two little boys talking about girls. They were about eight.

Boy 1: 'Do you two kiss? You have to kiss your girlfriend like a million times before you get married. And then once a day when you're married.'

Boy 2: 'No, twice a day. One when the husband comes home from work and one when you're in bed.'

Boy 1: 'Oh, and one when the wife gets home ...'

Overheard by Lauren, Shankill
Posted on Friday, 25 May 2007

I love the respect my boyfriend has for me ...

I'm a scouser and when I was working in Italy my Dubliner boyfriend was over to visit me. We were having a lock-in in the bar where I worked and my boss was telling us a delightful story about when he had crabs!

So, he was explaining all about the creatures and then stated, 'The female crabs are actually born pregnant.'

Quick as a flash my boyfriend asked, 'What, like scousers?!'

Overheard by slick, bar in Italy, with Dubliner
Posted on Thursday, 24 May 2007

Pyjama party

Overseen not overheard.

While queuing to cast my vote in the general election today at St Attracta's National School polling station, I couldn't believe my eyes.

Two girls about 20 years old in front of me in the queue — both wearing PINK PYJAMAS!

Absolutely no shame! I wish I had my camera phone.

Overheard by Vinny, St Attracta's school, Dundrum
Posted on Thursday, 24 May 2007

Great comeback

A bus stops with its front wheels slightly inside a yellow box at a junction. A guy with a flash girlfriend and a flash convertible car pulls up beside the bus.

The flash guy shouts out his window at the bus driver,

'Yellow box, yellow box!'

The bus driver opens his window and says back to him,

'You'd better get her to the clinic!'

Overheard by Anonymous, junction on Malahide Road
Posted on Thursday, 24 May 2007

The Mile High club

Recently got a flight to the UK. The pilot came on board to say the usual, introducing himself etc. He finished by saying,

'Hope you enjoy the flight, have a drink, relax, listen to some music, or feel the leg of the person sitting next to you ...'

Put everyone on the plane in a good mood for the rest of the flight!

Overheard by Sarah, Aer Lingus flight
Posted on Thursday, 24 May 2007

Times are hard

Was waiting at the pedestrian crossing at College Green last week. Nice sunny day, a gush of people waiting to cross.

A taxi pulls up at the lights (2004 BMW 5 series), driver's arm hanging out the window. Lad shouts over to him,

'No money in taxiing, eh? ME BOLLIX!'

Overheard by Bazmo, College Green
Posted on Tuesday, 22 May 2007

The smoking ban in Dublin

Not overheard but overseen.

Outside the Coombe Hospital while walking in to visit a family member. Along the wall, two big 'No Smoking' signs, and below them were two wall-mounted ashtrays!

Overheard by Anonymous, Coombe
Posted on Monday, 21 May 2007

462

Smokey & the Bandit

On the Westport to Dublin train recently. The train was just pulling out of Tullamore when the driver came on the intercom to make the normal announcement in a real Dublin accent:

'Could I have your attention, please! Would the person with their arm out the window drop the cigarette ... next stop Portarlington.'

Overheard by indcar, Westport to Dublin train
Posted on Monday, 21 May 2007

A hard case of the Ballymun Blues

A few years ago a friend of ours was bragging about the new hard-shelled guitar case he had just bought. He was telling us about how it was so strong that ... 'You can climb to the top of the Ballymun towers, drop it off the edge and it wouldn't break when it hits the ground.'

My friend chirps in:

'Yeah, maybe you're right, but I betcha it wouldn't be there when ya get back down.'

Overheard by Derek, Dublin pub
Posted on Friday, 18 May 2007

Bus to the moon

I got on a no. 83 bus just at the top of Booterstown Avenue. I was a bit tired so I checked whether the bus went to Stillorgan. The smug, sunglass-wearing, ridiculous moustached, angry bus-driver replied,

'No! It goes to the f**kin' moon!'

Wanted to reply, 'One to the moon, please,' but his tattooed knuckles said not to.

Thanks, Dublin Bus.

Overheard by Ian, no. 83 bus
Posted on Thursday, 17 May 2007

Xenophobia on the Luas

Three French tourists were on the Luas from Tallaght. Every time we stopped, they mimicked the Irish translation of the stations.

Voice: 'The Four Courts ... Na Ceithre Cúirteanna.'

Frenchie 1: 'Naccera corchinna.' (laughs)

Dub: 'I'd like to see yis laugh if the next stop was Darndale, ya frogs!'

Overheard by Sam, Luas from Tallaght
Posted on Wednesday, 16 May 2007

Full-time bus driver and part-time comedian

Getting on a bus in Crumlin, a would-be passenger enquires of the driver,

Woman: 'Do you go to the shopping centre in Tallaght?'

Driver: 'No, love, I normally shop locally.'

Overheard by Richie, Crumlin, on a no. 77 bus
Posted on Sunday, 13 May 2007

Doing a domestic

Was out shopping with a mate yesterday, buying stacks of cleaning equipment. Leaving the shop, an aul' one turns and asks, 'Doing a bit of cleaning, lads?'

Quick as a flash my buddy turns and says, 'Nah, it's my girlfriend's birthday!'

The look on the aul' one's face — classic!

Overheard by BB, Bakers Corner
Posted on Thursday, 12 April 2007

All he could do was laugh

At work in the local factory today we were all sitting down waiting for work to finish. The boss comes by and notices a lad at the end of the line not doing anything, so he shouts over, 'Here, wot dya call this?' then points to his imaginary watch.

The young lad replies, 'Yer wrist?'

Overheard by Stevie, factory in Monkstown
Posted on Friday, 11 May 2007

Not quite the charitable type ...

Having left Eason's on O'Connell Street, I turned right towards Grafton Street.

I noticed a stereotypical northsider talking to one of those chuggers from Concern or somewhere. Passed just in time to hear him say,

'Wha? Jaze, I thought youz were gonna give ME money! Forget it, pal!'

Overheard by Jonny, O'Connell Street
Posted on Thursday, 10 May 2007

Tackling the matter

Sitting in the stand in front of two archetypical middle-aged Dubs at a recent soccer match in Richmond Park, I was privy to their debate regarding a particularly aggressive midfielder who was playing at the time.

'Sure, he'd break yer leg,' exclaimed one of the men, disgusted. His friend reflected for at moment on the accusation.

'He would not,' he calmly disagreed, 'He'd break yer *two* legs.'

Overheard by Odd Slob, Richmond Park
Posted on Wednesday, 9 May 2007

Labour

I was coming home from Skerries when I saw an election poster for the Labour Party. It had been vandalised with the usual stuff (goatie, glasses, etc.) But in a speech bubble it said,

'Help, I'm in Labour!'

Overheard by Brian, on the road from Skerries to Rush
Posted on Monday, 7 May 2007

She's no good ...

Overheard in Fallon & Byrne recently, man with English accent talking into mobile:

'... and the worst thing is, she doesn't drink at all, so she remembers all my lies!'

Overheard by nefariousfaery, Fallon & Byrne, Exchequer Street
Posted on Sunday, 6 May 2007

Could only be said by a Dub

Guy: 'I hit him so hard on the top of his head, I broke his bleedin' ankles.'

Overheard by francy, on the no. 19 bus
Posted on Saturday, 5 May 2007

Bring on the exams!

I was in Biology class in sixth year and we were talking about the eye, as part of our revision for the Leaving Cert.

Our Teacher: 'What happens to our eyes when it gets dark?'

Student (deadly serious): 'Your night-vision comes on.'

Overheard by Lauren, Tallaght Community School
Posted on Wednesday, 2 May 2007

Tabloid Talk

Two women talking about Posh and Becks' move to LA:

Woman #1: 'Jayus, when they go over there, the pavarotti will be all over them!'

Woman #2: 'The what?'

Woman #1: 'You know, the newspaper people that follow you around!'

Overheard by Anonymous, pub in Portobello
Posted on Wednesday, 2 May 2007

Croker joker

Coming out of Croke Park a couple of years ago after a Dublin and Kildare match, the usual after-match crowds not moving very much. Then over the banter comes a shout,

'Don't mind those bleedin' traffic lights up there — keep on movin'!'

Overheard by wolftone, Croke Park
Posted on Tuesday, 1 May 2007

Sayin' me prayers

Run up to Christmas, Arnotts, busy. Long queues to pay. I come to the top of the queue with my presents. There are two women at the desk. The first (quite young) wrapping and calling out the items, the second (middle aged) keying the necessary into the cash register. Conversation as follows:

Young One: 'Four Galway crystal tumblers.'

Auld One: 'Wha? Will ya speak up so I can ear ye.'

Young One: 'I said four Galway crystal tumblers. Can't help it; I got a sore throat.'

Auld One: 'What's dat to me? How'd ye ge dat? Down on your knees again?'

Young One: 'Yea, sayin' me prayers.'

And they carried on without blinking an eye.

Overheard by Thomas, Arnotts
Posted on Monday, 30 April 2007

Warranty? Yeah right!

I was walking down O'Connell Street last week on a fine sunny day and stopped at a stall where this bloke was selling knock-off designer sunglasses. A young lad about 12 comes up to the guy and says,

'Hey, Mister, I bought these glasses about 20 minutes ago and they are way too big, do ya have any smaller ones?'

The bloke replied, 'Jung fella, it's not smaller glasses ya need, it's a bigger f**kin' head — now piss off!'

Overheard by bob, O'Connell Street
Posted on Monday, 30 April 2007

DART darlings

Heading to town on the DART on a Saturday evening, two D4 girls having a chat:

Girl #1: 'I mean I already pay, like, €50 a week rent, and I mean I only have one meal a day there and, loike, just sleep there, and he asked me for another €20? I couldn't believe it — I mean I only earn €500 a week you know?'

Girl #2: 'Oh my god, that's so unfair, my Dad wouldn't even ask me for money for anything ...'

Good to see these girls are prepared for the big bad world!

Overheard by Anonymous, the DART
Posted on Monday, 30 April 2007

Anto at the panto

At a pantomime in the Gaiety a few years ago with the family, and the usual scene happens where the villain creeps up on the star of the show. All the kids are screaming the whereabouts of the bad guy, when the kid sitting next to us gets into it, and starts shouting

'He's ahind ya, he's bleedin' ahind ya!'

Overheard by Derek, Gaiety Theatre Panto
Posted on Monday, 30 April 2007

Sore head

Waiting in the check-in queue in Manchester Airport for a flight back to Dublin, a Sikh was in front of us, wearing traditional turban. Young Dublin boy around six or seven shouts out,

'Dad, I really hope that man's head gets better soon.'

Innocence of kids ...

Overheard by Anonymous, Manchester Airport
Posted on Monday, 30 April 2007

Go home ya culchie

Walking down Grafton Street one day, an old man (in his 80s at least!) starts singing at the top of his voice,

'TAKE ME HOME THE COUNTRY ROOOAD TO THE PLACE I KNOW BEST'

And next thing a skanger shouts across at him ...

'Well then go home ya bleedin' culchie, we'd be better off without your bleedin' howlin'.'

The man quickly replies,

'Who the f**k are you callin' a culchie? I was born and bred on that road down there!'

Only in Dublin ...

Overheard by Kaz, Grafton Street
Posted on Sunday, 29 April 2007

Selfish society

Girl: 'Spare a minute for Concern?'

Guy: 'Sorry, I'm not concerned.'

Overheard by Jay, bottom of Grafton Street
Posted on Sunday, 29 April 2007

Chocolate muffin!

My Mum comes back from Dunnes after doing the weekly shopping. She'd bought chocolate muffins for my brother as a treat.

She brings a muffin in to my brother and says,

'Stick your teeth into that big brown muff.'

Needless to say, my brother and I were speechless!

Overheard by Shelly, at home!
Posted on Saturday, 28 April 2007

Clothing has no morals these days!

'Jaysus the prices of these T-shirts here, they bleedin' rape your pocket!'

Overheard by Geraldine, clothes shop, Temple Bar
Posted on Saturday, 28 April 2007

Evolution in the social conduct of the no. 50 bus

I overheard an interesting conversation.

Person #1: 'Well, I am a little stuck for money at

the moment and this sounds like expensive stuff, besides getting needles and all!'

Person #2: 'Come on, we can share a needle then.'

Overheard by Even, de 50 out'ta tallah!
Posted on Saturday, 28 April 2007

A Ryanair welcome to Dublin!

Ryanair flight from Lubeck to Dublin. I'm sitting at the window. Coming in to land there's turbulence, fog — you name it. Very bumpy.

After a rough landing, genuinely relieved pilot announces over the intercom, 'Clear of the active runway, sir, thank f**k, I hadn't a clue where I was going ...'

Fifteen seconds later ...

'My apologies there, ladies and gentlemen, I, errrrr ...' (pause)

Fifteen seconds later ...

Other pilot: 'Ladies and gentlemen, welcome to Dublin!'

Overheard by Anonymous, Ryanair flight
Posted on Friday, 27 April 2007

Ditzy Dublin blondes

Guy says to friend, 'Oh, I saw your twin today!'

Friend says, 'Oh, really? What did she look like?'

Testament to think before you speak!

Overheard by Anonymous, in the ATM queue
Posted on Friday, 27 April 2007

Compassionate Kid

We had a group of kids, about 10 years of age, making their way into one of the buildings at DCU. As I started walking through the automatic revolving door, one of the kids hit the big red 'emergency stop' button at his side. The door came to a stand-still with me 'trapped' halfway around, between the two panes of glass.

Rather than just push the door, I start clutching my throat and pretend to be choking, dropping to my knees, giving it an Oscar-winning performance. Some of the kids started laughing, others weren't quite sure if I was joking or not, when suddenly the child who hit the button in the first place walks up to the glass, presses his face against it so I can hear, and shouts:

'Ah, will ye ever ge' outta dat, ya bollix!'

I laughed myself to tears.

Overheard by Fred, DCU Research Building
Posted on Friday, 27 April 2007

Behave

I was in a supermarket and a kid was running around and getting in other people's way. The mother looked at the kid and said,

'I have two words for you: Bee Haaave'

Needless to say, the child didn't behave at all!

Overheard in Tesco, Stillorgan
Posted on Friday, 27 April 2007

Mother's advice

On a DART, overheard a snippet of a conversation.

Guy #1: 'It's times like this that I wish I had listened to what my mother said.'

Guy #2: 'Well, what did she say?'

Guy #1: 'I have no idea — I didn't listen to her.'

Overheard by Anonymous, DART
Posted on Friday, 27 April 2007

I can't believe I said that!

At my brother's wedding some years ago. Towards the end of the mass the congregation was invited up to receive communion. It had been a while for me, but I went and did my duty. As the priest said, 'Body of Christ', I said, 'Oh, cheers — thanks!'

Overheard by Anonymous, church
Posted on Thursday, 26 April 2007

The Dublin mating ritual

I was walking through a car park outside a newsagents in the humble area of Coolock. There were two separate groups of about 10 people, one all girls and one all guys between 12 and 14. As I walked past the girls I heard one of them shout over to the group of guys,

'Here, will ANY of yous meet ANY of us?'

Overheard by Beddy, Coolock village
Posted on Thursday, 26 April 2007

Good manners

Standing in the ATM queue in college one day, there was a girl in front of me taking out money. The machine seemed to be taking its time giving the money and she was looking around blankly, as if off in her own world. Eventually, the money comes out and she takes it, saying to the ATM, 'Thank you!'

Overheard by Elmo, UCD
Posted on Wednesday, 25 April 2007

Great answer

A few years back, we were in Biology class of adolescent 14-year-old boys, dissecting insects. The teacher asked, 'Can anyone tell us the difference between the male and female stick insect?'

Quick as a flash, the class wag pipes up with,

'Miss, the male has a bit more stick!'

Overheard by Mick, school
Posted on Wednesday, 25 April 2007

I spy with my little eye something beginning with IDIOT!

I was waiting at the bus stop at Eden Quay. A group of girls started playing 'I Spy' to pass the time.

Girl #1: 'I spy with my little eye, something beginning with E.'

Girl #2: 'Eroplane!'

Overheard by Anonymous, Eden Quay

Posted on Tuesday, 24 April 2007

Bogger in sauna

In the sauna in DCU after soccer. This guy we know from Clare came in and sat down the front. He started to get a bit agitated, and after about five minutes jumped up and said to us,

'Jaysus Christ, lads, can we open the door — it's f**kin' roastin' in here ...'

Overheard by TP, DCU sports centre

Posted on Saturday, 21 April 2007

Where women never look!

In the pub with my brother-in-law discussing my sister's birthday and the cake. I asked where he would hide it so she wouldn't find it, to which he responded, 'In the oven, sure she'll never look in there.'

I fell over with laughter — and that's exactly where he hid it!

Overheard by Surprise Surprise, pub in Dublin 9

Posted on Thursday, 19 April 2007

I thought they only came out at night

Driving to work the other morning on a sunny day, I was stopped in traffic just outside my area. A car on the other side of the road drove by and I beeped to a friend of mine, who waved back.

As I went to drive off, my passenger door opened and a lad in site gear went to step in. We looked at each other, he turned and said,

'Ah shite, I thought you were me mate, sorry bud,' and as he was closing the door I heard him under his breath say to himself,

'For f**k's sake, John, you're only out of bed and you're embarrassing yourself.'

I laughed all the way to work!

Overheard by ST, old airport road
Posted on Thursday, 19 April 2007

Erecting the Spire

Back some time ago, I was observing the Spire in its earliest stages of construction, the first section having being just slotted into position.

The middle-aged man beside me was unimpressed,

'Isn't very big.'

To which his more optimistic friend replied,

'Wait till it gets horny ...'

Overheard by Odd Slob, O'Connell Street
Posted on Wednesday, 18 April 2007

Nelson for the Aras?

Was on the no. 10 bus to work, which also goes to Phoenix Park. Anyway about 20 proper 'langers' from Cork in their teens got on the bus and headed straight for the back seat, full of joy and excitement. One of them made a comment about someone famous living in the Phoenix Park but they couldn't remember who it was.

A reply came from one of them, 'Ah yea, it's your man, what's his name, that guy Mandela!'

'Oh yea,' they all said in agreement. Except for one of them.

She then confronted them: 'Will yas don't be stupid, it's the president fella, Bertie O'Hern!'

I wanted to jump out the window ...

Overheard by Anonymous, no. 10 bus
Posted on Wednesday, 18 April 2007

Cuisine de Dunnes

I was walking past an older couple in the supermarket the other day. As I was passing, the man turned to his wife and said, 'Cock oven?'

'Coq Au Vin!' replied his wife with a sigh.

Overheard by Peter, Dunnes Stores, St Stephen's Green
Posted on Wednesday, 18 April 2007

Too much time to think

A load of D4 heads on the way to Dundrum.

D4 #1: 'Oh my God, like, how do we know it's Tuesday? It could be Saturday or something?

Like, what do days go by?'
D4 #2: 'You're such an idiot, it goes by the sea!'
The rest all agree ...

Overheard by Kate, the bus to Dundrum
Posted on Tuesday, 17 April 2007

Charm school dropout

In a taxi on my way to work after a particularly hard night, I told the taxi man I was feeling a bit rough. 'Oh,' he says, 'you've no need to tell me, I can see it.' Deciding to take it in the humour that (hopefully) it was meant, I laughed. Then he says,

'Ah jaysus, love, I didn't mean to offend you there. I know you're laughing and all, but I know you're offended really. I know the way you women work — I was married to a pig in lipstick for twenty years!'

I wonder why the marriage hadn't worked out!

Overheard by Anonymous, in a taxi in Dublin
Posted on Tuesday, 17 April 2007

Our future sports stars!

Umpiring at the back of the goals at a GAA match last night and all the play was at one end of the pitch. The two corner backs, bored to tears, were just passing time talking to each other when one says to the other,

'Jaysus, I hope that f**king ball doesn't come down here, I can't run for shite.'

The other one replies, 'You'd want to give up them smokes then wouldn't ya?'

They were 12-year-old girls!

Overheard by Gerry, at a GAA match in Dublin
Posted on Tuesday, 17 April 2007

Head wrecker

Two women were talking together in a café on Thomas Street. One of the women's little boy started getting fidgety and wanted to leave. He kept pestering his mother to go until she lost her patience and turned to yell at him to shut up. Then she turned back to her friend and said,

'Jayzus, that fella would give a bleedin' Anadin a headache!'

Overheard by clio, a café on Thomas Street
Posted on Tuesday, 17 April 2007

The good auld days ...

This happened Saturday night, standing waiting to use the urinal while it was being used by my Dad and another man. Both of them are doing their business and the man next to him started talking:

'I remember the days when you were able to use the underground toilets in O'Connell Street. You'd go down, do your business and no one would bother you.'

My Dad agrees and then the man pointed over to one of the toilet attendants and said in a very

loud voice, 'Now you can't walk into the toilet
without them wanting to wipe your arse!'

Overheard by SB, Russell Court

Posted on Monday, 16 April 2007

Life's a beach and then you die ...

Woman on a packed train to her friend:

'Oh, I love dolphins, we saw one when we were
on holidays last summer. It was beached, but we
took some photos anyway ...'

Overheard by Andy, on the train

Posted on Sunday, 15 April 2007

Tinted windows

Went for a spin with a friend of mine who had
just bought a new car. My (blonde) friend was
sitting in the passenger seat and had bought a
new pair of sunglasses that day. She turns to my
friend who's driving and asks in all sincerity, 'Are
your windows tinted?'

We all burst out laughing at the look on this
blonde's face when she realised that no, in fact
the windows of the new car were NOT tinted —
she was wearing her new sunglasses!

Don't know how we didn't crash!

Overheard by Anonymous, in my friend's car, driving in Dublin

Posted on Sunday, 15 April 2007

Transfusion confusion

I was in Beaumont Hospital recently, visiting my Nana who had fallen and broken her hip. There was a really loud guy two beds up from her who had to get blood. The nurse was putting the bag of blood up on the drip and he asked, 'Here, where does this blood come from?'

The nurse replied, 'People donate it.'

The guy says back really loudly, 'Ah right, I thought it was coming from some animal.'

Overheard by Karona, in Beaumont Hospital
Posted on Saturday, 14 April 2007

For the birds

My sister asks my Dad, 'Dad, have you ever seen an owl?'

Quick as a flash my Dad answers, 'An aul' what?'

Overheard by Anonymous, in my Dad's car
Posted on Friday, 13 April 2007

The kids are alright

An old man and woman were talking on the bus about the youth of today. The two of them smelled of booze and it was obvious that they were after having a few drinks. The bloke was giving out about lads and she was giving out about girls.

He says, sounding sad, 'All that these young fellas want to be doing is playing with their Playstations and fighting with knives.'

In a disgusted voice she replies, 'And all the young ones are interested in these days is nightclubs, boozing and the mickey.'

Overheard by I am the resurrection, on the no. 40 bus
Posted on Friday, 13 April 2007

Ulcer says No!

Overheard in a ward in the Mater Hospital the other day.

While visiting my father in a small three-bed ward, man being admonished by his visiting daughter in a broad Dublin accent:

'C'mon, Da, you have to take these tablets, they're for your Ulster!'

Cue stifled giggles as myself and father struggle to compose ourselves and not give the game away.

Overheard by Colm, Mater Hospital
Posted on Thursday, 12 April 2007

Slow Learner

Was getting a lift home with a female friend from college one evening. I noticed that her L plate was on the outside of the windscreen and I asked her why.

She told me 'It was backwards when I bought it, so I had to put it on the outside ...'

Overheard by Kev, front seat of a Nissan Micra
Posted on Wednesday, 11 April 2007

Place your receiver in my USB port

I was working the weekend in a pub in the city centre. The place was surprisingly dead for the bank holiday Monday, only the few auld lads in for the big race at 3.55, the Irish Grand National.

During the build-up to the race, the speakers started acting up and the commentary turned into screeching feed-back, deafening everyone. At which one of the men — true Dub — shouted,

'Whoh, whoh, whoh, jaaaaaaysus, f**king turn it down! Sounds like a bloody computer having sex with a telephone ...'

I nearly died laughing!

Overheard by Anonymous, city centre pub
Posted on Tuesday, 10 April 2007

zzzzzzzzzzzzz

After an extremely dull first 30 minutes at the Ireland v Wales football game in Croke Park, a man a few rows in front of me leaves for the toilet. He passes a man at the end of his row who stands up to let him by, and asks,

'Sorry, did I wake you?'

Everyone around us bursts out laughing!

Overheard by Anonymous, Croke Park, Ireland v Wales
Posted on Monday, 9 April 2007

Smooth

Was out drinking with the mates in Brogan's. A
friend was putting the moves on this girl all
night long, and eventually after a few hours and
a few more drinks it looked like he was in. So he
leans in for the kill when another mate yells
over,

'YOU'RE IN THERE, MATE!'

Instant mood kill — and bloody hilarious!

Overheard by Pól, Brogan's
Posted on Friday, 6 April 2007

Now that's good marketing

Outside the ladies bathroom on the arrivals floor
in Dublin Airport, there's an ad for some
business lounge in the airport or a nearby hotel.

The slogan is, 'Do your business in comfort.'

Genius!

Overheard by Anonymous, Dublin Airport
Posted on Thursday, 5 April 2007

Viniculture

Eating in the posh part of Bon Appetit restaurant
in Malahide. Most of us are so intimidated by the
surroundings that you can hear a pin drop.
Everyone ear-wigging everyone else.

Maître d' asks a gentleman at the next table if Sir
would care to choose wine. Sir asks Maître d' for
a recommendation. Maître d' explains in exotic

(French?) accent that the sommelier will be over shortly and walks off.

Sir's dinner partner asks what Maître d' said. Sir explains that Maître d' didn't know the wines so he's 'sending up a Somalian ...'!

Overheard by Stephen, Malahide

Posted on Thursday, 5 April 2007

It's for me!

My Dad works as a taxi base controller and I was visiting him last night in work. A call came through from a young woman trying to make a booking. When my Dad asked for her address, her reply was, 'It's for me!'

My Dad tried to explain that he needed her address, but she continued to say, 'It's for me in Meath Street!'

My Dad went on to explain that his company does not cover that area and gave her another contact number to call.

This confused young woman said, 'Yes, I called them and told them the taxi is for me but they gave me your number!'

At this stage my Dad was doing his best to hold in the laughter. He advised that he would need an address to secure a booking. The reply he got though was ...

'I don't think you understand, the taxi is for me!'

Overheard by E, taxi base, Clondalkin

Posted on Thursday, 5 April 2007

Hey bud

Walking home alone at the dead of night through a rough housing estate after a night out, when an upstairs window swings open.

'Hey, bud,' a voice from the window calls out.

I arch my head to the window and a guy appears, wearing a vest, and asks, 'Got a smoke?'

I shrugged and answered, 'No.'

Next thing he produces a smoke and asks,

'Got a light?'

Overheard by The rounder, in an unnamed rough neighbourhood
Posted on Wednesday, 4 April 2007

Haggis

In Biology last year, somehow we got onto the subject of haggis. One of the lads in the class asked our Scottish teacher (a real joker) what haggis actually was.

488

The teacher gave us a load of crap about it being a small animal that lived in the Scottish Highlands which ran around mountains until one leg was shorter than the other (much to the amusement of most of us).

He kept the joke up for about 10 minutes before he put the lad out of his misery and told him the truth. We all laughed about it as the lad looked revolted.

Then five minutes later, one of the less intelligent girls in the class piped up:

'What was the little animal, then, if it wasn't haggis?'

Overheard by CoolKitty, at school
Posted on Wednesday, 4 April 2007

Someone obviously isn't taking honours Maths

A few weeks back, I was travelling on a bus into town when I overheard two guys talking about their Leaving Cert study plans.

'My friend said you're supposed to do 29 and a half hours of study a week.'

'Wow, that's like nearly three hours every day ...'

Overheard by Dave, the bus
Posted on Wednesday, 4 April 2007

More Maths genius ...

In Maths class last week the teacher was giving out homework.

Teacher: 'I want you to do questions nine and ten for homework.'

Girl (blonde hair of course): 'Is dat nine and ten, or nine to ten?'

Overheard by Joey, school
Posted on Tuesday, 3 April 2007

Don't be sorry, Dolly!

At the Dolly Parton gig last night in the Point, Dolly apologised to the people of Cork for the cancelled Millstreet concert at the weekend.

Some voice from the audience pipes up, 'Dolly! It's for the best! They're all a bunch of langers down there!'

Overheard by Anonymous, Point Depot
Posted on Tuesday, 3 April 2007

There's an injured person in trouble somewhere

On the Red Line of the Luas, a Dublin lad gets on with a pair of crutches, both different. Next stop his friend gets on and asks why he's got two different crutches.

'One o' them was robbed off me, so I just went and robbed this one!'

Overheard by Hugh, on the Luas
Posted on Tuesday, 3 April 2007

Leaked email

Bloke I work with was in charge of sending all
the emails this morning for late deliveries,
apologising to the customers, and he sent out
about 50 stating:

'Sorry for any incontinence caused by this
delay ...'

One person wrote back saying, 'Thanks for
giving the whole office a smile on a Monday
morning, but I should probably warn you that
there's a big difference between inconvenience
and incontinence ... a big difference. Have a nice
day.'

He hasn't lived it down!

Overheard by ST, at work
Posted on Monday, 2 April 2007

You want a reason?

Man talking to woman walking through Trinity:
'Cos whenever you get drunk, you get naked!'

Overheard by joetrinners, Trinity College
Posted on Monday, 2 April 2007

Stating the obvious

In my mother's house on Saturday, my Granny,
who was staying over for a few days, was on the
phone to my Aunty who lives in Canada. The
conversation was going on a few minutes when
there was obviously some interference on the
line.

After a few seconds of Granny repeating my
Aunty's name down the phone and getting no
reply, she turns to me and my old man and says
in all seriousness,

'She seems very far away!'

Overheard by Ted, parents' house
Posted on Monday, 2 April 2007

P45's in the post, pal!

I was working for a car dealer a few years back.
In the valeting department there were two guys
working, Jimmy and new arrival, Simon. Jimmy
was your average middle-aged Dub, tough as old
boots, quick witted and a tongue as slack as a
road worker during rush hour! Simon on the
other hand was Chinese, poor English, timid and
learning the ropes.

They were working away one day when the boss
(who was a real hard ass but had a soft spot for
Jimmy) came strolling along. Immediately, Jimmy
dropped what he was doing and got the boss in
a headlock, and they proceeded to mess fight
with each other. After a few minutes of
handbags, they broke up and the boss walked
away.

Simon, who found this all very amusing on his
first day, gestured towards the Boss and asked
Jimmy, 'Who daaaaa?'

'Whooo him? He's only a little bollix,' and got
back to work.

The next morning Simon was standing in the
showroom outside the boss's office, when in
walks the man himself and walks past Simon.

'How are you?' asks the boss.

Simon turns around and says, 'Hawow littew bowox!'

Overheard by wetblanket, at a car main dealer
Posted on Saturday, 31 March 2007

Beer goggles

A couple of years ago after a christening, my mate was having the afters back in his well-to-do girlfriend's Ma and Da's house. Everybody was having a good time, with the drink flowing. We were all warned to be on our best behaviour and not show him up — all 'please' and 'thank you', and so on.

Our nice but dim buddy, who can't hold his drink, two hours later had to be warned about his behaviour and was told to sit down and chill out. In the lounge were four people including the collared priest who had done the christening that afternoon. He started making polite conversation to my drunk mate, asking what he did for a living, etc.

My mate in a drunken haze replies, 'So, Father, what do you do yourself?'

Overheard by Estaban, first time over in posh Dublin area
Posted on Friday, 30 March 2007

Always keep your eyes on the road!

Was in Blanchardstown last weekend with my sister-in-law. As we walked back to the car park, we noticed this young couple (around 15) kissing by the wall, in clear view of everyone in the multi-storey. All of a sudden this 'boy racer' in a Glanza done up to bits came spinning up on to the level. Just then, all I heard was, 'Getta bleeeeding room!' followed by a big crash ...

When we went to investigate closer, this muppet in the Glanza had smacked into the wall, while his head was out the window making smart comments at this lustful couple.

All we could do was laugh ... serves him right!!

Overheard by E, shopping in Blanch

Posted on Friday, 30 March 2007

New diagnosis from a taxi driver

Was in a taxi on the way into town last week and had the taxi driver tell me how he was relieved that the clocks were going forward.

He went on to say how he gets depressed during the dark winter months and explained, rather patronisingly, how he was diagnosed as having a relatively unknown disease called 'Mad disease'.

I didn't ask him where the name came from or if he was really a cow, but had to tell him that I thought the name of the disease was SAD (seasonal affective disorder).

Needless to say taxi drivers are never wrong: 'Sure I'm the one sufferin' from it! I should know!'

So after that I had to submit to him that he was right and that correct name for Seasonal Affective Disorder is actually Mad disease.

Overheard by Cossie, taxi

Posted on Friday, 30 March 2007

494

Lycra ladder

While walking from the bus to college the other week, I was passing by a building which was being renovated. A group of builders stood hanging over the scaffolding.

In front of me there was a woman in her early 20s wearing a denim mini skirt with black tights underneath. As she walked by the builders, the usual whistles started, until one of them shouted, 'You've got a ladder in your tights love!'

In true northside fashion, without even thinking, she spins around and shouts up at him,

'So why don't ya climb up it and kiss my arse!' followed by giving him the finger!

Genius!

Overheard by Dane, D'Olier Street
Posted on Thursday, 29 March 2007

No passport needed

I flew out from London Heathrow (after going through UK customs, getting my picture taken, passport checked about four times and questioned and searched).

Landed in Dublin and made my way to passport control, only to discover I couldn't find my passport. I say to the garda behind the desk that I can't find my passport. He pauses for a minute and asks me where I'm from. I tell him I'm from Dublin, to which he says,

'Ahh, feck it, go on through then.'

Only in Ireland!

Overheard by Fuzzy, Dublin Airport
Posted on Thursday, 29 March 2007

Clap your hands for Jesus

I work as a photographer and was in work one day when this woman brings her kid in to get his photos done. He's sitting there, refusing to smile, and she's trying to get him to clap his hands, which apparently makes him smile, when she comes out with this gem:

'Clap your hands for Jesus! Clap your hands for Jesus — or I'll smack you.'

Overheard by L, in work
Posted on Tuesday, 20 March 2007

Lost

I saw this in the ladies in college some time ago at the top of the door. It said,

'I lost my virginity' and at the bottom it said '... but I still have the box that it came in!'

Overheard by DIZZYDUB, graffiti in the ladies toilets in Cathal Brugha Street DIT
Posted on Tuesday, 20 March 2007

Dirty minds

In the lift in work the other week, I was going from the ground floor to the fourth floor of the building. A few other people in the lift with me and some from my office. The lift didn't go straight up to where we wanted to go, firstly going to the car park, then stopping again at the ground floor and second floor, letting people in and out.

When the lift stopped again at the third floor, one of the girls from my team turns to me and says,

'Oh my God, it looks like we'll never get back to our desks. I think we're destined to spend the rest of the day riding in the lift.' Cue me and everyone else left in the lift bursting out laughing — and her turning bright red.

Overheard by Johnny, lift in a building in the IFSC
Posted on Tuesday, 20 March 2007

Giz 20 Blue

I was in the Spar the other day buying cigarettes and this kid (no more then 12) comes in, skips the queue, and goes, 'Here, chung one, giz 20 Blue.' The girl at the till goes, 'Do you have ID?' Getting in a right mood, he spits on the ground and goes, 'Do I look like I have any bleedin' ID?'

Overheard by Anonymous, Glasnevin
Posted on Monday, 19 March 2007

Toilet humour

In a pretty run-down gents toilet in Ballyfermot College, I was reading the usual graffiti ('Up the RA', 'Liverpool rule', etc.) in one of the cubicles when I came across this gem:

'Sinead Conway is a ride.'

Directly underneath that:

'No I'm not!'

Overheard by Donall, Ballyfermot College
Posted on Monday, 19 March 2007

Scallops

Standing beside an extremely drunk guy in a Chinese take-away one night I heard him ask about the scallops. It went like this:

Drunk: 'What's no. 15?'

Waiter: 'Is scallops.'

Drunk: 'Yea, but scallops of what?'

Waiter: 'Is scallops, is scallops!'

Drunk: 'Yea ya dope, but scallops of what ... pork, chicken or what?'

Waiter: 'Is scallops, please, is scallops ...'

This went on for about 10 minutes, till the drunk gave in and said:

'Yea, well, I'll have it — but make it a mixture of scallops!'

Overheard by Anonymous, Chinese in Bray
Posted on Monday, 19 March 2007

Stirring the pot

Overheard at the bus stop:

'Bisto are bringing out a new line in honour of our rugby team. It's called "Laughing Stock"!'

Overheard by Anonymous, bus stop, Parkgate Street
Posted on Monday, 19 March 2007

Karma?

I'm walking down Collins Avenue and there's a guy (probably a student) a few paces in front of me, smoking. Group of hoodied 'yung fellas' on bicycles squeeze by me and cycle next to him.

Hoodie: 'Oi mista, can I have a lighter?'

Student: 'Ah ... okay ... here ...'

Hoodie lights his cigarette and starts cycling away with lighter.

Student (somewhat resigned to the fact he's lost it): 'Ah ... you can give me that back now ...'

Hoodie (cycling across road at speed with his mates, laughing obnoxiously): 'Hahaha, ya thick bollix, I said *have* not *borrow* ...'

Right at that moment — as if by divine intervention — Hoodie drops his packet of fags, and they end up crushed under the wheel of his mate's bike.

Overheard by Fred, Collins Avenue by
pedestrian crossing at DCU
Posted on Monday, 19 March 2007

Religion, from a five-year-old's perspective!

Was with my five-year-old nephew and his little friend going for a walk. Little friend kept running ahead. My nephew put up with it for a few minutes, then roared at his friend,

'Bradley, will you stop running out on the road, or we'll end up with a dead body like Jesus!'

Overheard by eimer, small town outside Dublin
Posted on Monday, 19 March 2007

Racist and confused

Was in a chemist in town recently when a young girl tried to walk into the shop. The black security guard quickly stopped her and told her she was barred and not to even think about going in, to which she confidently replied,

'F**K OFF YOU BLEEDIN' CHINK!'

Overheard by Anonymous, Henry Street

Posted on Sunday, 18 March 2007

Product recall!

I nipped out for a sandwich at lunch today. As I was passing by the Specsavers shop on College Green, a guy walked out of the shop. He was looking the opposite way to where he was walking, and barged straight into two builder types on their lunch.

One of the lads says to him, 'Here, Mister, I think you better go back in there and get a stronger pair of glasses — ya lampy bollix!'

Overheard by RonBurgundy, College Green

Posted on Sunday, 18 March 2007

Ignorance breeds contempt

Overheard in Hartigan's, Leeson Street, the night Ireland played Georgia in the Rugby World Cup. A Georgian player was being interviewed in English by RTÉ. Quote random punter:

'That guy works in Spar!'

Overheard by 73man, Hartigan's Pub, Leeson Street

Posted on Sunday, 18 March 2007

Putting your foot in it

In a pretty exclusive golf club in Wicklow a few years back, they held the world amputee championships. My friend was working in the golf shop at the time.

The manager of the shop is a real talker. Loves chatting to people who come into the shop. I used to work there too so I know what he's like.

There's a million and one stories but this one really stands out!

After the event had finished, the world amputee champion came into the shop. General chit-chat for a while, then this guy (American with prosthetic limbs) asked about getting a taxi to the airport.

Without blinking an eyelid or thinking, the manager of the shop replied,

'Ah, you don't want to get a taxi nowadays, sure it'd cost ya an arm and a leg from here!'

The American didn't know what way to take it — and promptly left!

Overheard by Bobby, Wicklow (not Dublin but close)
Posted on Sunday, 18 March 2007

County Cork: a skanger summary

On the no. 39 bus to Blanch. Real Anto and Dermo just behind me.

Anto: 'Stooooory, Dermo, where were ya over the weekend, bud?'

Dermo: 'Ah, I was in Cork, bud.'

Anto: 'Any good, bud?'

Dermo: 'Deadly buzz, man! All the girls are sluts and all the blokes are muppets.'

Overheard by theirishgrover, on the no. 39 bus to Blanchardstown
Posted on Sunday, 18 March 2007

Randomness

Man on phone: 'Go and ask the back of me flute!'

Overheard by Peter, at a bus stop on O'Connell Street
Posted on Sunday, 18 March 2007

A line to remember

Was standing out in the smoking area of a club one night, minding my own business. A true Dub chanced his arm as he walked past and tried to chat up a foreign girl; she was some sort of European.

After a moment or two, the boyfriend appears, another Dub, and says, 'Here, mate, I hope you're not tryin' to chat my bird up?'

To which the chancer replies, 'It's not your bird, mate, it's just your turn!'

Overheard by Si, Dandelion, St Stephen's Green
Posted on Saturday, 17 March 2007

Horses for courses

Was waiting for a train in Heuston Station last week, and there was a drunk guy pestering people for money. He spotted a very pretty girl, went over to her and said,

'I don't want any money, love, but I wouldn't say no to a ride.' Without batting an eyelid she replied,

'Stick around, there's a train to The Curragh along shortly.'

Overheard by Anonymous, Heuston Station
Posted on Saturday, 17 March 2007

Poultry in motion!

Overheard this slagging match by two skangers:

'I bleedin' wish I was a pigeon and you were a statue.'

'Oh yeah, tell yer aul' one to shave her back next time,' came the reply.

Overheard by Derek, at the back of the no. 27 bus
Posted on Saturday, 17 March 2007

Water and glass not so clear anymore?

Was in the canteen in work with the lads and one of them — we'll call him Karl (because that's his name) — was drinking a glass of water. All of a sudden he flips the glass upside down, spilling water all over the table and our lunches.

J: 'Why in f**k's name did you do that?'

Karl (surprised): 'Awh Jaysus, sorry, boyuz. I wanted to see if there was anything on the bottom of me glass!'

Overheard by Tongue-Bar McGowan, work canteen
Posted on Saturday, 17 March 2007

Amazing sheep!

While travelling to Dublin on the train for the day some years back with a few friends, we happened to pass a golf course. Noticing that there were sheep on the green, my rather dim-witted friend turned to her boyfriend and asked why this was.

Quick as a flash, he retorted that they were, 'trained to pick up the stray golf balls and return them to the club house'.

The rest of us all cracked up, while she responded, 'Really? That's amazing!'

She hasn't lived it down to this day!

Overheard by Anonymous, on the train
Posted on Saturday, 17 March 2007

Dogs' life

I was waiting with my two dogs for my fiancé outside the local Londis. Five scumbags came running down the street towards me; three ran into the shop and started causing hassle with the Polish security guard. One started making racist remarks, another started threatening to stab him and pulled out a rusty nail (I don't know what caused this).

While all of this was going on, the two scumbags outside struck up a conversation with me:

Scumbag: 'Nice dogs, Missus, where d'ya get em?'

Me: 'The Dog Pound.'

Scumbag: 'The Pound? What happened to 'em?'

Me: 'They were abandoned.'

Scumbags: 'Jaysus, some people are awful cruel, what's the world comin' to?'

I wish this were made up!

Overheard by Roisin, at the Londis on Parkgate Street
Posted on Saturday, 17 March 2007

Empty head

Long story short ... Mate A is as thick as a breadboard and he's on holliers. Him and Mate B are chatting up these two English girls in a bar and it goes as follows:

Girl: 'Where are you from?'

Mate B: 'Dublin — capital of Ireland.'

Girl: 'No, it's not!'

Mate B: 'Yeah, it is! Here [to Mate A], where's the capital of Ireland?'

Mate A: 'I dunno!'

Mate B: 'Ye plank! Ye live der!'

Mate A: 'Ahhh, Whitestown!'

Overheard by Steve, pub
Posted on Saturday, 17 March 2007

Bang and the scumbags are gone

On the no. 56a bus a few years ago, upstairs, approaching Cocos, minding my own business when all of a sudden a brick comes smashing through the window.

The driver jams on the brakes, and soon after comes upstairs to ask,

'Did anyone see those unholy bastards?' to which someone quickly replied,

'What channel was it on, bud?'

Everyone who heard it cracked up!

Overheard by peter, the good aul' no. 56a bus
Posted on Saturday, 17 March 2007

Stupid question

Was having dinner in an Italian restaurant recently. I wanted to order what I'd had the night before. The waiter told me twice it was number 39, the chicken dish. Stupidly, I asked what did the chicken come on. He looks at me funny and says, 'A plate ...'

Overheard by DAVE, Little Caesars, off Grafton Street
Posted on Saturday, 17 March 2007

Toilet tennis disappointment

Not technically heard in Dublin, but in a house full of Dubliners one summer in Chicago. Sitting down on their toilet, I see to my left the starting point of what looks like a normal game of toilet tennis. After reading 'Look right,' I turn my head to see scribbled on the opposite wall, 'Toilet tennis has been cancelled due to foot and mouth.'

Quality!

Overheard by Stanny Boy, Chicago
Posted on Friday, 16 March 2007

The unfamiliarities of technology!

On the weekend I was sitting down with my Dad having the aul' relaxing Sunday chat. Anyway, I tried explaining the pros and cons of Limewire to him (as ya do), and with that my Mum goes,

'I don't like you using that thing, Chloe, cuz you can attract viruses to the computer!'

And with that my Dad pipes up,

'Are they contagious?'

Overheard by Chloe, at home
Posted on Friday, 16 March 2007

Amateur spray painter

Seen on wall rather than heard. Young skanger must have been caught in the process, but managed to spray paint 'GRADA SCU'!

Overheard by Anonymous, Tallaght
Posted on Friday, 16 March 2007

North or south — I dunno!

A man walking down the street along beside the DART track, hears a DART going by but could not see it, so he asks a local. The conversation went as follows:

Man: 'Sorry, excuse me ...'

Local: 'Yup.'

Man: 'Did you see that train that went by there?'

Local: 'Yup.'

Man: 'Was it going north bound or south bound?'

Local: 'I dunno, I'm not a bleedin' compass!'

But he found out in the end.

Overheard by Thomas, Seapoint DART station
Posted on Friday, 16 March 2007

Scumbag in training

I saw a small boy about four years old trying to give some skangers in a car the birdie — he stuck up his index finger.

Skangers to boy: 'What's that supposed to mean?' His father then shows him how to do it properly! As the car drives off the boy shouts,

'F**k off, ye bastards,' as his Dad cheers him on.

Overheard by Jono, Finglas
Posted on Friday, 16 March 2007

Famous Dublin landmarks

Two English guys in town, walking along the Quays, just coming up to O'Connell Bridge, obviously trying to find their bearings.

1st Guy: 'Oh look, I remember that bridge there' (pointing at O'Connell Bridge).

2nd Guy: 'Oh yeah, you're right, this is near where Abrakebabra is.'

I just wonder what we're coming to, when Abrakebabra is a more famous Dublin landmark than O'Connell Bridge!

Overheard by Rosi, Aston Quay
Posted on Friday, 16 March 2007

Not so much unheard as unseen!

Advice from the National Consumer Agency to disgruntled holidaymakers:

'Write everything down, keep a record. For example, if there is a problem with the swimming pool — or if there is NO swimming pool as promised — document it with a photograph!'

Overheard by Anonymous, last night's *Evening Herald*
Posted on Friday, 16 March 2007

The pen is mightier than the laptop

Snippet of conversation I overheard ...

Flatmate: 'Well, we'll make a list, then run up to Tesco's and do some shopping.'

His stupid D4 girlfriend: 'Good idea. Hold on ... I'll just get my laptop from my bag. Oh, but I've no printer with me. Do you have a printer?'

Flatmate: 'Uh ... we'll just use a pen.'

Overheard by Fred, in the kitchen
Posted on Thursday, 15 March 2007

Pet name?

On the no. 18 bus a while ago, sitting upstairs, a father was at the very front with his young daughter, around three, sitting beside him, and two other children on the seat across.

He and the youngest were talking to the mother on the speaker phone, and the young girl was shouting down the phone to the mother. The girl said they were at a certain point and everyone on the bus could hear the mother say, 'Okay, I'll see you in a while.'

The husband says goodbye, then the young girl shouts down the phone, 'See you, big tits!'

Overheard by Anonymous, the ever reliable no. 18 bus
Posted on Friday, 16 March 2007

Albert Book, inventor of the novel ...

I was in the basement of Eason's with a mate of mine who was looking for a map of Dublin. While I was wandering around, a gaggle of Three Stripers passed me by. As they passed, one of them said (and I'm quoting his EXACT words heard):

'Sure, what do yez want to buy a book for? Books is the stupidest invention ever!'

Sweet Jesus ...

Overheard by Icecream, Eason's
Posted on Thursday, 15 March 2007